One fire burns out another's burning
One pain is lessened by another's anguish...
Romeo & Juliet

Chapter 1

Siren wailing and the metallic clang of its bell, our 1953 Rolls Royce, Dennis F 8 Pump, screamed flat out in second gear as we turned into Washburn Street. Confronted by clouds of black putrid smoke billowing from shattered first floor windows, this was my first experience of a large city-centre fire as a Probationary Fireman.

I was nearly twenty and I lived with my mother in a small rented back-to-back, part furnished terraced house. A month before I was born Mother scrambled for safety from a war-torn Germany. Arriving at last in England, she suffered from several abusive attacks, having to uproot us and move home several times. Eventually we settled in Torridge City, a city with a population of nearly half a million people where we struggled to be accepted.

My school days were hard and difficult. Money was always short and so Mother took all kinds of jobs to make ends meet washing, cleaning, working evenings in the local off licence shop. At school I struggled with all forms of theory, especially arithmetic, and cruel childish racial taunts taught me to trust no one.

Leaving school as early as possible I tried several jobs until Mother, in her guttural English, read out an advertisement one evening from the local paper which said, 'young men wanted to join Torridge City Fire Service'.

1

"Sicherheit and a pensionable future," she told me.

Security and pension at my age? I would be twenty in a few months; the very thought of a pensionable salary was of no interest to me. But as winter approached, the thought of continuing to work in cold damp buildings, churning out never-ending mountains of wet plaster for an ever hungry and demanding craftsman made the thought of another change welcome. I was an inch short of the specified five feet eight inches but even so I posted a letter for an application form.

A reply to my letter arrived, telling me to attend an appointment with the Police Surgeon for an examination at Torridge City Town Hall. This included a brief medical interview with a doctor. My chest was sounded by stabs from the freezing end of a stethoscope; I quickly looked through a thick and well-thumbed book with numbers hidden amidst dots of different colours and finally answered questions about an eye chart hung at a crazy angle on the back of a door.

At half-past nine in the morning, four days later, I walked with some trepidation into the headquarters of Torridge City Fire Brigade. I was wearing my best and only suit. I was about to take the entrance exam.

My dark green suit had been purchased second-hand, its trousers shortened by my mother. It showed polished crease marks pointing forwards, a result of constant steam pressing. The winter was cold, very cold, turning to be one of the coldest on record.

Divisional Officer Chad, tall and gaunt, was in full uniform, complete with a very impressive cap which displayed a white silver band on the peak. He introduced himself. His jacket, he explained was known in the Fire Brigade as the undress uniform. As a Divisional Officer he was entitled to wear rank markings, consisting of a large impeller, like a miniature pyramid encircled by a laurel wreath, fashioned in shiny metal and standing erect and proud as they rested snugly on his shoulders.

His cap, pressed firmly on his head, and had a half-inch of silver braid on the peak.

"An impeller is a miniature copy of the internal workings of our water pumps," he explained.

He removed his cap, leaving a red ring indented under his grey hair. From a piece of paper he proceeded to call out our names. He swung his pencil like a baton as if he were a conductor.

"Stephen Saury?" Dipping his pencil in acknowledgement of the answering.

"Yes Sir," Stephen answered.

"Michael Edward Fairn? Yes," I answered.

I stepped forward to stand alongside Stephen Saury. (Mother had altered our surnames in her attempt to prevent any recurrences of racial problems.)

"Yes, Sir," Divisional Officer Chad gave his instruction shouting as though I were deaf.

Out of the six names the Divisional Officer called out, one man had not bothered to turn up and as the remaining five of us answered, he ticked off our names with an emphatic swing of his pencil.

Then we were ushered into a long thin room with a row of desks arranged in neat lines.

"Just a few measurements to check your application form," said a stumpy man with a squeaky voice. He was dressed in a brown pin-striped suit and like mine had obviously seen better days. A dirty white tape measure hung around his neck.

"Follow me! Stand against the wall," he squeaked.

As each of us stood against the wall, the man held a ruler on the top of our heads and stretched to his full height before marking the wall surface behind us with a small stub of chalk.

When my turn came I could not help noticing the heavy odour of tobacco oozing from his clothes. Unaware of the stench he carried, he held the ruler in a level position as I moved away.

"You aren't tall enough," he informed me.

"You should be five-feet and eight-inches! You're an inch short." My heart sank.

"You'll have to try again." His voice went up an octave.

Once more taking a deep breath, I stood against the wall.

"Stand up a bit, on your toes."

Gaining an extra inch or so in this way I achieved the minimum height required.

"Now your chest measurements."

Almost as quickly as the tape measure went around my chest the necessary two-inch expansion was accepted.

"You'll do. Next."

After each of us had quickly gone through this charade, we were told to sit at the desks. We were given a clean piece of white lined paper and the Divisional Officer began asking general knowledge questions. He pulled an old crumpled exercise book from one of his uniform pocket and began.

"Name of the Prime Minister? Longest river in the world? Capital of Egypt?"

The questions came fast. We scribbled down our answers. More followed. My page slowly filled. Papers handed in for marking we were then ushered outside into a cold and icy morning for the practical side of the entrance examination. Two on-duty firemen waited impatiently to demonstrate the requirements to potential recruits. One of the firemen, a huge chap in pale-blue overalls, which were more, washed out than true blue, picked up the second fireman like a rag doll. He bounced the fireman across his shoulders and proceeded to amble casually up the back street just as if he was carrying nothing at all. He walked twenty yards or so turned and trotted back before dropping the fireman from his broad shoulders to the ground. His warm breath shot out from his mouth, blanketing his face in clouds of steam.

"Pick a mate!" Divisional Officer Chad instructed.

Dutifully we paired off. I looked for a partner I thought I could lift.

"Right get on with it. Let's not be shy."

From the officer's manner it appeared that we did not have a great deal of time. I looked carefully at my opponent. He looked about my size. Thrusting my right arm around his waist, I made him lean forward and bend down slightly from his hips. I managed to support the man across my shoulders and as I straightened myself it not only felt uncomfortable but also top heavy. It is easier carrying bags of plaster, I thought. Perhaps there was a special technique carrying a live body? Unsteadily I trod carefully up the street, turned and with my legs shaking hurried back and deposited my partner eagerly on the ground.

"Next!"

Another couple went through the same procedure.

"Go a bit further," Divisional Office Chad shouted as this pair turned, trying to shorten the distance.

When it came to my turn, to be carried, I felt distinctly odd, upside down and across someone else' shoulders.

A ladder appeared, and the two firemen demonstrated our next task. Placing the ladder against a wall, one held the base securely as the other climbed about fifteen feet up. He put one leg through the ladder rungs and, using just his leg to grip, he let go with his hands and leant outwards.

"This is a leg lock," the Divisional Officer told us, "so we can tell if any of you are frightened of heights."

The first applicant to stand at the bottom gripped the sides of the ladder. He was stopped immediately.

"Rest!" the Divisional Officer, shouted.

"In the Fire Brigade we hold on to the rounds, you'll no doubt think of them as rungs. The sides of the ladder are known as strings."

The big fireman stepped forward and began another demonstration.

"Use your left hand, left foot, right hand, right foot."

He began to scale the ladder. It looked so easy.

I felt confident and volunteered to be next. Used to climbing ladders on building sites, I too climbed the ladder as if I was carrying a hod of ready mixed plaster gripping both sides of the ladder. But this was not what was taught in the Fire Service.

"You a window cleaner?" the big Fireman grunted.

"Window cleaners do not use rounds because of getting muck on their shoes," he told me.

"But they are not likely to carry anything other than their shammy-leather," he continued.

"At all times a round, or in your words a rung, must be gripped in one hand."

He could not resist showing again his talent for climbing as he climbed the ladder once more. But on his way down he deliberately slipped and fell. His feet fell away but he hung with one hand quite securely. He had proved his point.

With the practical examinations completed, five of us were sent in the direction of the canteen for much needed refreshments. They were welcome after the bitter cold temperatures outside.

The Police Fire Brigade originally used Torridge City Fire Station, a hotchpotch of buildings. Built at the end of the nineteenth century, through the decades an assortment of dwellings gave the place a higgledy-piggledy untidy appearance with the ancient Police Headquarters now converted into the main office block. The large four bay engine house was adapted from the horse drawn steam pump era to accommodate today's petrol driven appliances.

The canteen, to be found up a flight of well-worn stone stairs, looked like a church hall. Its high ceiling, its large wooden beams and its stone floor did nothing to reduce the bitter cold of the day. In one corner a Radio Rental speaker, played apparently to itself. Sounds of a new group of musicians and the words 'love me do' blasted out into the room.

"Come for a drink of tea?" A voice carried over the music from a small hatch cut into the far wall. Nervously the five of us crept towards the questioner, to be confronted by a small dainty woman wearing a large white coat that fell to within an inch off the floor. Her hair was draped in a bright red and yellow flowered patterned scarf.

"And something to eat?" she asked. Coming from inside her kitchen and screwing her hands tightly through a white towel, she went to turn down the Beatles.

"Maurice always has this thing on too loud. Then he goes out, leaving it blaring away. I'm Blanche Spurling. Now lads, what do you want?"

She shuffled back into her kitchen. Her long white coat brushed the floor as she walked.

"Bread and dripping!" called a voice from somewhere inside our group.

She stood alongside a large copper water heater, straining up to reach the handle. Boiling water spluttered out from the spout into a large aluminium teapot. Clouds of steam danced upwards.

"Come to join the Fire Brigade have you?" Blanche Spurling asked, as the teapot slowly filled. She plonked it onto an enamel tray, which held a bowl of sugar. Five white plastic mugs followed in quick succession before she lifted the tray in both hands. We followed her sheepishly to a table. Without further ado she was back in her kitchen and, reaching for a large knife, proceeded to cut into a loaf of bread.

"Sit down, don't just stand about!" she ordered.

We each nervously selected a chair. Through the door a man wearing a brown overall coat entered.

"Maurice?" the canteen lady greeted him, "some new recruits."

Maurice never said a word. He went over to the Radio Rental speaker and, twisting the volume knob, filled the room once more with loud music.

Carrying a large plate stacked high with slices of bread three quarters of an inch thick and plastered in dark beef dripping, Blanche Spurling sat down with us, her feet dangling under the chair. Treating us as if she were a mother hen she began.

"Before you finish this morning, providing you have all passed, Chief will want to see you. He'll ask, "Why do you want to join? Whatever you think," she went on, "don't say it's for the money! Alan Bass, the Chief, doesn't like to think men join just for the money. I have known him for many years, since well before the war began. Now he's Chief, and he still speaks to me!" She clucked on at us.

She commanded our attention, going through our expected interview step by step.

Divisional Officer Chad returned to collect us after we had eagerly devoured Blanche's full plate of dripping sandwiches and had downed her mugs of sweet tea. Blanche rose, from her chair, collected our empty plates and cups and went off into her kitchen.

"All five have passed the entrance examination," Divisional Officer Chad said in a dull uninterested tone.

"One or two of you need to brush up on your general knowledge. Harold Macmillan is the Prime Minister. And the capital of Egypt is Cairo," a sly smile cracked his face into two.

"Not to worry," he added, "you can all read and write. Now the Chief and the Assistant Chief need to interview you all before you are accepted," he told us as we followed him out of the canteen.

Five of us followed the officer back down the stone stairs and along a corridor to a new and as yet unseen section of the headquarters.

"Wait here," he said.

We stood outside a large brown polished door as he tapped gently on it and entered. The door did not have time to close before it sprung wide open again and the first of us was asked inside. As the rest of us were left idle, standing outside, I attempted to make casual conversation. But before I could exchange anything more than the day's cold weather, the large door opened and we were told to make less noise.

This is just like the hours spent outside the headmaster's study in my school days, I whispered to myself.

The interviews lasted only a few moments and since our names were taken in alphabetical order I did not have long to wait before the call came for Fairn. I entered through the big door. The room looked dark and sombre. Chief Officer Bass sat behind a large leather topped-desk. His uniform looked impressive with masses of silver buttons and markings of rank.

Two red lines pointed downwards on his lapels. Alongside him another Officer sat dressed similar. To his left sat a civilian in a brown suit.

He was the man smelling of tobacco we had met earlier when he had been taking our measurements. Behind the three men a hot blazing fire glowed from a huge fireplace, sending waves of comfort into the room.

"So you want to be a fireman?" The Chief's words were brief and clipped.

"Why?"

I thought of the canteen lady, Mrs Spurling.

"The job offers security," I answered.

"Not the money?" the Chief turned to the Officer at his side. "Blanche must have been giving advice," he muttered. Obviously a man of few words, he sat back in his chair, leaving the other officer to continue the interview.

"My name is Richard Albert Carp, Assistant Chief Officer. This is Mr Parr the Brigade clerk," he began.

"Just a few questions about you," he spoke quickly.

"How old are you, laddie?"

"Nineteen," I answered.

"Now laddie, when are you going to be twenty?"

"April this year. Sir. The twentieth," I added as an afterthought.

"You start at 9 o'clock next Friday morning."

Chapter 2

Beginning work on a Friday is different to being in the outside world. Most work places finish their week on a Friday, or Saturday; for some obscure reason Torridge City Fire Brigade begins its week on a Friday!

"So you were ill with sickness and diarrhoea?" the owner of the plastering firm where I had being working said with malice in his voice, "so how come we received a letter from the local Fire Brigade today wanting references?"

The Torridge City Fire Brigade had sent a letter to the firm I was working for.

"So 'Kraut' wants to join the 'Feuerwehr'?" The owner mimicked what he thought was a German accent, displaying a prejudice no doubt derived from his war service.

"You can finish now. Today," he added.

My employment terminated immediately. I collected my bundle of old working clothes from the workshed and my old pedal cycle, fetching it from the array of cycles under a corrugated shed. I pedalled home slowly feeling harassed and dejected and short of four day's pay.

Mother was shocked at my sudden appearance. A smile darted for a fleeting second across her well-worn creased face and revealed her inward pleasure for a second before she composed herself. The smell of bleach drifted from her hands and wafted after her as she darted off to the scullery and proceeded to rattle a few pots in the sink.

I removed my thick duffel coat and moved closer to the fire, where a few embers struggled for life. Mother had deliberately allowed the morning fire to die in an effort to save fuel. The times were hard and my new appointment as a fireman with a weekly starting wage of eleven pounds and one penny would mean a further loss; I was earning £14, and sometimes £15 a week mixing plaster.

"You need a job with a pension," mother shouted from her kitchen.

Pension, I thought! Who thinks of a pension at twenty years of age?

On Friday, still dressed in civilian clothes, I arrived back at Torridge City Fire Station ready to begin my new life. Dressed for a keen frosty morning, with two thick woollen jumpers covered by my working duffel coat, I leaned my Old Faithful bicycle against a wall.

"You can't park that there!" The voice boomed with authority as I meekly whispered an apology.

"You new?" The voice went on.

"Park that thing over there," he ordered. I moved the bicycle obediently.

"Please can you tell me where to go?" I aimed my question at the voice giving all the orders. But the Fireman in uniform simply turned and walked away without answering my question.

Another fireman, tall thin and smart, intervened. Even the sleeves of his black uniform jacket supported straight creases and the peak of his hat was polished to look like glass; it reflected the view.

"Come this way, kid, take no notice of the old moaner. He's always grumpy after being on nights. My name is Norman Sterlet and I'm a Union official. We've just finished a fifteen-hour night and we're ready to go off duty now. The day crew will look after you," Norman Sterlet told the other newcomers and me. I joined the other familiar faces from the previous week's interview. We all looked nervous, overawed by the number of men jostling about. At nine o'clock the Station changed shifts from night to day crew. Both crews assembled and formed up in two lines. We stood and watched as the morning parade began.

"Parade 'Shun!" Someone shouted.

Two rows of firemen straightened, standing to attention.

"Off-going watch is dismissed."

Turning smartly to the right, a group of Firemen walked away.

"On-coming watch stand at ease. Red watch answer your names."

It all seemed very efficient, if rather alarming.

The Station Officer in charge of the Red Watch day crew, dressed in a white shirt with two chrome impellers on the shoulders of his uniform jacket, introduced himself and told a Leading Fireman to look after our needs.

"Follow me to the stores," he said.

Deposited at the entrance to the stores, we were greeted by a white-haired gentleman wearing a grey-white coat, not dirty but washed until it was grey; his hair looked whiter than his coat. A man of few words, he whistled continuously; it was not a particular melody but just a constant drone up and down the musical scale. As he whistled, notes from his mouth steamed out in narrow

13

tubes as his warm breath hit the cold air. He unlocked a door, using a large key on a chain fastened underneath his coat. We followed him inside where, lit by a single light bulb hung from the centre of the ceiling, the stores-man laid a sheet of paper carefully onto a table top.

"Who's Fairn?"

Was his first utterance, as he read from the list of names on his paper.

"This will be your pile of clothes."

"Who is Saury?" He went down the list, calling out our names. We all stood obediently alongside our allotted places as he kept disappearing to the shelves and returning with armfuls of clothing. The piles of kit on the table grew and grew.

"Try these for size." He first looked, made a guess handed us what he thought would fit. We ended up with

An old fire-helmet.
A new leather belt, pouch and fireman's axe.
Two new pairs of serge fire-trousers.
Two fire-tunics, both second hand.
A new pair of leather fire-boots.
A pair of used leather fire-boots.
Two new pairs of socks.
Two new shirts with detached collars.
A new black tie.
New set of overalls.
A second hand undress jacket.
A new uniform cap.
One new pair of undress trousers.
Two new pairs of shoes.
Two new pairs of grey woollen socks.
A new pillow.

Three new grey woollen blankets.

One gas mask complete with canvas shoulder bag.

"No raincoats, old greatcoats will have to do," he muttered as he folded our thick black, uniform greatcoats on the floor in front of us.

"No underwear?" the ginger-haired Stephen Saury enquired.

The stores man heard him. He looked at Saury and momentarily stopped whistling, but said nothing. Choosing to ignore the question, he carried on, pursing his lips and continuing to whistle the tuneless melody.

"No underwear?" Repeated Stephen Saury, not prepared to have his question left unanswered. His freckled face pleaded for an answer.

"The Army supplied everything, even vests and underpants," he added. But there was no acknowledgement. The shrill whistle just continued without interruption.

The uniform cap, shirts, tie, socks, shoes, pillow, blankets and fire-boots all looked new but the rest of the equipment seemed to be second hand.

The fire-helmets had definitely been used before. Made of leather, they resembled the helmet Britannia wore on a penny piece. A large curved pinnacle protruded and arched over the top and obviously a World War One issue. The gas masks in its canvas bag were supplied for the next World War and the threat of nuclear fall out.

"Fire-helmets are expensive," the stores man told us.

"You'll get a proper one if you stay the distance." A few brief words had at last interrupted his tuneless drone.

The Leading Fireman, the first rank after a promotion, returned and took us to what he called the hose room. We felt like heavily burdened packhorses. We climbed up a long steep staircase before entering a low ceiling room lined with racks full of lengths of hose. "After you're dinner, all this equipment needs marking with your number," he told us.

It was midday already. The morning had already disappeared. Following the Leading Fireman through an array of stairs, alleyways, passageway, and yet more stairs, we eventually arrived at the canteen which looked like a church hall. The day watch duty crew sat, already eating and the room briefly hushed as we entered.

Blanche Spurling, the petite canteen lady, greeted us with the motherly affection she had shown at our first meeting week earlier.

"You'll want something warm to eat?" She asked. Her fresh stiff white coat circled her like a white tube.

"It's fish and chips, always fish and chips on Fridays."

Her strong positive manner belied her small frame. It did not seem possible one so small could speak so firmly. She produced five dinners, which she had already prepared.

Large white plates, with a huge piece of fried cod surrounded by dozens of finger thick chips, appeared from her kitchen. A dollop of mushy peas, ladled over the tail end of the fish, sat motionless like green wet concrete. The plate felt heavy as we carried off our dinners and found places to sit and eat. Rice pudding followed the fish, looking like the mushy peas, only white!

"Enjoy that?" Blanche enquired as she collected the empty plates; their emptiness answered her question.

We followed the Leading Fireman and the rest of the duty crew, and were introduced to the recreation area. The Leading Fireman explained, almost lovingly, the history of the Fire Station. We sat around him and digested every word. Built in the 1880s, he began; this Fire Station grew through two world wars from the old horse-drawn era of a Police City Fire Brigade to the present day.

We sat in the long-room. This was the area where firemen spent their leisure stand-down time. All four walls were covered by frescoes, showing the marvels of the world; Chinese Geisha girls, Paris, Venice, and the Great Pyramids had all originally been designed and painted by an artistic fireman. In the middle of one of the long walls was an enormous fireplace. There was no shortage of fuel here. The heat from the fire was immediately noticeable as the warmth struck our cheeks. The massive red-hot glowing coke-fired grate blasted hundreds of therms into the room. Its welcome was overpowering.

Dinner hour ended, and it was a real effort to move after such a large meal and after half an hour under the spell of a furnace. But the cold air outside cruelly brought us to reality as we gathered for the marking and numbering of the kit issue from the morning.

Each of us was presented with our Brigade number, which was to be our identification for the rest of our service in Torridge City Fire Brigade. Using a well-used stencil I duly labelled every item. 'M.E.FAIRN, T.C.F.B. C435' the white painted lettering eventually adorned every article of my uniform. We obediently stamped metal and leather objects, axe, belt buckle, boots with steel punches.

"What is the C for?" I asked sheepishly.

The Leading Fireman looked straight at me but said nothing.

Remaining mute in answer to questions, seemed endemic.

Cold grey daylight turned to pitch darkness as home time arrived.

"Take home with you a shirt, tie, trousers, shoes, and socks and report tomorrow, Saturday dressed in uniform." This order was the Leading Fireman's final word.

Struggling with my brown paper parcel precariously balanced on the crossbar, I pedalled home.

"Been to any fires yet?" Mother asked in her guttural accent.

I sat down for tea. Mother produced a plate of fish and chips. Always fish on Fridays, she had learnt, an English custom. I was keen and excited about my new job. There was so much to tell; Mother listened interestedly as my second fish dinner that day vanished.

On the following morning, Saturday, I struggled to fit the detachable collar to the blue shirt. Stiff as plywood, even with proper collar studs, produced magically by my mother the separate collar did not like the idea of living on a shirt.

Worrying about being late for duty I left home to collect my old push-bike normally that was kept twenty yards down the street in our outside toilets. But there was no bicycle. It had gone, stolen during the night. There was nothing to do but to walk and run to the Fire Station. My new uniform felt strange and uncomfortable. The new shoes pinched, the undress jacket was too big, the cap was too small and the uniform trousers needed a pair of braces to hold them in place.

"No cap-badge in your hat," an officer shouted at me. Met by yet another Station Officer, the change of watches took place and a new crew began on duty. The officers wore a uniform that was different from that of the firemen; it was tailored with outside pockets and a small material belt with a gleaming buckle, which sparkled, from the front.

None of us five recruits had been given cap-badges. This was another expensive item to be issued later.

Saturday morning was packed with more indoctrination, this time from another Leading Fireman who introduced himself as Geoffrey Sardelle. He explained his family had connections with Torridge City Fire Brigade going back for many years. His Grandfather, who served at the beginning of the century, had worked in the Brigade when horses drew fire-pumps. He went on to say that in those days firemen worked almost a continuous duty and the average turn-out times for horse-drawn pumps, fully equipped, was fifty seconds by day and seventy seconds by night.

In those days they all lived in houses built around the Station, each house having its own alarm bell. Many of these houses still existed and were still used by Firemen and their families. Today they provided cheap handy accommodation. Like his father before him, Geoffrey Sardelle was born in one of these houses. His father, who worked when Fire Brigades throughout the country were amalgamated in 1941, forming a National Fire Service during the Second World War, was a victim of an enemy bombing raid after being mobilised from Torridge City to cover the blitz on the dock land areas suffering fatal injuries. I grimaced at mention of a German enemy, chewed my inner lip, and said nothing.

His knowledge of and insight into the present day Fire Service was full of depth and personal feeling; he spoke about it with such pride and cherished memories. He explained that there were three shifts, or watches, known as Red, White and Blue. One of the colours was on duty

0900 to 1800 hours. The second watch worked nights from 1800 to the following morning at 0900 hours, a total of fifteen hours on nights! The third shift enjoyed rota leave and had three days off duty. Every three days the system changed; the watch working days went onto nights, the night crew went onto rota leave and the crew off duty began their three days on. The long nights with fifteen-hours on duty began after the introduction of shorter working hours. It was considered important to have Firemen available and working through the night for continuity. Many fires occurred during the night and changing crews over in mid-shift was considered impracticable. Because of these long nights, firemen were allowed to sleep in the Station; it was cheaper to keep men in bed than to keep them occupied and awake subject to immediate turnout by the station alarm bells. Geoffrey Sardelle explained turnout times on nights were faster than those in the day. Sleeping times, called 'boots off', lasted between the hours of midnight and reveille at 0645 hours.

The long duty periods that Geoffrey Sardelle's predecessors endured created many hours not regarded as working time but still kept the men confined on station and ready for fire-calls. Sundays, Saturday afternoons, evenings, and any bank holidays were considered stand-down periods, times when station-working routines were relaxed.

Down the years, these stand-down periods were often filled by recreation pastimes. Ball games, football, cricket, and a crude form of tennis were all played outside, on the back street. A licensed bar provided drinks and a social get-together during the leisure periods, though the bar was now restricted to an hour on night shift and to the midday breaks on Saturday and Sundays.

By the time Geoffrey had completed his historic account it was midday and we had reached the end of our day and a half induction. His offer to stay and have a drink at the bar was most welcome; pint of mild beer went down well. The white creamy froth clung to the sides of the pint glass as the dark brown nectar quenched our avid thirst.

I had been given a glimpse of an entirely new world.

Chapter 3

Monday morning arrived. Rising in darkness before an idle January sun blessed the morning with its light, I struggled into my Fire Brigade uniform. The blue shirt with an attached stiff collar, bit deep into my neck. The black tie was fastened so tight I struggled to breathe. Uniform-trousers supported by a pair of braces hung like heavy curtains. New unbroken and pinching black shoes completed the cladding. I felt and looked like a stuffed dummy.

For a week, as five raw recruits, we received basic instruction. Every morning this consisted of handling ladders, running lengths of delivery hose, connecting the brass couplings and extending our hose-line up the backstreet of the Fire Station. Every afternoon we joined the duty crew and were introduced to the Station routines. Cleaning the Station occupied many hours as we waited for the station alarm bells to ring we were shown the 'mop and bucket'. I was soon to learn these items were to be a fireman's most important companion.

The following Monday a new shift, White Watch and Station Officer Finnan the officer in charge, began their three-day, three-night tour of duty.

Station Officer Finnan spoke with a marked Scottish accent. At first I found it was difficult to understand him, but he seemed kind and reassuring. He explained that as recruits we could be posted to any of the five Fire Stations in Torridge City. We gathered in his office where he produced a piece of paper and sat down. The five of us shuffled around his desk, which was in a room six-foot square. He removed his cap, revealing black hair plastered down with hair cream and glistening under the electric light bulb. Down the centre of his head an immaculate parting divided his scalp exactly in half.

"Michael Edward Fairn is posted to this watch, Torridge City Station," he said to me.

The other four recruits were detailed to other Fire Stations dotted about the city. We trailed outside as all their equipment; blankets, helmets and fire-uniform were stuffed aboard a red Ford Thames van. The four recruits clambered in the back of the van with all their uniforms and blankets. The van sped off down the street as if turning out to a fire.

With his rank markings (two impellers sprouting from both shoulders all fashioned in shiny steel looking like four shiny nipples) Station Officer Finnan stood and watched the van as it left. The impellers, a design used in all officers' rank markings, consisted of a knurled steel knob, the size of a large button, with its central design imitating blades found inside Fire Service water-pumps.

"Thinks he's a racing driver, tells me he wants to drive to fires!"

His words were quiet and more to himself than spoken out loud. Replacing his cap he nodded for me to follow. I trailed close behind. The officer in charge of White Watch, Station Officer Finnan, possessed a kind and friendly face.

He told me he controlled his men with kindness, respect and fairness and in return he demanded total commitment. Educated by life's experiences, his round plump face had the ability to express pleasure or annoyance by a single glance. I stood in front of his desk as he sat down. Removing his cap once again he carefully undid every chrome button on his jacket. Taking it off he draped it over the back of his chair. He sat down slowly to reveal an officer's white shirt, sectioned by maroon braces and split by a black tie. He began.

"A fireman's job can be compared to driving a nail into wood. Everyone seems to know the correct size, the type of nail and the correct type of hammer, even the proper trajectory and force needed. The manuals are full of this sort of theory, all perfectly true, but," he leaned across the table and looked at me closely, his face showing a hint of a smile, which quickly changed as he went on, "ultimately it needs someone to pick up the hammer and actually hit the nail!"

This brief introduction over, he called for Fireman Bleck to act as my mentor and protector for the next few days. Barry Bleck, tall, thin and wiry with tight curly red hair crowning his head, had eleven years service in the Fire Brigade.

"Get your fire-helmet, your axe, belt, boots, and tunic and I'll find you a peg." Barry told me.

Burdened down like a struggling packhorse I followed him into the muster-room. The muster-room was the hub of the Fire Station. It was a dimly lit room, even during daylight hours, the centre of operations and sited next to the engine house. On one wall was a crew-board, the size of a small window. Painted in red, white and blue, two sliding doors left the list of on-duty crew visible. Barry pointed to it. Down one side of the crew-board the titles of every fire-appliance on the Station were inscribed in black letters. Alongside every appliance was a line of small hooks and from these hooks hung small round steel discs, known as tallies! Each member of every watch had their own tally with their name written on it. Even the tallies were in the colour of the appropriate watch. I was impressed.

"This crew-board must be checked at all times," Barry Bleck standing alongside, fondling the tallies as he made his point.

"How we man the appliances rests on these names and when the bells sound it needs to be checked."

The tallies rattled and swung as his fingers brushed them. I looked at the numerous names, trying to commit some to memory.

WHITE WATCH

Pump One   **_Stn.O. Finnan: Lfm.Loche: Fm.Tailor: Fm.Cale_**

Pump Escape   **_Sub.O. Gardon: Fm.Scar: Fm.Bleck: Fm.Ronchil_**

Pump Two

Turntable Ladder **_Fm.Twaite: Fm.Grundel_**

Emergency Tender **_Fm.Margot: Fm.Capelin_**

Detached Duties **_Fm.Partan_**

Off Station   *Sub.O.Latchet:*   *Lfm.Weever:*   *Fm.Bley*
Fm.Dory Fm.Ray

Annual Leave *Fm.Kingstone*

Sick Fm.Milter

Named tallies hung against every title except Pump
Two.

"Pump Two isn't usually manned during weekdays.
There aren't enough men," Barry said.

Opposite the words 'Off Station' hung several tallies.

"These men are on duty but are off the Fire Station,
working as tradesmen and doing repairs," Barry explained.

I learned that every watch should have a contingent of
twenty-one men, when at full strength: Sixteen firemen,
two Leading Firemen, two Sub-Officers and one Station
Officer. With somebody always on holiday, or as they
called it in the Fire Brigade 'annual leave', the number of
men on duty should have averaged eighteen. But these
numbers were rarely achieved.

The muster-room also housed everybody's fire-
uniforms. Each member of the Station was allocated a peg
on which he hung his fire-tunic. Above this peg on a shelf
rested his fire-helmet, and below it, on another shelf, a pair
of fire-boots were ready for collection the moment the
bells sounded.

On another wall hung the indicator board listing the
full compliment of appliances. When the alarm bells rang,
lights behind this board showed which appliances were
turning out. Men allocated to that machine collected their
fire-uniform and went to the appliance.

"This will be your peg," Barry told me.

He placed the fire-helmet I had been issued on the shelf above the peg and my gas mask in its canvas bag on the peg. Over this he hooked my fire-tunic and then my axe on its leather belt. Carefully folding the fire-tunic around the belt, Barry formed a neat curled parcel. On the lower shelf, conveniently situated directly above some central heating pipes he placed my pair of leather fire-boots and told me.

"Because our uniforms are always on show, always make sure that your boots, your tunic, and your helmet are always left clean and tidy." My fire-uniform now hung neat and tidy alongside the rest of the Station's crews.

"Until you have a proper tally this will have to do," Barry said as he scribbled my name Fairn on an inch-square piece of cardboard and hooked it on one of the tiny hooks alongside the appliance named Pump One.

"But always check before we turn-out!"

I followed behind Barry as closely as possible. He bounced through a pair of swing doors to the engine house. I followed in hot pursuit. The line of fire-appliances I saw looked impressive; and they gleamed.

Two identical machines stood in the first two bays. They were early 1950s Dennis F8s with Rolls Royce engines and open-backed pumps. Each appliance carried a thirty-five foot ladder, a hose-reel and eighty gallons of water. Barry opened the lockers to display the contents: rolls of delivery hose and specialised equipment in different lockers.

A Dennis F12 Pump Escape sat gleaming in the third bay. On its back there was a fifty-foot ladder. Above, the fully enclosed cab housed a ladder attached to two huge carriage wheels, which protruded from the rear. One of the two large wheels spun easily as Barry brushed the steel rim with his hand.

In the fourth bay was a 1955 Dennis F17 Turntable Ladder, again powered by a Rolls Royce petrol engine. A Turntable Ladder was a self-supporting mechanical hundred-foot ladder, I learned.

I was still only a foot behind Barry as we passed the Brigade Control Room door. This small insignificant door, Barry informed me, led into a secret room where all messages were received from the General Post Office. Strictly out of bounds to firemen, exclusively women manned Control. He whispered as he gave me this information.

Finally he took me to the rear of the Station to show me an additional appliance, the Emergency Tender. I was very impressed by the large amount of specialised equipment carried on this appliance. Barry opened drawer after drawer and locker after locker, revealing all manner of equipment. The machine was packed tight with such things as spanners, cutting gear, breathing apparatus and emergency electric lighting. Barry told me that the Emergency Tender turned out to road accidents and any special incidents requiring this impressive array of equipment.

There was so much to digest it was probably a good thing the Station bells did not sound on my first full day!

Tuesday began as Monday had with morning parade and roll call. This time my name was actually called out on parade and I was detailed to ride on Pump Two. A freshly painted white tally was produced with my name Fm.Fairn. It hung neatly alongside the appropriate appliance on the crew-board.

Despite the severe frosty conditions, part of White Watch performed a drill outside, on the street at the back of the Station, which was used as the drill ground. The crew moved fast, leaning the ladder against the drill tower effortlessly. I could only stand, stare and once more be impressed.

Now the induction period was over I was re-introduced to the routine duties. One of these important tasks was for a fireman to heat the Fire Station. The fireman carrying out this particular duty was called 'The Yards and Fires Man' and I was detailed to seek out Fireman Brian Ronchil. His waist solid like a thick tree trunk, Brian gave me a guided tour of all the boilers dotted all over the Station. His task for the three days on duty was to keep these boilers producing heat and hot water for the whole station. Using large shovels I assisted Brian as we thrust coke into the ever-open mouths of the many furnaces.

"Big Bernice is the biggest," Brian explained, "she supplies heat to the engine house and eats five tons of coke a week."

On Monday afternoon and on nearly the whole of Tuesday I continued to assist Brian coping with the demand from insatiable boilers. Still there was no sign of any turnout, but late on Tuesday afternoon, bells sounded at long last. This happened just as I was washing and getting ready to go home. With soap on my face I panicked and rushed out of the washroom and ran as fast as I could towards the muster-room.

The tinkling of one station alarm bell in the washroom had sounded like a bedside alarm clock. Outside, with several bells joining in, a cacophony of noise filled the night air as everybody on duty dashed forwards. Men appeared from all directions joining together as we banged through the well-bruised and polished entrance door into the muster-room.

In the rush I tried to locate my tally on the crew-board but with men coming in all directions, charging back and forth some collecting their fire-uniforms, I could not get close enough to see the my name.

"Pump Two," someone cried.

"Grab your gear, you're on Pump Two," Barry Bleck shouted, finding me looking puzzled.

"Don't forget your helmet," someone else yelled.

I struggled, my arms full, through swing doors from the muster-room into the engine house. Pump Two had an open rear platform, which allowed us to climb on board easily. Our officer in charge, Sub Officer Gardon, collected his fire-message from a woman standing outside the Control Room. His fire-helmet was already on his head. (Sub Officer is one rank above a Leading Fireman and one rank below a Station Officer. Sub Officers had two chromium half-inch bars on their shoulders and their black fire-helmets displayed two red bands.)

The driver, Fireman Trevor Tailor, and the Sub Officer climbed aboard through their individual cab doors at the front. Their doors slammed shut.

Trevor was about forty. His blonde hair cut to no more than half an inch in length; cover his head like a field of standing corn. He brushed a hand constantly through this harvest in a repeated mannerism.

The engine roared into life. The engine house doors crashed open and in a second we were rolling forwards. I held on tight. The single blue light turned slowly on the roof as we chased off.

I watched as the other two members of the crew got dressed. The helmets went on first, and then arms were thrust into tunics. Sitting on the polished wood bench seats they yanked their shoes off before slotting each leg into their leather fire-boots.

"What's that you got on?" Barry shouted above the screaming engine.

"That thing on your head?"

My fire-helmet was already perched on my head. It resembled that of an ancient Roman soldier.

"Is that the best you can do? Good job its dark," Barry laughed.

Confused by all the rush and now feeling embarrassed, I dressed as best I could.

Our appliance hit the rush hour traffic. With siren wailing and bell sounding we darted in and out disturbing other traffic but avoiding it as easily as if we were in a dodgem car. Barry went forward into the cab, removing his helmet to reveal his tight red curls. He clambered through the two open sliding doors that separated us on the outside from those in the front cab.

"We're backing up Weaver Road Fire Station to a house fire in their station area," Sub Officer told Barry.

Weaver Road Fire Station was one of Torridge City's outer Fire Stations; its district stretched to the outskirts of the city. Our driver continued through busy traffic with the ease and aplomb of a man with great experience and confidence. The dark cold winter air rushed by, as we raced on. My two fellow crew-members stood on the narrow rear platform. Gripping onto handrails, their situation looked precarious as we swung from side to side. The passing scenery flashed by so fast it was difficult to be sure in which direction we travelled. At last we arrived, our bell still clanging but the noise of the siren petering out. Another fire-appliance, presumably from Weaver

Road Fire Station, stood outside a house. We pulled up alongside as firemen from the other appliance ambled down the garden path.

"Mickey," it had been a malicious fire-call they shouted.

All that rush and excitement for nothing!

On the journey back to the Station I felt drained. It had been so pointless and wasteful. Rest of the crew cursed anybody who made such calls.

"Here, wear this!" Barry said when we arrived back.

From one of the pegs in the muster-room he produced a modern helmet borrowed from one of the appliance drivers. Drivers, Barry told me, only wore flat caps and tunics when turning out and always left their fire-helmets behind. Now I looked like any other fireman.

The third day of my first tour on duty Wednesday did not bring another turnout. Fires, Barry tried to explain, did not come with any particular regularity.

"It's usually all or nothing," he said.

Our three weekdays on duty ended on Wednesday evening; our three nights began Thursday 1800 hours.

Barry advised me to bring some sheets to protect and cover the rough grey blankets, which were supplied when I first joined. A change of underwear was also recommended. I obediently brought these as he had suggested I should and stacked my spare clothing in the personal locker I was given. At every change of watch every appliance needed checking. Still working alongside Barry Bleck, I followed his every move like a lost lamb. We opened every locker door on the Pump Escape as our fifteen-hour night began.

After checking the appliances we had an hour's drill. It was a cold dark night, so we assembled inside and prepared to listen to an officer reading from the Manuals of Firemanship books. These were our gospel. First published in 1943 by the Home Office, each of the nine manuals covered every subject describing every aspect of the service in minute detail. The warmest room on the Station was the long-room. The open coke fire had been allowed to burn down, but strenuous efforts were made to load the fire up again with several buckets of coke, which crackled and spit as the flames slowly took hold. Sub Officer Gardon, who had thinning grey hair and a face with eyes that bulged out from his sockets, was designated to do the reading. Droning on a single note he began.

I sat with the rest of White Watch as the Sub Officer droned on, reading every word from the Manual of Firemanship Part, 6b. He regularly interrupted his reading by producing a small silver tin from inside of his uniform jacket. Taking a pinch of snuff between his thumb and first finger, he placed it first on the back of his wrist and inhaled the powder with gusto and relish. After these brief interludes he resumed, still reading in a boring manner. As he reached the bottom of the second page, the words 'eye-eye' went unnoticed. Page 'eye-eye-eye' caused a little amusement to those bothering to listen but when he reached page four, 'eye-v' caused uproar.

He ignored our laughter. Pausing to take more snuff, he carried on regardless. By the time he finished in his boring drone at seven o'clock, reaching 'eye x' (the Roman numerals) the reading session had proved entertaining if not educational.

Following the lecture we were allowed to stand down. Again I followed Barry closely, not knowing exactly what was expected.

"Stand down," he explained, "is the time left to us when all the routine work is completed."

Most of White Watch had disappeared. Some watched television, some played snooker and some sat around the coke fire. The warm and friendly atmosphere matched the heat from fire. By nine o'clock the fire glowed white hot making the room more like a games room than a place of work, and this was even more so when a sliding shutter door opened at nine o'clock to reveal a licensed bar.

"Don't drink on your first few nights," Barry advised.

Station Officer Finnan appeared for the first time since the parade only for the hour when the bar was open. He noticed the glass of lemonade in my hand and smiled in approval.

'Boots off' came at around midnight. My bed was in the main dormitory, itself a room converted from a wartime air raid shelter. I laid out my cotton sheets on the bed and covered them with the three grey blankets. The single metal-framed beds were positioned close together and covered with a horsehair mattress. The beds were so close together that you could easily reach out and touch your neighbour.

"You'll need your three blankets. It feels like another cold night," Barry told me.

I listened with one ear for the alarm bells, and it was a long time before I slipped into a shallow sleep.

I awoke sharply. Bells clanging and light from an electric bulb dragged me from my slumber. Men all around instinctively dropped their legs into their ready boxed-boots. Boxed-boots were made by feeding a pair of trousers over a pair of fire-boots leaving the tops open and ready for leaping into.

I was sleeping in my shirt and socks and underwear. I slotted both feet into my fire-boots, pulled up my trousers and with the braces over my shoulders I was dressed and ready. No one said a word while all this was going on.

I followed the others as we dashed from our dormitory outside down the street and finally into the muster-room. Most firemen slept well away from the engine house but Pump One crew always slept on portable beds in the muster-room and manned the appliance turning out regardless of any orders given during our parade at the beginning of the shift! It was considered faster and more efficient to have a crew sleeping immediately next to the engine house and our individual tallies so carefully positioned alongside the detailed appliances at 1800 hours was just ignored during sleeping hours. A practice, I was told, originating from the distant past when turnouts required harnessing the horses!

The Pump Two indicator light shone brightly from the board. The crew-members sleeping in the muster-room were already in the process of turning out. The appliance left the engine house, leaving behind it an empty bay thick with exhaust fumes.

We waited patiently in the muster-room for their return. At three o'clock in the morning I found myself struggling to stay awake. Yet still no one spoke.

Two of our officers, Sub Officer Gardon and Station Officer Finnan, eventually appeared from Brigade Control.

"Midden on fire, Mount Ribble Flats," Station Officer Finnan explained.

At last a rattle on the engine house doors signalled the return of Pump Two. Eager to learn about the turnout, I excitedly questioned a fireman but he only said.

"Time they got rid of those rubbish bins." It was an anti climax as everybody trailed off back to bed.

The dormitory now resumed its silence disturbed only by an occasional cough and the regular rhythm of someone snoring at the far end of the room. I was unable to drift off to sleep again listening to every noise. But I was startled as lights came on and bells started ringing. I was already awake and so I was into my fire-boots before anyone else moved. Amid groans of disbelief we all dashed out, ran outside and down the street taking us from the dormitory towards the main part of the Station, and once again lurched into the muster-room where we found that Pump One and Pump Escape were to go to a house fire.

For us, detailed as crew on Pump Two, it was our duty again to wait. During boots-off period we were the crew that did not turnout initially but were required to sit and wait in the muster-room in case of other turnouts.

We smelt the sweet cocktail of fire, which drifted when both crews eventually returned. The crews re-stocked their appliances, but still produced nothing by way of conversation.

"Teach them to smoke in bed," someone said, almost in passing.

Once more we all trailed off back to bed. When reveille arrived at six forty-five precisely I felt shattered. Disturbed nights, I discovered, were not easy. And with my first tour of duty ended there was still no exciting story to relate.

As our three days and three night's tours of duty multiplied, I felt more at ease. All the White Watch crew appeared friendly and I was able to put more names to faces as time progressed. It took time to meet everybody since someone was always on holiday, and with groups on leave spread across the whole calendar, it was rare to find the whole crew on duty at the same time.

As the new boy on White Watch I was fodder for practical jokes. Initiation ceremonies for new boys were common. As I had previously worked on building sites, such things were not entirely unknown to me. Now when going to the toilet I commonly expected objects to fly over the door. If the door was open then flying mops buckets or anything else to hand could be seen before they hit the unsuspecting stooge going about his business. One of the old hands on White Watch, with over seventeen year's service, Fireman Jeffrey Twaite, guided me through the maze of these potential hazards.

Jeffrey had served several years in the Royal Navy in submarines before joining the Fire Brigade all those years ago. Jeffrey's face was now tight and rarely broke into a smile.

"There are no such thing as toilet doors in submarines," he told me.

I was already reluctant to go to the toilet and such stories made me even more so. Should alarm bells sound, what was I to do? But long hours on duty meant there must be a time when nature called.

"If you really must go," Jeffrey warned, "then use the toilet nearest the engine house and keep the door open!" he added.

Jeffrey, a large framed man who was almost bald, had to believed. I took careful note of what he said. As nature called I selected the particular toilet he suggested and sat nervously with the door wide open. Nothing untoward happened. It was a little draughty but seemed safe from flying objects. However, I was to discover that I should not have believed him, for when the time came to pull the chain I first heard a muffled flushing noise and looked with horror at the basin as white creamy foam began to fill it to the brim. I watched with dismay as it began to overflow, but still the foam multiplied. It cascaded onto the floor, over the top of the basin and over the toilet-seat. A large creamy-white blanket spilled out of the cubicle and smothered everything in its path. Jeffrey, of course, just happened to be passing. A glint in his eyes and a large smile covered his face producing lines like creases in an old used shirt. Using two chemicals, aluminium sulphate and bicarbonate of soda, which were used in our foam extinguishers, he had placed one of the chemicals in the basin, and the other in the header tank. Brought together, they produced carbon dioxide gas and thick creamy foam.

As winter eased into spring tours of duty gathered momentum, turn-outs became a common place occurrence. At long last issued with a cap badge I slowly became an accepted member of White Watch.

As the daylight hours lengthened, the dread of attending Brigade Training School for the twelve weeks Recruits Course became a talking point for the members of the watch.

Training School, held at another of Torridge Stations, Ellen Approach Fire Station, was something to be feared. I heard rumours of the horrors of hook-ladders, of the exhausting and demanding breathing apparatus training and the dread of the carry down. All these terms were as yet unknown to me, and they were told with a good deal of intimidation and with a certain amount of glee and satisfaction.

Torridge City Fire Brigade adopted a policy of allowing recruits to serve three or four months on a Fire Station before being given this training. For these months we were watched carefully on the Station to see if we were made of the right material and were worthy of the cost of further training.

I suppose I must have passed this entry test since I was given May, just four months after joining, for my twelve weeks course.

As May came closer I became more and more familiar with station life. Arriving on duty early at 1730 hours, I changed into my uniform. At 1800 hours the usual parade and roll call designated me again as a crew-member on Pump Two. As I was opening every locker and accounting for every piece of listed equipment, the station bells sounded. Out of the small door from Brigade Control a woman appeared.

"Job Out, City centre. Off Washburn Street." Her voice was almost drowned by the sound of alarm bells.

"Another 999 coming in," she raised her voice.

The engines of Pump One, Pump Escape, and Turntable Ladder started, adding to the noise and excitement. Within seconds these three appliances shot out of the engine house. Their bays were left vacant. We closed all the engine house doors as residue from the exhaust of the appliances filled the engine house. Bells and sirens diminished in the distance as all three appliances disappeared down the street.

Prepared and dressed in our tunics and boots, and me still with the borrowed fireman's helmet in my hand, we gathered outside the Control Room door and waited. Sub Officer Gardon opened the Control Room door, forbidden territory for us, and went in. The tension grew as we peered through the crack of the open door.

At last one of the two women control officers grabbed a hand microphone. A garbled message spluttered through the radio system.

"From Station Officer Finnan at Washburn Street. Building well alight. Make Pumps five."

Make Pumps five meant additional appliances were needed at the fireground. With two Pumps already in attendance, the officer in charge requested a further three Pumps.

With siren wailing and with bells clanging our Pump Two, screaming in second gear, turned into Washburn Street, which was blocked by clouds of black, putrid smoke coming from a building at the far end of a block of shops.

This was to be my first experience of a large city centre fire.

Chapter 4

As we entered Washburn Street thick black smoke was belching out from a second floor window and then curling majestically upwards. Sitting on the back of our Pump Two, we had arrived at the scene of a major fire in response to a 'Make Pumps Five', a further call for assistance. The thick smoke blocked our path.

A Leading Fireman, wearing his black helmet with its single red-band around the rim, emerged from the smoke and ran towards us.

"Water! We need more water," he cried.

A length of delivery hose from a stand-pipe poking out from the centre of the road snaked in a large bight before connecting into the Pump Escape. This was one of the two appliances that had arrived at the scene, answering the initial call. The delivery hose was of sufficient diameter to enable firemen to transfer water in quantity from one place to another.

Station Officer Finnan, his white helmet tilted at a crazy angle, approached our Pump as we shuddered to a halt.

"Kevin. We need more water," he screamed to Sub Officer Gardon, the officer in charge of Pump Two who was sitting in the front cab.

"It's a wholesale paint store! The buildings are full of fuel just waiting to go up!" he continued.

"There are more Pumps coming. Try the 'fire-tank' down Swale Road!" These were the Station Officer's final words before he spun round and half-walked, half-ran back towards the smoke, which now engulfed everything in its path.

Our Pump Two, complete with its crew of four, lurched forward and bounced over a length of hose on the road. Several Firemen from the two appliances already in attendance scurried around. It looked totally confusing.

We raced down Washburn Street, past the front of the burning shop. The heat from the fire hit our faces like heat from an opened-oven door. The oil-based paint was already feeding the fire.

We jerked to a halt in Swale Road, and Sub Officer Gardon sat alongside our driver, Fireman Robert Ray who was in the front cab, climbed down after flinging open his door.

"The fire-tank-lid is somewhere around here," he said.

Fire-tanks were underground holes in the road. Built for war-time-blitz conditions, these specially built brick lined caverns were positioned close to large size city-water mains. There were over fifty such tanks dotted all over

Torridge City and their exact location often became a test question asked by the experienced firemen.

"That's it. Over there!" someone shouted, recognising a square steel lid in the middle of the road. Our Dennis F8 Pump Two stopped; it's rear-end sat over the lid.

"Tank lid keys, somebody?" came a query.

I knew what tank lid keys were, steel handles with a square end for fitting into a lid. There were stored in the nearside locker with rest of the water gear. Lifting the locker door and locking the safety catch which locked it in place; I reached inside for the two keys. Grabbing them I ran back to the fire-tank.

The driver of our appliance, Fireman Robert Ray and the Sub Officer struggled to get both keys into the two square holes in the lid. They were solid with grit; the handles would not fit.

"Float it off!" Robert suggested, his dark ginger hair falling over his eyes.

Suddenly a large dull explosion made us all look back to the fire. The paint shop front display window exploded. Large flying pieces of glass hung in the air refusing to fall. Hanging, almost floating they slowly crashed, then hit the road and bit into the lines of delivery hose. Dull muffled bangs echoed from within the fire, as further stocks of paint exploded. Flames fuelled by a sudden entrain of air escaped from the shattered window and water sprayed out from the damaged hose.

"Get this lid off!" Someone screamed.

With the inlet water valve for the tank turned on, air began to hiss out of the road surface around the edges of the lid. As air pressure built up inside the fire-tank, the hissing increased. Water seeped out. Then as the mains water filled the underground tank its lid gave way suddenly and ever so gently bobbed on the surface of the water. The lid was now loose and free, and a sideways push exposed the inside of the tank. Water oozed out from the chasm.

With guidance from our driver and crew I helped to fit two lengths of hard suction hose, stiff tubes with large brass screw fittings on each end, to the Pump inlet. A brass strainer screwed on to the end of the suction hose completed this part of the operation. Thick black tubing, looking like an elephant's trunk, now linked the water in the fire-tank to the Pump inlet.

The driver primed our pump, removing all the air from suction hose. Robert, the driver pushed the hand lever, situated next to the throttle lever, down firmly.

The engine laboured as the primer created a vacuum in the pump and the lengths of suction hose. With one end of the suction hose now underwater, all the air in the pump and suction hose was soon replaced by water from the fire-tank.

"Help me run out some hose." Robert panted. He peered at me through the strands of hair covering his eyes. Overwhelmed by all the commotion I followed him and did precisely what I was told.

We ran lengths of hundred-foot long and two and three-quarters inch in diameter delivery hose to the fire-ground. Joining several lengths of delivery hose together, we snapped the male and female brass couplings into each other until at last Pump Two, situated over two hundred yards away, and were finally connected to the Pump Escape positioned at the fireground. Robert ran back and opened the outlet valve on our Pump. The flat delivery hose swelled and expanded with the internal pressure. Water now filled our empty hose. Snaking and weaving, the delivery hose curled in large loops up the road. As I saw this happening a loud ringing bell disturbed me. I looked up.

A Turntable Ladder with a huge brass radiator at the front of a long bonnet with the word 'Leyland' in large letters charged towards us, up Swale Road. A large shiny brass bell hung from nearside of an open cab. The officer in charge, sitting on the left of the driver, shook the leather handle of the brass bell vigorously to clear a path for the arrival of a second Turntable Ladder.

"Get all this hose pulled to one side." I heard a shout and looked up to see a very senior officer indeed, the Assistant Chief Officer, Mr Carp. He was tall and thin and dressed in a flat uniform cap. His tunic, which had full chrome epaulettes on both shoulders, was unbuttoned.

"You, YOU, young 'laddie'," he shouted at me.

"You can be the monkey, laddie!"

I assumed he wanted me to climb on the ladder.

The Turntable Ladder stopped on the opposite side of the road. The driver dismounted from his open cab quickly and proceeded to lower the supporting jacks. I watched as he swung each of the four hinged jacks out, away from the body. They clanked against their stops. He placed a thick piece of wood underneath each steel foot and turned the handles to let the four supporting feet down to the road surface. Finally he tightened each of the four jacks, and expertly turned all the screw handles until the heavy Turntable Ladder rested evenly on the road surface.

"Get yourself a belt" he said to me gruffly. The driver looked old, and the ordeal of bringing this monster of a fire-engine from Weaver Road Fire Station, which was a good six miles away, had obviously taken a great deal of physical effort.

This particular type of turntable table ladder, a 'Leyland Merryweather', was one in the UK distributed by the Home Office at the beginning of World War 2. Previously these Leyland appliances had Metz (German) ladders fitted but on the onset of War, English manufactured Merryweather ladders were commissioned.

Under the seat I found a thick belt with black and red stripes and with a large hook attached to it. The belt supported two sets of straps and buckles and took a few seconds to be tightened and fitted around my waist.

The self-supporting ladder was elevated, lifting away from the housed gantry and extended, shooting upwards. Its head continued to be extended until it stopped high above the road, and positioned away from the burning building. I glanced at the blazing shop. Radiated heat hit us from the fire just twenty yards away. Black heavy smoke enclosing ribbons of red flame curled upwards from the broken windows.

I was now belted and dressed and ready to climb up the ladder. The delivery hose supplied from a nearby Pump snaked around the base of the Turntable Ladder and went straight up to the top. It swelled as it filled with water.

"Wait until the water arrives at the top of the ladder," the driver told me, "then walk up slowly. If it gets too hot, stop and come down. But if you get to the top, fasten yourself with the hook."

I accepted every word without question. I knew it was dangerous to propel a man up to a fire on an extending ladder. Hidden pockets of heat and unseen objects made it far safer to climb the ladder after it was in position.

I experienced difficulty at first as I climbed from the four-foot high operator's platform to the base of the ladder. I swung myself out before I could catch hold of the sides of the ladder. Once I was on the ladder, the rungs were not easy to find. The delivery hose running up the ladder snaked and zigzagged over its whole width, making it difficult to climb. From the base of the ladder each of its four extensions narrowed. I struggled upwards until I reached the head of the ladder.

On the last and the final extension, the ladder narrowed to shoulder width. I located a small ring, but I needed to lean in close to allow the hook on my belt to fit on to it. Leaning out and waving at the driver operator below, I indicated I was now hooked in position. A voice squeaked into life from a round metal canister below my left shoulder.

"Drop the platform and show your heels," the driver told me.

I looked at my feet. A steel platform was bolted to the side of the ladder next to my left boot. I undid the bolt and as I moved my feet in turn the platform at last fell into position. Now standing on the platform, both my heels stuck out and were visible to the driver below.

This indicated to the operator below that my toes were safe. Should the ladder need to be extended or lowered; my toes remained free and would not be trapped in any moving parts. The driver began to train, or turn, the ladder. It jerked to the right and turned closer to the building.

A jet of water shot out of the brass nozzle at the top of the ladder and crackled as the air trapped inside was forced out and forwards under pressure. Water leaked from the joint on the nozzle and trickled back down a large wooden handle. The large handle provided ample vertical movement but allowed only a small movement to the sides.

Fastened securely, seventy foot up in the air, the ladder slowly moved closer over the fire. Water shot out from the head of the ladder as I experimented by moving the large wooden control handle up and down.

I could see firemen scurrying about on the ground below. Huge crowds of spectators had gathered in the street. The police were trying to marshal the crowds away from the danger. Fire appliances, looking like small red toys, stood together. The roads were glossy with water.

A slight rumble drew my eyes back to the fire. Smoke percolated through every seam in the slate roof tiles which were still intact. The noise reached a crescendo, but still it increased. The roof began to move. Slowly, almost too slowly, slates began to peel away, sliding down before reaching the guttering and flying off to the ground below. A single flame pierced the gaps left by the disappearing slates. Suddenly, without warning, half the roof caved inwards. More slates slid off over the edge and hurtled to the ground. I could only watch as the Firemen below, alerted by the rumbling from inside the building, and ran from the now impending danger.

I felt the stab of hot air strike my face. A squeaky voice crackled through the communication system.

"All right," it asked. I muttered that it was getting hot.

The ladder now trained to the left and slowly edged away from the roof. Flames shot out from the open roof and almost immediately a gush of hot air struck the side of my face. Water, now leaking from the nozzle, was very welcome; it kept my face cool.

The ladder was trained back once more over the fire. I looked down.

Assistant Chief Fire Officer Carp, now dressed in a black helmet with a chrome rim and a big black oil-skin knee length jacket and green waders, made his way slowly up the ladder which flexed and dipped slightly back and forth as his additional weight altered its balanced position.

"What's your name, laddie?" he asked when he reached the top. I told him.

"Now Fairn," he said shouting to be heard above the noise of the water jet shooting out in front of us and climbing higher. He forced me forwards against rungs of the ladder.

"Keep that jet of water on that adjoining wall. The shop and building have gone." His words spilled out.

"We have to stop it spreading next door." He stood close behind me, pressing me tight against the ladder and breathing on my neck under the rear brim of my helmet.

"Forget about the flames. Just keep that jct of water hitting that wall."

I tried to turn round to see his face, but we were too close to each other. His hands gripped both sides of the ladder, pinning me down. Thinking I was doing so well by attacking the flames, I had never thought of preventing the fire spreading.

After studying the area the Assistant Chief began his climb back to the ground. He parted from me with words of encouragement.

"You're doing all right," he said, his words tailing off as he descended.

The roof had now gone completely and each floor followed in rapid succession. Debris showered all around. Bricks, slates, wooden beams all crashed many landing onto the street below. My jet of water continued to pour from seventy foot up on to the adjoining wall.

The leak from the nozzle continued. A trickle of water ran down the inside of my tunic sleeve, down my trouser leg, and finally into my left boot. Shuffling to one side only filled my right boot. As daylight turned slowly to dusk I was still directing the water jet onto the adjoining wall. Some water even went down some of the chimney pots on the next building; scarred by fire, they looked like massive salt and pepper cruets. Gallons of water from my jet continued to drench the party wall. Eventually the jet lost its pressure as the water was finally turned off.

"You can come down now," the speaker crackled and the words were welcome.

"You've been up that ladder nearly three hours!" The driver greeted me as I reached terra firma at last. I was wet, cold and stiff.

"Good job. Well done lad!" He told me.

Chief Officer Bass, in charge of the whole incident, sent a stop message, indicating that no further appliances or assistance were required, by radio to the Brigade Control.

This large City centre fire was considered serious enough to warrant our Chief, Assistant Chief, eight Pumps, and two Turntable Ladders being involved. Ten Pumps were the maximum Torridge City could muster. Any more appliances had to be called from outside Torridge City, but this was never encouraged. It cost money for another Fire Brigade to give assistance, and anyway calling for such outside help was an admittance of defeatism.

The shell of the building, where the fire had been, steamed and died. It was gaunt and dead, but the surrounding property had been saved from the fire, which was prevented from spreading. Now the long damping-down procedure commenced.

Sub Officer Gardon found me and explained that Pump Two and its crew were to return to the Station for a quick change of clothing.

Since the Pump Two we turned out with originally was still connected to the fire-tank we found another appliance, and returned to our Fire Station. We washed, changed our underwear, and donned fresh trousers and dry fire-tunics as well as a fresh pair of fire-boots. After a gulp of hot sweet tea we were back at the fire within the hour, our glory now long gone.

The huge crowd, which had gathered to witness our battle, had now dispersed, and the unenviable task of damping down for the next few hours began.

The building was completely gutted. The front wall had collapsed completely. The rear and one of the sides was severely damaged, but the shop on one side looked intact. Protection from my jet from the Turntable Ladder had perhaps helped in some way and stopped the spreading fire. From my position high above the fire-ground I had witnessed tremendous team-work as the crews below gained control over such a major incident. As more supplies of water were obtained, the sheer workload and the strenuous effort carried out by all was a credit to everyone involved.

Heat from the body of the shop, which had been destroyed, was considerable. Most of the roof and upper floors had collapsed into the cellar, where steam from the jets of water aimed into the cellar indicated there were pockets of fire hidden beneath the tons of rubble.

Midnight passed and still, four Pumps with twenty men remained, carrying out damping-down duties. We continued to pour gallons of water into the steaming cellar before being relieved at 0430 hours. We returned to

Torridge City Station, tired and wet. Our Pump Two, which had been rescued at last from its position at the fire-tank, needed re-equipping with clean delivery hose. Every length of delivery hose which had been used at a fire needed washing before it was hung up to dry in the heated hose tower. This would be done later since our Station carried sufficient lengths of spare hose to re-equip each of the Pumps twice over. The appliance also needed to be filled with petrol and to be washed down before anyone could relax.

In the early morning hours it took some coaxing for us to move our aching bones and weary bodies. It had been a long, long night. I had a glimpse into the amount of hard work and courage that Firemen had to have. When they were called on, they performed without hesitation.

Arriving home that morning after the end of my long night on duty at 0900 hours, being able to slide between clean sheets into a comfortable bed was shear pleasure. For a few seconds the excitement of the night was re-enacted before the pull of unconsciousness dragged me into a deep and welcome sleep.

On the next night and back on duty, all members of our watch retold own stories and relived the night of our large fire. Morale on the Station increased noticeably. A busy Station is a happy one, I learned.

With my bulging kit bag filled with two pairs of boots, tunics, a borrowed chrome axe, overalls, uniform cap, undress jacket and trousers, it was time for me to attend Brigade Training School at Ellen Approach Station. Sadly I parted company with White Watch; I had been working with them for four months. I hoped to be back if I could pass the rigours and pitfalls of the Training School requirements.

Chapter 5

Snivelling-Monday arrived.

It was my first day at Training School. Torridge City Fire Brigade Training School was situated at Ellen Approach Fire Station, and provided facilities for the training of recruits for Torridge and also for the surrounding County Borough Fire Brigades.

Thirty-six of us cowered beneath a glass canopy, sheltering from the incessant drizzle.

We met the Assistant Divisional Officer, the Commandant of the Training School and three Sub Officers; all four were to grill and drill us for the next twelve weeks.

One rank above a Station Officer, Assistant Divisional Officer Grayling his uniform cap pressed firmly on his head, marched amongst us. His three large impellers on each shoulder looked like six steel nipples pointing up. An impeller was a distinction used in all officers' rank markings. It was the size of a large button and one of its features was taken from the internal workings of the Fire Service water pumps.

He looked kind, almost benign. He stood tall, smart and erect in his immaculate uniform. We shuffled nervously, straining to get our first glimpse of the full entourage of training officers.

Sub Officer Roach, the second in command, carried the reputation of being a tyrant. This reputation was fuelled by rumours that he was a no-nonsense man and a strict disciplinarian. His military service record was exemplary, and the mere thoughts of being taught by the loudest drill Sergeant ever, sowed seeds of fear and dread in us. On his left stood Sub Officer Hussar who was rumoured to be an eccentric professor, with idiosyncrasies that burdened on the insane. On his square face, under his thin pointed nose, he sported a pencil-lined moustache. His head repeatedly jerked rapidly to the right.

Two paces behind these three stood Sub Officer Brill, younger and new to the Training School. Until recently he had been a Leading Fireman on Torridge City Station's Blue Watch. He had taken this new position in order to reach the second rung on the promotion ladder. With a grin that grew and creased his cheeks he seemed young, and almost out of place compared with the rest of the ancient instructors standing in front of him. Suddenly the snivelling Monday sky blubbered. Raindrops the size of glass beads rattled and bounced off the floor of the drill yard. I stood nervously with the rest of the squaddies, taking shelter from the deluge. I extracted my bulging kit bag from the enormous pile, which looked like elephant seals mating under the glass canopy.

Twelve of the thirty-six recruits like me were from the City of Torridge. The other twenty-four were from other City Fire Brigades. Their respective Brigades paid the fees for their own recruits. These fees helped to finance the running costs of the school. Of the five recruits who had enrolled with me in January only two now remained. Many men joined the Fire Brigade, but other employment was easy to obtain, often with better pay and no night work, so most of them did not last through the three months induction period.

"What's this? You look like a flock of shaggy sheep!"

Sub Officer Roach's voice boomed at us. One point of the rumours proved correct.

"Get fell in outside on the drill ground."

Like sheep we shuffled into the deluge.

"YOU, YOU" he screamed at someone close to me.

"Yes, YOU!" he yelled even louder.

"Stand here. The rest of you fall in alongside!"

"This is a uniformed and disciplined service." His voice rose louder and louder. We moved obediently into position.

"From the right, dress!"

We shuffled into position. I looked and at those who knew and copied them. My arm was outstretched and my knuckles touched those of the next fireman to the right.

"Open order, march!"

The men alongside me stepped forward one pace. Belatedly I copied them.

"Right. Your names?"

Roach marched along the line. His shoes gleamed; his uniform was smart, immaculate. The rank markings of a Sub Officer sparkled with the raindrops that dropped from his uniform cap onto his shoulders. As each of us answered to our name he looked at his list and detailed our squad colour and our instructor.

"Fairn," Sub Officer Roach shouted in my left ear, "you're in Red Squad."

Sub Officer Brill, one pace behind Roach, grasped a brown cardboard box whose lid deepened in colour as rain soaked into the lid.

Tilting the lid to protect the contents, he presented each of us with a small metal tally, which he removed carefully from the box. This was our personal identification number for the duration of the course and was to be worn at all times. As I unclipped the safety pin and struggled in the wet to locate the clasp I noticed the number ten in flaking blue and painted roughly on the well-used disc.

Assistant Divisional Officer Grayling was at attention patiently waiting in front of the line of bedraggled men. Rain still drummed down from a heavy sky.

"My name is Assistant Divisional Officer Grayling," he began.

His uniform cap positioned with precision and perfectly level, supported a small puddle on its top. Growing with every drop of rain, the puddle threatened to overflow.

"The reputation of your Brigade is at stake," his voice went on, soft and delicate. Straining to hear, I expected at any moment that the water would cascade all over him.

"During the next twelve weeks you will pass or fail. If you pass you'll be a basic fireman. If you fail you'll be a civilian again looking for another job."

He turned smartly to the left and marched away. In total defiance of all normal rules of gravity the pool of water never moved off the top of his cap as he disappeared from our sight.

"Fall out!" Sub Officer Roach shouted.

We turned to our right and shuffled like wet rats from the soaked drill ground; we were now to collect our kit bags. With steam rising from our sodden bodies we entered the corridor and went to our lockers. We passed a large glass fronted notice board on the way.

"Study this notice board at all times," Sub Officer Roach suddenly stopped us and ordered.

Those at the front, keen and eager suddenly halted. Those of us following behind then crashed into each other. Our heavy bulky kit bags fell with a damp thud to the floor.

"By reading it you will find exactly what you should be doing and what you must wear." He marched on.

Looking through the glass panel we strained to see our instructions and to learn the details of every lesson in the first week.

For all drill sessions we were to be in flat caps, tunics and boots. Walking-out uniform, the so-called undress uniform, was to be worn at meal times and for classroom lectures, and during the morning and afternoon break times. Routines and cleaning periods were to be carried out in overalls and flat caps. With precise organisation, no two sessions followed which required the same dress. Every change meant a dash to our lockers to re-dress in the appropriate gear and a mad dash back again.

Every morning would begin on the drill ground with an hour's squad-drill; we had to be dressed in overalls, shoes and flat caps. There was something special every Wednesday morning, requiring us to be dressed in our best tunics, flat caps, polished leather boots, belt and axe. On that day every week, Assistant Divisional Officer Grayling would inspect us.

Picking our kit bags up again, we all left the all-important notice and went to the locker room. We changed quickly from our soaking clothes into dry overalls. By the end of our first day any dry clothes were now thoroughly soaked as a result of constantly changing in and out of wet uniforms.

"Quick. Quick," a voice, now easily recognisable, barked at us again and again.

Recruits from all the visiting Brigades slept at the school in dormitories converted from rooms, which served as lecture rooms during the day. As favoured Torridge City men, we were allowed home for the night. For this privilege we were given extra cleaning routines to be carried out before we left. We also provided waiter service, dishing out the meagre food allowance to the school of hungry recruits.

The first day over, I arrived home damp but still keen. I thought Mother would be keen to hear my story. But she had retreated into one of her silent moods. Her full history remains an enigma, even now. She never discussed the reason we came to England when she was struggling, heavily pregnant with me. Although she still retained an accent, she otherwise spoke and understood English perfectly. Occasionally, especially when she was upset, she chattered away to herself in German, but she always insisted that I spoke English. Regardless of many taunts and racial abuse, she worked hard taking in washing, cleaning, and doing anything to make enough money for basic living. She never complained.

The Fire Brigade wages meant a drop in my weekly wage packet from my previous job, but I gave her all I had. Mother and I were very close. I understood how she felt, sat and ate my dinner on my own.

Day two. The rain still poured down from a dark miserable sky. Morning parade was followed by an hour of marching. Dressed in the appropriate rig as detailed on the notice board overalls, flat uniform cap, we were subjected to more shouting from Sub Officer Roach and to another soaking from the relentlessly crying sky.

Louder and louder the commands kept coming.

"You are a complete shambles! Stand in line!" Roach's face grew crimson with rage.

Marching and squad drill was new to me. Pressure was on those who served their national service to bring rest of us, born too late for compulsory conscription, into line. The Fire Service followed the Navy for the style of saluting, standing to attention and marching. Our undress uniform with double-breasted buttons down the front was also similar in colour and design to that worn by some Navy personnel.

We were told that 'Squad Shun!' meant that we must stand with our heels together and feet turned out at an angle of forty-five degrees. Our knees were to be straight, our bodies erect, and heads up. Shoulders were to be level and square to the front. The palms of both hands had to be turned and positioned towards the thighs with the hands partially closed the thumb close to the forefinger. We were to look straight ahead.

When we were to stand at ease, we were to move the left leg twelve inches to the left, put our hands behind the back with the back of one hand in the palm of the other and grasped lightly with the fingers and thumb. This allowed both arms to hang easily at their full extent.

We tiptoed through the Fire Service Drill Book, learning to stand easy, number off, size a squad and to take each pace the correct length. We marched in quick time, in slow time; we stood and marked time. We marched in a squad. We had to do all this with precision and detail.

Those of us who were inexperienced and found difficulty with the marching held a broom handle which reached to the man in front. These were issued to co-ordinate the left leg and right arm, and resembled connecting rods from steam engines. A distant noise of railway engines puffing away came from within the ranks. This was not appreciated.

"If I find the man responsible for these childish noises, he will be playing trains permanently," Sub Officer Roach screamed at us.

Our first Wednesday arrived. The rain ceased at last. In full dress uniform of fire-tunics, fire-boots, belt, firemen's axe and flat uniform caps, we were ready for our full inspection. This was to be taken by Assistant Divisional Officer Grayling.

Every detail of our appearance was minutely inspected. In anticipation our hats were brushed and their peaks gleamed, our tunics were pressed, our buttons were clean and shiny and even the Torridge City coat of arms insignias on the buttons needed to be correctly aligned. Our belts were polished, the buckles expected to shimmer. Axes were held at arms' length, the handle bleached white and the axe head polished to shine like glass. Our trousers had to have knife-edge sharp creases and our boots had to be polished to resemble mirrors.

On that first Wednesday, most of our standards were well below requirements. I glanced down the line of recruits as the Assistant Divisional Officer and Sub Officer Roach, his notepad and pencil at the ready, stopped at each man in turn. Every item found not up to standard was noted and our numbers were taken.

Eventually they stood in front of me.

"Is that a borrowed axe?" Grayling asked.

My bright chromed fireman's axe, held proudly out in front, was indeed borrowed. Prior to training school one of old hands back on the Fire Station had lent me his specially treated axe to save me time in endless hours trying to bring the normal dull metal surface of the axe blade to that of a mirror.

"Where is your identification tally?"

There was no identification tally fastened to my tunic.

"Take Fairn's number, Sub Officer."

"What is your number?" Roach screamed. He wrote down 'ten' for further punishment.

Assistant Divisional Officer Grayling was not pleased at what he had seen. Things would have to improve. Those who had their numbers taken would suffer extra cleaning duties.

Classroom and a lecture always followed the morning squad drill and required yet another change of clothing. The lecture room was cramped for the thirty-six of us and thus created another mad rush to change from one set of clothes to another and to get a decent seat. From my schooldays I knew that there was always less chance of questions being directed to those at the front, than those sat at the back. I carefully made for an unpopular front seat.

"All change," 'Professor' Hussar announced as he entered the class room to give us his first lecture, following an hour's squad drill and change of clothes from overalls to undress uniform.

"Sit as per your recruit numbers starting at the back of the room," he jerked his head sideways. So I found myself seated at the back of the classroom after all the pushing and moving of chairs. He began his first lesson on hydraulics.

For as long as I could remember I had struggled with sums and arithmetic. Now all the dreaded rules and formulas from my schooldays were resurrected. He mumbled on, his voice always at the same level, and boring. He brought a pile of old notes to every lecture and read every sheet of paper from top to bottom. He then turned each tatty sheet and kept them, no doubt for the next recruits' course. When and only when, the final sheet of paper had been read carefully from top to bottom did he finish his lecture.

To add colour to these dreary proceedings, the recruit who sat on my left suggested we counted the amount of twitches he made in any given lecture. At each jerk he jolted his face to the right. His right cheek was screwed up and folds of skin were creased to form a hideous mass of wrinkles from his hairline to his cheekbone.

"Forty-three!" I counted.

After the lecture we changed once more into the correct attire and went back onto the drill ground. This brought relief as classroom theory gave place to practical exercises. Tuesdays and Thursdays were the nights for the Torridge City men to perform menial tasks, our tasks for the concession to being allowed to go home every night. We had to clean every floor, working on our hands and knees; even the Fireman's friend, the mop and bucket was considered too easy. We also had to polish every brass fitting in sight and make them gleam.

One of the floors we had to polish was in the canteen area, which was also part of the operational station. The operational canteen man on duty, Fireman Chevin, knew our routine and offered us assistance secretly. Kenneth 'Gripper' Chevin was a legend in the Brigade and well known through the efficient grapevine that transmitted all snippets of gossip. He was known to be strong, as befitted an ex-boxer. Strangely he spoke in a high, squeaky voice, but we trusted him in spite of this.

"Someone needs to keep a look out," he sang to us with a glint in his eye as he produced a mop and bucket to make our task easier. In no time the floor was mopped and cleaned to perfection.

Sub Officer Roach was certainly not impressed when he returned suddenly, unannounced. He emptied the contents of our mop bucket onto the floor and stood hovering as we cleaned the floor again, this time by hand.

As that first week continued, we began basic hose running. All drills in the Fire Brigade Drill Manual were explained in detail. Each individual crew-member was given a number; numbers did everything. Numbers, we were told was essential to enable each man to perform a specific task.

Working through the official drill book, basic delivery hose drills began. The delivery hose was made from a heavy canvas outer skin and lined with thick rubber. Although it was only twenty-feet in length it weighed over forty pounds. The male coupling at one end and the female coupling at the other were made of solid brass. Cleaned to look like gold, we were told that these couplings were not to be thought of as brass, but of glass!

Changing numbers at every drill, we each learned to ship a standpipe. We removed the steel hydrant lid, screwed the large clumsy brass standpipe on the screw thread onto the water main, ran out three lengths of hose, fitted a large size nozzle into the female outlet and shouted the order 'water on'.

When we were given the order to Knock Off and Make Up, we rolled the hose back into a neat Swiss roll, unshipped the standpipe, replaced the hydrant lid and stored all the equipment neatly on the drill ground. Rubber lined hose was never designed to be neat and it always looked untidy.

As the crew's number one, I reported to Sub Officer Brill.

"Drill completed, Sir," indicated we had completed our allotted task.

"Carry on number one," Brill ordered.

I ran smartly back to join the other crew-members.

"Hose not rolled up properly. Roll it up again!" His smile, was it deceptive?

After another try the end result looked no better, but the second attempt seemed to satisfy him.

As the first week ended, Assistant Divisional Officer Grayling's parting speech did not give a very good picture of our performance. Things would have to improve, he announced.

The weekend, free of Training School restrictions, gave a welcome breathing space to the numbers game and to the strict regime, with someone watching and criticising every movement.

With an effort I attended the second week. My dread of another eleven weeks of such painfully slow instruction and unquestioning blind obedience brought grave doubts whether I should continue. I was bored. Already having served on a busy operational Fire Station and riding to fires and incidents, I had experienced the job at first hand. I had lived and ate with firemen who, for the first time in my life, treated me as an equal. Because of this I did find sufficient reasons to continue.

All the equipment we trained with was old and obsolete. Scaling ladders, sixty foot wheeled escape ladders, trailer pumps, all were unknown in modern Fire Stations. Wartime appliances, more suitable for a museum than for modern day instruction, often struggled to get themselves out of the drill shed. One old Leyland Pump Escape, with an open cab and a heavy sixty-foot wheeled escape ladder, perched on its back, needed hand starting every morning. Plenty of volunteers raced forward to wind the starting handle and show their strength, only to find the compression from its six, cylinder; longstroke engine was too much to turn. Usually this farce concluded by all hands push-starting the monster into life.

In the classroom, under the auspices of our Sub Officers, we recorded pages and pages of information on the size, construction, and manufacture of ladders, hose and pumps, all in minute detail.

"The outer rims of the large wooden carriage or coach wheels, that carried the fifty and sixty-foot escapes, were made from wych-elm, the hubs in oak, and the spokes and felloes made from ash." I diligently recorded every precious word.

Once again in the prescribed dress on the drill ground, the numbers game continued. Detailed crew-numbers, which were changed until everyone eventually, had done each task in the drill.

Yet another ancient appliance, a 1940 Leyland Cub Pump, appeared on the drill ground. Twelve of us were divided into three groups of four.

I shouted my appropriate crew-number, three.

"Number One crew fall in!"

We ran smartly, positioning ourselves three paces away, facing the rear of the appliance as we were ordered.

"Mount!" was the order.

As instructed we climbed aboard the appliance smartly.

Number One in the left hand front seat. Number two in the driver's seat. Number three and four sat in the rear. Then came the order.

"Change round!"

Number one jumped out from the nearside front, crashing his door behind him and climbed in the rear to become number three. Number two jumped out from his driving position, ran around the front of the appliance, opened the door, climbed aboard and slammed the door shut, becoming number one.

Number three shuffled across the cab seat and became number four. Number four jumped out from his position, opened the driver's door and became number two, closing yet another door with a bang.

This ritual of changing round from different positions and slamming doors must have been some use to somebody somewhere, but from our viewpoint as we charged from seat to seat it was hard to see any practical benefit derived from it!

But not all drills were of such poor quality. Wet drills when we used water were more realistic, and climbing ever-higher ladders gave us more confidence, which increased as the ladders got higher.

Our third week began, and we started the dreaded introduction to the hook-ladder.

A wooden hook-ladder was carried easily by one man from the drill shed and placed carefully on the ground in front of us. It looked simple in design. It was thirteen feet nine inches in length and weighed thirty pounds. From head of the ladder a large hook hinged out and locked in position. Sub Officer Brill picked up the ladder placed the protruding hook on to the first floor window-sill of the drill tower. The ladder hung only by its hook. Leaning away from the wall he proceeded to climb the ladder. His outstretched arms relayed his weight through his feet to the toe-pieces, two small protruding metal brackets on the bottom of the ladder. It looked anything but safe.

Sub Officer Brill climbed with confidence and entered the first floor window. Feeding the hook-ladder upward through his hands to the next window-sill, the ladder was suspended, once more, from its single hook. Climbing out of the window he scaled the ladder and entered the room on the second floor; his technique was impressive and he returned to the ground just as easily as he had gone up.

My first attempt was disastrous. The ladder swung off to one side.

"Your arms ought to act as if they are made of string!" The Sub Officer said, his grin just managing to part his lips.

The hook-ladder fulfilled its reputation. As our squad took it in turns to copy the excellent example of the Sub Officer we found the hook-ladder was a difficult piece of equipment to master. Most of the other drills involved working as a member of a crew, and if things went wrong the whole crew was suspect. But the hook-ladder relied on the individual to perform correctly. It was regarded on Fire Stations as not a practical piece of equipment but only as a training tool; anyone who could climb hook-ladders could climb anything.

For a brief period I was no longer bored and looked forward to the sheer challenge of hook-ladders. But this surge of interest did not last long. Both in the classroom and on the drill ground things progressed far too slowly. With so much effort placed upon detail, with our constant changing into different dress and with the evening cleaning routines which had to meet such high standards, any useful knowledge became lost among the mass of trivia.

Occasionally, however we were given examples of real dangers.

For one of these, Sub Officer Brill organised a session away from the prison compound of the drill yard and took us to a small stream. Two lengths of delivery hose from the delivery outlets of the pump ran out along the grass bank and were left unmanned. Water from the stream was boosted through a trailer-pump, which allowed the pressure to increase until the nozzle outlet thrashed about. Like a venomous snake's head it banged and thrust itself against the ground. Its full weight and power demonstrated the danger of being hit as the nozzle thudded in anger on the grass. Sub Officer Brill proceeded to tame the nozzle by following the line of the delivery hose from the pump. He crawled towards the raging outlet, and as he slowly crept towards it the thrashing decreased. Reaching the outlet he obtained full control, and although he got thoroughly wet in the process he tamed the angry python.

This was a splash of colour during a dreary six weeks.

We were half the way through the course, and the ordeal of revising for the midway examinations loomed.

Chapter 6

Slowly, painfully slowly, the weeks dragged by.

We faced the prospect of the halfway examinations and of another late Thursday when we stayed back to do the cleaning. The work was not hard but it was boring, tedious and only completed when the clock reached 1830 hours. All training school brasses, standpipes, hose-couplings, stored in the Training school drill hall needed to be regularly polished, until the finish looked like gold.

To demonstrate the application of 'Brasso', the metal polish, which was a fireman's constant accessory, our tyrant Sub Officer Roach, took time to rub and polish a single hose coupling.

"The trick of using Brasso is the actual putting on the liquid and rubbing it in," he told us, his hand working a Brasso dampened-rag on the coupling until a black wet gunge completely covered the surface. Left to dry, it became a white-grey powder, which rubbed off to reveal a glistening coupling. This was an example for us to copy.

"I'll be back in an hour," he promised. He walked away leaving shelves stacked high with brass implements with which to follow his example and reach his standard.

All the old appliances used for our instruction and drill were stored in the Training School drill hall. Among these ancient training school fire appliances stood several Home Office Green Goddess appliances, gathering dust. Kept in case of a future nuclear war and manned by volunteer auxiliary firemen, and firewomen, several of these green painted appliances were stored bumper to bumper along a rear wall. There was so little room that all the Training School Appliances competed for any available space.

Both our old Pump Escapes appliances carried wheeled escape ladders, their large carriage wheels hanging high and free and turned round easily. We were bored as we waited for the belated return of Sub Officer Roach.

"Spin the wheel," someone suggested. It was a daring challenge to occupy our time. The technique was to hold onto these large wheels by both arms, with legs wide apart. The hands gripped the spokes of the wheels; the legs were pressed firmly against the inside rim. The wheel was sent spinning; the greatest number of revolutions decided the winner. The challenge began, but one of the Green Goddesses was parked too close to another for its large carriage wheels to spin freely.

"Move it," someone suggested.

As quick as lightning I leaped into the cab, released the hand brake and with a big heave by willing hands, the green appliance lurched forward. I slammed on the foot brake only to find the pedal going flat to the cab floor. The appliance had not been used for some time and there was no air in the braking system. Before I could pull on the hand brake the machine kissed the wall.

Sub Officer Roach, as if by magic appeared at that moment. Examining the front mudguard for damage, he glowered at me.

"Another mark against you, number ten. Report to Assistant Divisional Officer Grayling, Fairn," he warned, able to put a name to my number as I emerged from the cab of the Green Goddess.

With the training course at the halfway stage, the Breathing Apparatus lectures began. Giving us the history of men wearing protection against smoke at fires, Sub Officer Hussar demonstrated an early example. From an old wicker basket he produced a pair of leather bellows, a big red mask and a length of canvas covered rubber tubing. Men outside and well away from the fire worked the bellows, forcing fresh air through the tubes to the recipient wearing the hood inside a fire and relying on this help. He passed the heavy leather red painted copper riveted mask around for us all to examine. I pulled the hood over my face. The inside stank of stale prehistoric air.

There had been some improvements since those days and the oxygen Proto Mark Five, with a supply lasting for an hour, was to be our main training example of modern breathing apparatus. Carried operationally on many of our appliances in Torridge City Fire Brigade, Proto sets were considered by many of the older firemen to be far superior to the new, recently acquired, compressed air-sets.

The Proto Mark Five weighed twenty-seven pounds and pressed heavily on the shoulders on two leather straps.

A large rubber bag lay on the chest and the black-oxygen cylinder dug into the base of one's back. The set was completely enclosed, and supplies of oxygen entered the system from a cylinder containing compressed oxygen. A reducing valve allowed oxygen under high pressure to flow gently into the set. The wearer's exhaled breath entered into a rubber bag containing soda lime, which absorbed the carbon dioxide.

A sealed canister containing calcium chloride helped to reduce the temperature of the hot exhaled breath before the wearer breathed in again through a mouthpiece.

The set was regularly taken to pieces ritually, and every last washers, spring, nut and bolt was removed, examined and re-assembled. Great emphasis was placed upon the workings of the reducing valve and the exact and precise diameter of the hole, which held back the spring and controlled the oxygen's entry into the chamber under high pressure. This we were informed was very, very important. Thirteen and a half thousands of an inch, we dutifully recorded this vital information!

As the mid-way examinations loomed our brains became filled to capacity with knowledge. I struggled to transfer the painfully memorised knowledge into written answers as we sat for a whole day in the classroom. Questions from the blackboard bombarded me. No one failed, however as the results, posted on the notice board, showed. In fact, some bright spark achieved ninety-nine percent. My name bounced off the bottom in theory but was towards the top in practical drills.

This was a cause for celebration and a night out. Never slow to indulge in drunken revelry, and since it was not one of our nights for extra routines, I dashed home, gulped down the meal Mother had prepared in record time, returned and waited for the rest of the course members at the local public house. Two drinks in front.

As our pints went down the atmosphere became more congenial and the desire to have had better examination results became obscured beneath an alcoholic screen.

"What's a one-man band look like?" Someone asked.

I thought everyone must have seen a one-man band.

"I've never seen one. What do they look like?" Someone insisted.

I began to describe thus showing off my expert knowledge about how the different instrument was positioned.

To demonstrate the cymbals between the knees, I knocked my legs together. To show a mouth organ between the lips, I imitated blowing imaginary notes, complete with noises to match. With a big mythical drum on my back I swung my arms and made a drum noise as I pretended to have a hand held trumpet held out in front. Before I knew it I was strutting up and down the aisles between tables, doing the appropriate actions and making the noises. The room exploded in hearty laughter. Unknowingly I was the centre of a bet.

"I can get him to strut up and down prank."

I saw bets being paid out.

With the part of the twelve-week course now behind us, the final weeks crept on. Like a breath of fresh air, the welcome arrival of Assistant Divisional Officer Stanley Gudgeon took place. Working partly for the Home Office, he was our Brigade's Civil Defence Instructor. One of his duties was to recruit volunteers to man the dull green-painted appliances, the Green Goddesses.

He introduced us to the realms of the possible total annihilation by a foreign nuclear attack. A full week of comprehensive Civil Defence Training would come later, away from home at Moreton-in-Marsh, an old wartime airfield. Mr Gudgeon's manner and presentation, mixed with a dry sense of humour, was a welcome change from the never-ending dreary hours of classroom drudgery.

Flamboyant in attitude, he treated the possibility of the country being wiped out of existence very seriously, but with a touch of sarcasm. He believed the future for any still left would be bleak. Gas masks were issued to every fireman and we carried them obediently in their small brown canvas shoulder bags on all operational turnouts. We were left to ponder their effectiveness in the case of a holocaust.

His lecture was followed by half-day drill, using a couple of the Green Goddess pumps. I looked for the one I had left with damage to the front wing but could not find it.

Organised at a nearby Home Office site in old derelict houses, we practised searching, rescuing casualties and removing them from a possible future nuclear bomb attack. This drill provided realism at long last.

The final two weeks at training school arrived. Every single hour was now counted with glee.

Carrying down, the fireman's rescue lift had initially been attempted from a ladder pitched up to the first floor. By our final weeks, using a sixty-foot wheeled escape ladder, we reached the fourth floor, a height of forty feet. Everybody had to go through the ordeal of carrying a colleague down from the drill tower using the fully extended escape ladder. Then we climbed the ladder again before being slung over our partner's shoulder and jostled and bounced back down to the ground.

Hook-ladder drills also got ever higher. Serious doubts existed over the very existence of this ladder in the Fire Service and attempts to remove it from operational appliances followed after serious accidents were reported. But I found hook-ladders satisfying to climb even if they were not considered practical. In stages we all scaled the ninety-foot tower single-handed, carrying the hook-ladder from floor to floor.

Breathing apparatus drills too became more intensive. Taking long walks round the school tested the amount of time during which they could be used. For testing endurance in heat and smoke, an old brick built chamber was filled with burning steel braziers manufactured from old oil drums and was fuelled by old tyres, wood and other rubbish, all of which were soaked in paraffin and set alight. We crawled round and round in the increasing temperatures and moved wooden logs from one end to the other. Pushed to extreme limits, the cooling properties of the calcium chloride became useless and our bodies and the contents of our lungs reached a critical temperature.

In these conditions the Proto breathing apparatus reached its working limitations. The rubber mouth insert were glued to the gums, our goggles pressed hard around the eyes, and the nose clips became welded to our nostrils.

As our training course reached the Friday of the penultimate week, we sat our final written exam. My fingers ached with the constant use of a pencil. Not since my secondary school days had I suffered so much; my index finger even showed signs of bruising.

When the last page of questions was almost completed, Assistant Divisional Officer Grayling entered and walked slowly to the front of the lecture room. He approached Sub Officer Hussar who was the invigilator. We stopped writing and looked up from our answer papers.

Mr Grayling spoke in a whisper. He walked slowly down the spaces between the desks. Every one hesitated holding their breath. Stopping in front of my desk he bent low and quietly asked me to come to his office. The room hummed.

With my brain in overdrive I put down my pencil and pushed my chair back slowly. The wooden chair legs of the chairs scuffed on the floor, disrupting the silence. As I turned slowly to the door I could see Mr Grayling waiting patiently, his face full of concern. I tried a quick smile but there was no response. This must be the end of my career, I thought. Was it execution time? Every misdemeanour I had committed during my weeks at training school raced through my brain.

I followed exactly two paces behind Mr.Grayling, across the drill ground. Not a word was said. After the long walk to his room I entered after him and slowly closed the door.

"Sit down Michael," he said in a soft and kind voice. He was using my Christian name. Not an executioner's attitude I thought.

In the far corner of the room stood a uniformed policeman, staring out of the window. He turned to face me, his helmet tucked under his arm.

"I have some bad news for you," he said, "some bad news about your mother."

Mother. Mother. Training School and Mother. I searched to try and understand the connection.

"Your mother has been involved in an accident." His sentence was short.

"She has been knocked down by a bread van. I am sorry to have to tell you," he paused for a moment, "she was dead on arrival at the hospital!"

Mother. Not possible, I thought.

In a daze the policeman in his car took me to the hospital. The entire journey was made in silence.

Ushered into a cubicle at the hospital, I was shown a trolley on which was a body covered in a white and spotless sheet. A nurse stood at one end of the trolley. It wasn't my mother, surely. The nurse slowly pulled back the sheet; the policeman opened his notebook. I looked at the face and then at the blue-grey painted wall. I nodded. The policeman noted the time on his wrist-watch and scribbled something in his notebook.

I looked again.

Mother looked so serene. Her face was peaceful. Gone were the tight crease marks that had once lined her forehead. Her lips were a smooth deep blue.

I had never experienced death at such close quarters.

Divisional Officer Mullet, one of our senior officers, was waiting outside to take me home. I sat in his red Hillman estate car, stunned. I was glazed and blank during the journey home.

"Is this your house?" He interrupted my nightmare.

Two men stood on the pavement knocking on our door. I recognised one of the men. He was the regular rent collector; a small pathetic weasel of a man and at his side, looming high above him was a solid thickset hunk of a man. I dragged myself out of the car and stood in front of them.

"I want you out of this house," whimpered the small weasel.

"You're not living here on your own. Your rent finishes in two weeks, be out by then." Bad news travels fast, I thought.

Divisional Officer Mullet climbed out of his estate car, fastening his belt buckle and placing his uniform cap on his head. He glowered at the two. The weasel cowered behind his minder.

"Two weeks." His words drifted off. He scuttled off down the street, his bodyguard at his side.

Inside, the house felt cold. The dining table was laid with just one place set for my evening meal. It must have been the last thing Mother did. Divisional Officer Mullet produced a fresh pot of tea from our scullery.

He talked to me and tried to be reassuring. It was a wasted effort. After a while he gave up and left, telling me to let him know if I needed help.

Saturday and Sunday passed in a dream. I tried the contents of a bottle of kirsch I found in the sideboard but it gave me no feeling of relief.

One week was left to do at Training School, and it provided a welcome relief to my sadness and anger. Mother, my mind churned over and over, was only forty-four years old.

The final day at long last arrived and on Friday we had our passing out parade. For this special parade a series of demonstration drills which we had rehearsed was planned. They were to be performed in front of an audience of Chief Officers from all the other Brigades, and the families and friends of the passing out recruits were all invited, to make the event special.

Two items on the agenda were a live rescue from the drill-tower with a carry-down using the sixty-foot escape, and a demonstration using the hook-ladder. I found, to my surprise, that I was to perform the hook-ladder demonstration.

The drill tower was to be scaled from the ground to the top floor. I lifted the ladder and placed the hook on each window-sill and then climbed up and up.

At the sixth floor, sixty feet high, the hook-ladder dangled from its steel hook. Going into the building over the horns meant first gripping the two strings of the ladder that protruded from the top of the tower, like two stubby thumbs and then climbing up the ladder until both feet were between the hands. Then I stepped onto the top of the tower.

Mother would have been proud.

A Chief Officer from another Fire Brigade gave a complimentary speech and we were dismissed. He left us feeling a sense of achievement.

My twelve weeks' basic training was completed at long last. Although there was a great deal of trivialization and an endless obsession for cleaning, there were also one or two useful highlights. The practical experience I had gained from working alongside actual firemen on a busy Station made me look forward to the next hurdle, passing my two years' probationary period.

Returning to a home full of blackness and sorrow I felt at odds with a cruel world. I still had to find somewhere to live. But my panic lessened; the pressure was too great to bother with mere panic.

I took another helping of kirsch, but again alcohol did not help my depression.

The next day I awoke in a daze, hearing someone banging on the outside door. I pulled the curtains back to reveal bright daylight. It was mid-Saturday. Unlocking and opening the door I found Barry Bleck and two other Firemen. Across the street I saw a red Fire Brigade van. Barry threw me a newspaper parcel.

"Here, get some food down you," Barry said as I caught the parcel.

"We've come to rescue you."

I opened the parcel to find a late breakfast of fish and chips. I consumed the fish and chips straight from the newspaper, only now realising how hungry I was. My three friends bustled about the house and packed three tea chests with the contents of all the drawers in the house, the pots and pans from the scullery, the crockery from the sideboard. They helped me to parcel up all the clothes and bedding which were stored in the landlord's wardrobe into two old battered suitcases. Our two old beds were dismantled and everything was loaded in the Brigade van.

All my worldly possessions were in a single van. Like a helpless child I was pushed about. When the van was loaded, we set off. Barry Bleck told me that wheels had turned to get me some alternative accommodation. Eventually the wheels stopped turning; someone knew someone else who knew of an empty flat above a green grocer's shop. We set off. The van wheels, too, were turning to rescue me.

We struggled through a shop packed with green vegetables, up a tight winding staircase to two small rooms and a partly fitted kitchenette with the two beds and the tea chests. All my possessions stood at last in a heap on the floor.

Barry produced a crate of ale and we proceeded to christen my new home well and truly.

Chapter 7

My new black leather helmet, pristine and brand new, nestled like a roosting raven on a sheet of pink blotting paper.

"Your school report's not good Michael," Station Officer Finnan said. He pushed my helmet slowly forward.

"I'm sorry about your mother," he added in his northern accent, as my helmet reached the edge of the pink paper.

"But I'm pleased to hear you have somewhere else to live."

Kind man I thought.

But immediately he changed his tone of voice.

"You have only just reached the pass mark at training-school. The Chief expects all his recruits to be in the top ten." He stood up, turned away and faced a small cracked mirror suspended from a nail on the wall.

"He'll want to see you."

He produced a steel comb from his uniform pocket, peered into the mirror and combed his hair. He arranged the centre parting with precise accuracy. I collected my new helmet and grovelled out.

Outside the Station Officer's office I tried my helmet for size. Made from compressed leather, it rested heavy on my head. My other helmet, forty or so years old, now went back to Stores to be re-issued to another raw recruit. With the smell of new leather lingering in my nose I pranced about proudly, brandishing my new headgear.

While I was enduring the three months away at training school, White Watch had gained another recruit, Malcolm Cackerel. His face was dotted with small red spots, and three pink plasters on his neck covered large bulging boils.

Malcolm greeted me in a lilting Irish accent.

"How difficult is Training School?" He asked.

"It's physically demanding and we were always hungry," I replied with the satisfaction of someone who had completed the course.

The food provided at Training School barely bridged the energy gap caused by the amount of exercise we took. Constantly on the move, I was forever hungry. The large stodgy dinner we consumed midday and a second dinner at home at teatime was still insufficient to replenish all the energy I had used.

"If you're not fit at the beginning, you will be at the end," I told him with glee.

A new boy on White Watch would ease the pressure on me,

Complete with my new helmet, I felt pleased and proud to rejoin my watch. Received by my colleagues, who reserved judgement about me, I quickly found that all the techniques I had learned in Training School, drilling by numbers, marching, and formulas for working out quantities of water belonged in the class room.

Wearing my helmet, I strutted about the Station. But the bells sounded interrupting my performance.

'Job Out! House fire, number seventeen Dart Terrace, off Scar Road'.

I grabbed the rest of my uniform tunic, fire-boots, and leather belt and with my axe in my arms; I barged through the two swing doors leading from the muster-room into the engine house.

I ran round the back of Pump One, dodging the other firemen converging in answer to the call out. Around the Pump Escape I gripped one of the two large carriage wheels as I ran past. The wheel spun freely. I opened the offside rear cab door and climbed inside the rear cab.

The engine house doors banged open. The engine started. Pump Escape followed Pump One out in front of the Station. We raced away. It was mid-morning on a Monday and the tarmac roads were black with fine drizzle.

Leading Fireman Henry Carp, the officer in charge sat on the left of our driver, Fireman Trevor Tailor. Tailor revved the engine and changed into a higher gear.

The newly promoted Leading Fireman Henry Carp had joined White Watch from Stour Crescent Fire Station, one of the four outer sub-stations of Torridge City, while I attended training school. Although he was only twenty-six years of age, Henry had attained the rank of Leading Fireman only four years after joining the Service. Breaking the normal eight or nine years' service others needed before their first promotion. His father was our Assistant Chief, and no doubt this had some bearing on his rapid ascent.

A younger version of his father, tall and thin with the same long thin face, Henry displayed the confidence and assured manner that came with knowing someone on high.

Pump One in front of us negotiated the main road traffic easily and disappeared from view. Pump Escape stopped suddenly to avoid a car whose driver ignored our wailing siren. We lost our momentum but soon picked up speed again and chased after Pump One. On the roof of the cab above us, the silver bell clanged and the chrome siren wailed, its note going up and down.

By the time we turned into Scar Road with its maze of terraced property and cobbled streets fanning off in all directions, there was no sign of Pump One.

"All the Darts are further along this road," Leading Fireman Carp said.

"Dart Mount, Dart Place," driver Trevor shouted, reading the small black and white name plates high on the red bricked house walls.

"These small cast iron name plates were not designed for easy reading," Trevor observed, as he stroked his crop of fair hair with his right hand. His left hand still steered the appliance.

"Dart Terrace!" Screamed Fireman Peter Margot, our fourth crew-member, wiping away steam from the cab window. Our Pump Escape shuddered to a stop as Trevor braked suddenly on the damp road. He yanked the steering wheel to the left and we turned into Dart Terrace.

A big buxom woman dressed in a full-length blue-flowered-pinafore dress, stood in the middle of the road. She was gripping a tiny girl by the hand; her other arm was folded tight against her chest. She hobbled towards us, dragging the little girl with her.

The small girl's face was dirty and rivulets of clean skin descended from her eye sockets where tears had flowed. Blood oozed from the folded woman's arm.

"Round the back, round the back," she screamed at us. As she moved her damaged arm, drops of blood flew into the air before landing onto the wet cobbles.

"Peter?" Leading Fireman Carp shouted from the front cab of the, "get the first aid box. Look after this woman." His words were brief.

Grabbing the black first aid box, Peter Margot leaped from our slowly moving appliance.

"Here luv, I'll see to you." Peter's voice tailed off as the appliance moved off, his door still open. It slammed shut as Trevor crunched the gear; the appliance jumped forward.

There was a small narrow alleyway at the rear of Dart Terrace. We saw smoke drifting from a downstairs window nine houses down. Pump Escape crept slowly with only inches to spare down the alleyway towards the smoke.

Crammed in the narrow back street opposite the smoking window, our cab doors would not open fully. Dressed in my uniform, with new helmet, my tunic, and my leather boots, I squeezed through the narrow gap, which the street allowed. My axe and belt-line, a small personal rope twelve-feet in length, which was rolled up neat and tidy, caught on the inside door handle of the appliance. However by undoing the large shiny buckle on my belt I managed to untangle the mess and get out, leaving my belt line flapping and dragging behind me.

Leading Fireman Carp climbed out of his cab window dropped onto the cobbled alleyway and ran around the front of the appliance to the high gate of the burning house.

"Hose-reel!" he shouted.

There was barely sufficient room at the side of the appliance. I reached up and grabbed the end of the hose-reel and pulled on the end holding the hose-reel nozzle. The red tubing unwound slowly from its drum.

Trevor squeezed down the side of the Pump Escape and managed to organise the pump's controls, which were situated down the offside. The engine raced now that the hose-reel pump was engaged. I tested the water supply from the hose-reel nozzle. Water spurted out in a spray and I threw the nozzle and hose-reel over the garden wall and climbed up the side of the appliance.

Dropping down into the back yard of the house I stood alongside Leading Fireman Henry Carp. We were immediately showered with objects flying from the window.

A white enamel bowl crashed down near our feet on the cobbles. Chips of enamel flew off it in all directions as it bounced several times on the hard ground. Plates, bottles, pans followed. Objects rained down upon us from the broken window. Dodging these we reached the rear doorstep and pushed hard on the door. Henry entered first, forcing the door wider open. I dragged more hose from the appliance until it curled in loops on the doorstep. I followed Henry into the room, squeezing through a narrow gap and clambering over a broken chair.

In the far corner of the kitchen, at the side of a white pot sink, a partly clothed man stood. Dressed only in a pair of trousers, he was throwing everything he could reach out of the window. At his elbows, the curtains merrily blazed away. Grey smoke drifted up and out of the broken window. Perhaps he was saving as much as possible, I thought.

Not fully understanding the picture I sprayed water on the burning curtains. Nothing else appeared to be burning.

The man was furious. Ranting and raving, he turned on Carp, shouting abuse at the top of his voice. His piercing voice turned the air blue. We stood mesmerised, not knowing the full situation. With a pair of braces over his bare shoulders and his fly gaping open he picked up a large pop bottle from the wooden draining board and swung the bottle crazily against the wall. The pop bottle would not break so he swung even harder. The walls cowered, but fortunately for us the screw top on the bottle remained firm and tight. Again he hit the wall but still the bottle would not break. Undeterred he swung the complete bottle menacingly in front of Henry. His verbal abuse grew louder.

In a brave attempt to calm things down Henry tried saying words of comfort. The man turned, threw the bottle on the floor and stormed off towards the cellar door. He was still screaming obscenities at us.

We dragged the curtains onto the kitchen floor. I rolled them into a bundle carried them outside, and dropped them onto the cobbled back yard. They were still steaming.

The fire had not done much damage except to the curtains but the kitchen was devastated. The table and chairs were smashed and bits of food decorated the walls. Broken pots and pans littered the room.

Peter Margot joined us. Panting, he reported the tiny girl had taken a severe beating from this man. Her Mother, attempting to protect her child, had stopped a flying carving knife with her arm.

"They are safe in a neighbour's house," Peter gasped.

"The ambulance's coming," he added, between breaths.

Eventually Pump One and Station Officer Finnan arrived. Scar Road was over a mile long and they had approached from other end.

Noticing all the damage in the kitchen, Finnan looked puzzled.

"Bit of a nutter, gaffer!" Henry informed him. "He's disappeared into the cellar." On cue, strong thuds against the walls below us emphasised the man's presence. The house shook.

"Better get the police to sort things out," our Station Officer suggested in his Scottish accent.

The ambulance arrived and the mother and child were despatched to hospital. The fire was a result of domestic upheaval and although when we arrived, Dart Terrace had been completely empty of anyone but the mother and child, neighbours now suddenly appeared from all directions, offering belated advice. They stood in small groups, huddled together in the back alleyway.

We replaced our equipment on the appliance and made ready to return to the Station.

A police car arrived and parked behind the Pump Escape. A diminutive detective dressed in a grey full-length raincoat, climbed out from the car and squeezing past our Pump Escape and across the back yard he came into the kitchen. He was small in size but huge in confidence.

"Where's chummy?" He asked. We told him.

Making his way to the top of the cellar steps he peered down into the darkness. The madman, who was waiting at the bottom of the stairs, flared up again. The house shook as a big heavy iron bar, he must have found, crashed against the cellar walls.

"I need a lamp and a rope," detective stated.

Henry gave him one of our big heavy hand held searchlights and I removed the line from my belt. Without hesitation the detective grabbed them and disappeared down the stairs. The iron bar banged, and the noise rang out furiously as the bar rattled from side to side against the wall. But not for long. A loud gasp was quickly followed by a scuffle and then by total silence.

Moments later the detective came out from the cellar.

"He's all yours," he said addressing two-uniformed policeman, who had now appeared, with another plain-clothes policeman. The kitchen was now crowded with people.

"I'll leave it with you, Henry," Station Officer Finnan said.

"Michael?" He added, "Come back with me. The Chief wants to see you. Best bib and tucker," he added without a smile.

Collecting my shoes from the Pump Escape, I climbed aboard Pump One and joined Malcolm Cackerel. He sat on one of the damp bench seats.

He was wearing an old fashioned fire-helmet similar to the one I had been given on joining. It was too small and sat perched high on his head. From under the large brim one of the plasters on his neck hung loose.

As we pulled away from the incident we witnessed two burly policemen man-handle the apparent madman out of the house and into a police car. Trussed up, with the belt I had provided, like a joint of rolled sirloin he was thrown unceremoniously into the back of the police car.

Malcolm chattered in his Irish accent all the way back to the Station. But the thoughts on my mind were about my visit to our dreaded Chief Officer. Malcolm's nattering did not help. Although he perhaps meant well, it was a relief to be able to rest my ears from his constant banter when Pump One finally reversed into the engine house.

"Chief rang down just before we turned out. He won't be pleased to be kept waiting," Station Officer Finnan said as he descended from appliance.

Borrowing a uniform from several members of the watch, and sporting a new cap, clean and pressed trousers and polished shoes I looked reasonably tidy. With trepidation I made the solitary walk from the locker room to the headquarters.

The administration block stood apart from the engine house but lay in the same direction as our canteen. I mounted the flight of stairs and went along the corridor and I nervously opened the entrance door leading into the headquarters. I noticed a strong smell of polished linoleum as I tapped timidly on Chief Bass's door.

"Come in," he boomed. Gingerly I opened the wide door and entered the room.

My instructions were to go in and salute. Chief likes to be saluted, I was told.

He sat behind his large desk like an overgrown walrus, and I walked up to the front of the desk.

As smartly as I could, I stood to attention and saluted.

"Is that the best you can do?" Chief growled.

"Get out and come in again."

I crept out, turned at the door and re-entered and saluted again.

"That's much better." The Chief glanced to his left where Assistant Chief Officer Carp smiled and nodded in approval.

"Now, Fairn, this school report says you acted the goat. Is this true?" The Chief was obviously not amused.

"Well, Sir," I attempted to reply.

"It's not good enough," he boomed, "you young lads think life's a bloody holiday camp! I've had words with Mr Carp and your Station Officer and they both say you perform well at fires. All my recruits are on a two-year probationary period. Get out. I don't want to see you in here again."

I beat a hasty retreat.

As I returned the uniform I had borrowed for the occasion to its rightful owners, White Watch immediately grilled me about my appearance in front of the Chief.

Not a popular man with the lower ranks, Chief Bass still possessed his followers. In the Fire Service for nearly thirty-four years, and past retirement age, he stayed on and seemed to have no intention of relinquishing his command. Those who wanted promotion treated him with apparent and obvious reverence and never uttered a word in opposition to what they knew to be his views.

I already understood that promotion was gained through fear, favour and a touch of nepotism. Never to upset the hierarchy and perhaps to win favour by carrying out trade work on the Stations (if you had been a skilled tradesman before joining the service) or having good family connections were the routes for advancement.

On Fire Stations, firemen collectively, unless they were the privileged tradesmen, were an embarrassment. Work-creating schemes, high in manual labour content, filled our days when we were not called out. But when they turned out to incidents firemen changed miraculously from being a nuisance to something essential and important. Once back on the Fire Station, however, we soon returned to the humdrum of station life.

The ranks of Leading Fireman and Sub Officer were the two first major steps on the ladder of promotion. Both ranks ate at different tables and never mixed with Firemen during station routine duty hours.

When men reached the rank of Station Officer, and higher, their shirts changed from our common blue to white. They all ate in the officer's mess, which was furnished with a carpet and small tables, adorned by white linen table-cloths. They were clearly a race apart.

Under this pyramid I was happy to live and work alongside very experienced firemen, many of who would never reach any chance of promotion.

As I settled down on the Station it was to these experienced firemen, at the bottom of the pile, I turned to for guidance.

Chapter 8

David Edgar Capelin now aged forty-five joined Torridge City Fire Brigade in 1947 after having achieved an exemplary war-record. It was whispered that he held a bravery award and now endured a damaged right hip as a result of his wartime exploits.

Fireman Capelin's silent unassuming manner attracted respect from everyone in the Fire Brigade. An ex-marine and a practical man, David showed an ability to turn his hand to anything mechanical. He was protected from having to do much heavy work and spent most of his time driving our Station's two special appliances, the Emergency Tender and the Turntable Ladder. David loved to provide advice to anyone willing to listen. He willingly shared the knowledge he had acquired, and took great pride in explaining how things worked.

As the number of appliances on the Fire Station grew over its eighty years, first from horse drawn steam fire engines to the first motorised petrol Model T Ford machine at the turn of the century and now to modern appliances, the Fire Station needed room to expand. A converted property at the rear now housed our Emergency Tender and a Home Office Green Goddess.

The Emergency Tender, a 1957 Commer pantechnicon crewed by two men, the driver and an officer in charge, carried a mass of equipment in addition to that carried on the bread-and-butter appliances, the fire fighting pumps. Acetylene cutting gear, vehicle bottle jacks in varying sizes, extra Proto oxygen breathing sets, oilskin coats, spanners, joinery tools, saws.

Minuteman, an automatic resuscitation apparatus were part of the Emergency Tender equipment. Perched on the roof were three heavy steel legs and a block and tackle for lifting. The road engine also powered a steel cable winch and a 110 volts generator for power tools and for electric lighting.

E.T. as it was colloquially known was designed and built to Torridge City Brigade's specifications and supported two rear sliding doors and a walk-through interior. David was inside and was leaning against the workbench for support as he slid open a drawer and selected a piece of equipment to demonstrate. He carefully unzipped a brown leather pouch and removed a set of compact hydraulic bolt cutters, which were intended to replace the heavy and cumbersome hand, operated bolt cutters we carried on the pumping appliances. The cutting jaws on this small model gradually closed as David pumped the flexible handle.

"But they're expensive," he commented, as he meticulously described the workings and strength tolerances of the cutter.

His enthusiasm never lessened as we went through locker after locker, drawer after drawer. Driving the Emergency Tender regularly, David experienced several serious incidents, road accidents and industrial injuries. He knew the feeling of pain and death, which he saw at close quarters.

Stories of a serious house fire spread through the brigade on the grapevine as we reported on the last of our three night duties. Red watch, the day crew, discovered an elderly couple and removed them from their burnt out bedroom. Complete descriptions of both bodies which were severely disfigured, were given.

I knew the Fire Service dealt with such human tragedies, but I wondered how I would cope when it arrived.

David, with his wealth of experience, offered advice and acted as a willing mentor. Sitting in front of the coke fire on a high firm-backed solid chair in the long-room, our recreational area when on stand-down duties, the smoke from David's pipe fogged the room as he puffed away. I listened to his every word.

"Death and serious injuries, which we treat with respect, become someone else's problem once we have done our job," he began.

"To carry the burden back to the Station does no good. Emotions, like blood on the road, must be left at the scene," he tapped his pipe on the fireplace, "it's better to find other outlets to relieve the trauma." Tobacco fell onto the red-hot embers and sparkled for an instant, like a burning star.

I thought of my mother, of her funeral, its aftermath. I remembered my pain and feeling of great loss. Death was so definite, so final.

For some months Torridge City Council had been constructing new sewer pipes along Baysdale Road, a busy arterial road carrying traffic in and out of the city. Every two hundred yards large cavities in the road joined the underground tunnelling. These cavities, surrounded by upright railway sleepers and protected at night by red paraffin lamps, dotted the roadside looking like wooden fortresses.

Bells rang just after 2200 hours on one warm summer evening. Message was 'Pump One and Emergency Tender to Road Accident near some sewer works. Outside a shop at 583 Baysdale Road.'

The night air was warm and humid. I was a crew-member on Pump One; Station Officer Finnan was in charge. I collected my uniform and climbed aboard and joined the rest of the crew, Leading Fireman Henry Carp and Fireman Peter Margot.

Peter had been in the Fire Service for ten years. He was loud, outspoken and brash. His carefree attitude to life was attractive to all young Firemen.

Baysdale Road, like a spoke on a wheel, splayed out to the city boundary. I shuffled about on Pump One, which was opened back, concerned and nervous at the possibility of an approaching tragedy. The single lamp on front of the cab roof cast a thin beam of blue as it revolved in the warm night air.

From the bench seat, looking back along Baysdale Road, we strained in the gloom to see if our Emergency Tender followed.

House numbers usually started at the city centre with odd numbers on the left and even numbers on the right. We looked for a number on the passing buildings. Suddenly 155 jumped to 271.

Chasing past the dark wooden sewer fortresses and the reported scene of the accident, we slowed down. Suddenly the road was blocked by stationary traffic. The Pump swung to the opposite side of the road before it slowed down opposite an accident. Glass, bits of metal and a single car wheel were strewn all over the road The rear end of a car poked out from a shop window, its rear wheels on the pavement and the engine and bonnet were buried deep inside a fish shop window.

The fish shop proprietor stood in the doorway of his shop. His white coat was blood stained. Henry Carp and Peter Margot leaped from our open backed appliance and ran to answer his frantic waving before our Pump stopped. I followed.

The shopkeeper's arms flapped in the air. Agitated, he gabbled away as he tried to explain how the car had first collided with the sewer works and then ended up in his shop.

The fish shop looked more like a butcher's shop than a fish shop. Bright neon tubes flooded the gory sight with strong harsh light. There was blood on the floor and blood was spattered over the white tiled walls. A groaning body, partly in the car and partly through the windscreen, moved slightly on the car bonnet. The head was covered in blood and red streaks ran down its face. One eyelid opened and an eye pleaded for some relief.

"Over here Michael!" Peter Margot shouted as he climbed over the debris that filled the front of the shop. The shop lights, unaffected by the calamity, left no doubts about the horrific sight. I picked my way through broken glass and over torn metal and saw another body.

Henry Carp joined us as Peter's hand groped inquiringly.

A mixture of bells and sirens outside the shop indicated the arrival of our Emergency Tender and an ambulance. Feeling the body for any signs of life we found no pulse, no response, and no movement. I helped as we moved an arm gently. The head suddenly jerked forward towards me. I reached out to prevent further movement, stopping the head with my hands. Blood, which felt warm and sticky, oozed through my fingers. I was amazed. It had never occurred to me that someone else's blood would be warm.

I looked more closely. The left side of the face was completely missing and a mass of dark red greasy substance hung loose from a deep wound gouged into the skull.

"There's not a lot we can do," Leading Fireman Carp stood up, his hands dripping red. Three of us joined Finnan and David who were working on the body poking out of the windscreen. The driver's door forced open by a crowbar.

David, draped across the front wing of the car, ignored any pain from his hip and held the driver's body in his arms.

"Got his leg caught on the steering wheel," somebody said.

"Get the new compact bolt cutters," David told me.

I clambered over the wreckage and ran to the Emergency Tender. Opening the rear doors and racing down the Inside Passage, I collected the brown leather pouch from an inside drawer and ran back to the shop. I handed the cutters to our Station Officer who had managed to reach the trapped driver by going through the passenger door and crawling beneath the dashboard. He placed the jaws of the cutter over the rim of the steering wheel and pumped the handle. With two cuts the lower half of the steering wheel came away. Ever so slowly the trapped hips of the victim were eased upwards and came free. The body slid slowly through the missing windscreen and onto the bonnet. David and Peter tugged from the outside and from inside the car I helped Station Officer to keep both of the victim's legs free of the sharp remains of the steering wheel.

Willing hands took the weight of the body as it came agonizingly free from inside the car. It was a woman. We lifted her off the bonnet and placed her gently on a stretcher and then carried her towards the waiting ambulance. We wrapped the second occupant of the car in a salvage sheet and lifted him clear of the wreckage. Man-handled from the corner over the car bonnet, the body was awkward to lift in the confined space. As we straddled the broken fish-shop window one leg fell out of the bundle.

"He's got no shoes on!" David joked.

"Look, he's got holes in his socks!" His distraction served the purpose, taking our attention away from the horror.

With both casualties removed, the car, once a Vauxhall Cresta was made safe. The bonnet was prised open and the battery disconnected.

"Is the fish going to waste?" Peter Margot asked the fish shop man who had resumed his position behind the counter.

"Just about to throw it all away," he said.

"I love fried fish," Peter said. He had been a chef before he joined the Fire Service and liked his food.

"Anybody else fancy some fish?" He asked. Everyone else refused. Blood splattered all over the white tiles did nothing for our appetites. Undeterred, Peter tucked into a large piece of battered cod.

"It tastes grand," he announced discarding a chunk mauled by his dirty fingers.

"We've done our best. The world must go on. If anyone can't stand the blood, then they are in the wrong job," he muttered between mouthfuls of fish.

The shopkeeper, already shocked and now looking decidedly wan, was not pleased with our seeming nonchalance and air of unconcern, but I was to learn this warped sense of humour and trivialisation was not meant to be disrespectful.

It was a relief valve.

An outlet for our feelings.

Chapter 9

White Watch meandered along peacefully under a decent and capable leadership. We were like a sedate, untroubled river.

A Station Officer always had to be in charge of our Station and with Station Officer, Alec Finnan, on annual leave his temporary replacement, the recently promoted Andrew Charr arrived. There was a rumour circulating throughout the Brigade that connected Charr's promotion with his uncle's tailoring business and the dubious supply of officer's uniform. Charr stood glaring at us during morning parade and with his reputation, of being a perfectionist meant that our once tranquil river situation was suddenly threatened by an impending tidal-wave of destruction.

White Watch's normal contingent of officers comprised of Sub Officer Latchet (who was off the Station working as the Brigade's electrician) Sub Officer Gardon (off-duty, sick), Leading Fireman Loche (Brigade's joiner) and Leading Fireman Carp who was on annual leave. Thus we were also short of junior officers.

To add more water to the rising river, Leading Fireman Bret joined us after his recent promotion. He stood alongside Station Officer Charr. With his fat grinning face, Barney Bret was the favourite nephew of Torridge City Chief Fire Officer, Mr Bass. Promoted from fireman to Leading Fireman, Bret came to us after his legendary brain operation. On the receipt of his chrome markings for his new rank this mythical operation was said to have implanted a phial containing wisdom and knowledge through a small hole drilled in the rear of his skull. Bret was another example of promotion through family connections.

"I'm in charge now," Station Officer Charr told us. Immaculately dressed in his new uniform, that fit his body like a handmade glove, his cloth peaked-cap, positioned with minute detail rested in perfect position, flat on his head. Manicured sideboards bristled with annoyance as his ears buckled slightly under the sides of his cap.

In his new Station Officer's uniform he looked like a tailor's dummy. His shoes were polished to such a high degree they no longer looked black.

Standing on parade on a station that was old, well used and worn out, he looked dressed for a wedding at a scrap yard!

"There are going to be changes! Everyone is going to be smarter. And everyone is to do their job smartly," he screamed at us.

Standing next to Charr, Bret grinned smugly, expressing agreement. Bret continued to shout our names detailing our manning for the day. Then we were inspected. Their eyes were everywhere.

Station Officer Charr's intentions were to flood our sedate river situation sufficiently so that those would note his presence on high. From a once peaceful watch we were now under amber flood alert.

"After parade and proper appliance checks, properly, and I mean properly," his face reddened with the effort of emphasising his order, "everyone, before they change into their working overalls, will see me in my office," his voice rose in a threatening wail.

The older members of White Watch smiled wryly. One or two had already served with Andrew Charr during his twelve years' service and witnessed his privileged ascent through the ranks. He had received his mythical brain operation six years ago, and then promoted to a Leading Fireman then a Sub Officer and now, prodigiously, a Station Officer in record time.

The outlook looked bleak. The river was still rising.

As we were still short of officers for each of our four appliances, I was detailed by Bret to ride as officer-in-charge on the Turntable Ladder for the day. Fireman Maurice Grundel, one of our senior firemen was the driver and operator.

We entered the engine house for our morning checks, as canteen man, Maurice immediately changed out of undress parade jacket into a full length brown canteen coat. Maurice always wore a brown coat as canteen man. We sat in the crew cab of our 1955 Dennis F17 Metz Turntable Ladder contemplating the rising troubles.

"Both of you to the gaffer's office now!" Leading Fireman Bret suddenly shouted at us.

I dropped out of the crew cab and followed Maurice across the engine house, down the three steps into muster-room, and into the Station Officer's office.

Station Officer Charr, his new hat still perfectly aligned, his ears still protruding, sat waiting for us. A white handkerchief hung down from his left sleeve. His shirt cuffs showed equal margins of white obviously measured with extreme care. Leading Fireman Bret stood prancing at his master's side.

On the desk in front of them stood piles of assorted buttons. There were all kinds of buttons. There were chrome buttons in three different sizes each inscribed with the Torridge City coat of arms.

There were black leather buttons for use on our overalls, even a pile of miniature trouser-fly buttons. Every button sat stacked high on the sheet of pink blotting paper in the centre of the desk.

"I noticed on parade that you have two buttons missing from the cuffs on your undress jacket," he looked me straight in the eye. Like Scrooge bequeathing pennies, he counted out the appropriate number. I obediently picked up my two chrome buttons.

"Get them on for tomorrow morning," he ordered.

"Maurice Grundel. Your brown-overall coat needs two buttons," Station Officer Charr kept the same intimidating tone of voice. Maurice stood, mouth open.

Selecting two brown leather buttons, Station Officer Charr pushed them deliberately across the blotting paper. Maurice glowered defiantly.

"I'm not sewing any buttons on," Maurice challenged the Station Officer.

"Then you must ask your wife to do it for you." Charr's order was insistent.

"If you think my wife has nothing better to do than to sew buttons on," Maurice answered stubbornly, "then you're off your trolley!" I had never experienced such open defiance.

"Not only will you sew these two buttons on, in future since you are canteen man, I want my cup of tea in this office at every tea break," Charr said.

"I'll bring it, if you'll drink it. But just don't go far from a toilet!" volleyed Maurice, scattering the two buttons onto the floor as he left the room. I too retreated still grasping my two precious buttons gripped in the palm of my hand.

Leading Fireman Barney Bret picked up the two buttons Maurice had thrown down and scurried out chasing him. Bret's tubby face glowed red with anger obviously supporting Station Officer Charr.

"Buttons Charr and Balmy Bret," Maurice shouted to the rest of White Watch who were all lined up in the muster-room awaiting their button issue. The sentence was halted in mid-stream as the Station bells sounded. The battle was suspended as all eyes turned to the indicator board. It demanded a full turnout, with Pump One, Pump Escape and Turntable Ladder.

I grabbed fire-helmet fire-tunic and fire-boots from my peg and moved towards the engine house. As officer in charge of the Turntable Ladder I needed the piece of paper with the fire-message.

I ran through the swing doors to the engine house jostling with rest of our watch.

I glanced at the message Control had given me. It read: 'Fire, Reeve's Shop, Otter Square, off Parret Place City Centre'. I took the piece of paper and dashed to the Turntable Ladder.

Maurice in the cab revved the engine. The engine house doors already open the appliance edged slowly forward as I threw my fire-uniform up onto the nearside seat and climbed up over the front wheel into the cab. I slammed the cab door behind me. As we moved out across the narrow footpath before turning sharp left and heading down the street I reached down to remove both my shoes and slide on my fire-boots.

Maurice suddenly hit the brake pedal. The Turntable Ladder jolted to a sudden stop and I slid forward off my seat. A dark green staff car had suddenly appeared and shot across our front. The car mounted the pavement to avoid colliding with our front bumper.

"He'll cause an accident one of these days." Maurice cursed the luckless driver.

Assistant Chief Fire Officer Carp receiving the fire calls in his office regularly raced appliances to incidents. His staff car now sandwiched between the Turntable Ladder and the Pump Escape joined the queue as we all joined the main road traffic.

I continued to dress. Fire-helmet on first. Then my arms were forced into the tunic sleeves. As the appliance gained speed I pressed hard on the two floor switches which made the roof of the cab thunder above our heads as the bell clapper rattled inside the bell. The noise of the wailing siren rose higher and higher until it became a high pitched scream.

My tunic at last fully buttoned, I thrust both feet into my leather boots before struggling to fasten the buckles on the thick Turntable Ladder belt. The large safety hook dangled loose from the belt on my left.

The early morning city traffic was busy and the streets congested. Pump One followed by Pump Escape and Assistant Chief's staff car cleared a path in front of us. We forced our way confidently through narrow gaps as the noise of our bells and sirens disrupted and stopped the normal flow of rush hour traffic. We raced towards Parret Place and Otter Square. When we arrived, the road was seized solid with traffic. Each appliance had to bounce across the pavement to avoid the congestion.

From a second floor window in Otter Square a sliver of smoke drifted casually upwards. Underneath a window, in bold red letters, a sign read 'Reeves, Agricultural Merchants and Seed Suppliers.'

Pump One and Pump Escape pulled up in front of us.

"There's somebody in that window!" Assistant Chief Carp leaped out of his abandoned car and screamed at Maurice through the windscreen of our cab. My foot was still pressed firmly on the button and our siren continued to scream. Maurice decided our Turntable Ladder needed to be closer to the window. He manoeuvred slowly around the abandoned Pump Escape.

Still dressed in his brown coat, Maurice yanked the hand brake lever on, before leaping out of the cab. I ran to join him at the back of the appliance. Furiously he turned a big wooden handle. Four supporting jacks which were held back under tension from internal springs, suddenly escaped and spun down. All four hit the road surface with a clatter.

"Get on," Maurice shouted to me.

I climbed onto the rear platform and straddled my legs over the small wall on the sides of the ladder before stepping down to the rungs. Along the top section of the housed ladder I hopped to reach the head. I quickly fastened the hook on my belt to the securing point. Thrusting my left arm straight out, I indicated to Maurice that I was ready.

Maurice working from the roadside, elevated, trained and extended the ladder working the three hand controls in unison. Working the controls with speed and dexterity the ladder came off the appliance and turned as it extended. Clipped to the top of the ladder I was propelled up, out, and forwards. I looked up. An old man's face appeared for a moment through an open window. Grey and black smoke billowed out from the window. The face fell back inside.

The head of the ladder moved closer to the smoking window. I glanced down. Crews from Pump One and

Pump Escape could be seen running inside the ground floor and dragging a hose-reel tubing after them.

The old man's face appeared again as the head of the ladder brushed against the window-sill. He still had his trilby hat on his head.

Maurice, even though he was a good sixty feet away, judged the distance exactly. I unclipped my belt and climbed up over the horns of the ladder. The sash window was partly open and I heaved the sliding wooden frame upward to gain more access. Smoke billowed out from the open window. Through the gap I dived in, head first. A voice moaned as I fell clumsily on top of the old man. I felt him wriggle underneath me. Grabbing the body I man-handled him to the window.

Assistant Chief Carp following me up the ladder shut off any light from the outside as he covered the window.

"Over here laddie," he said.

I pushed the grey haired old man towards the wall underneath the window. With an encouraging shove and a pull from our Assistant Chief, who was still outside on the top of the ladder, the old man clambered out. I followed him. With another fireman our Assistant Chief and the old man was guided slowly down the ladder.

The old man complete in his hat half-climbed half-fell into Maurice's waiting arms. Maurice bundled him onto a waiting stretcher. Two ambulance men wheeled him away.

Looking back at the window I saw that thick black smoke now covered the head of the ladder and spewed out. Maurice elevated the head of the ladder away and moved it from the smoke. Tiny fingers of flame muffled in black smoke suddenly exploded into a wall of fire. A sheet of flame shot out, licking and lashing the outside wall before curling over the facade of the shop.

I was then presented with a female coupling from the end of a dry delivery hose, fed to us from the Pump Escape. I climbed the ladder again.

Snapping the female coupling to a male coupling belonging to a length of hose already fitted on the ladder I climbed back to the top the ladder and waited. Almost immediately water shot out from the fitted outlet nozzle at the head of the Turntable Ladder. Water shot out straight through the open window and into the angry flames. Plumes of smoke cascaded out from the window as the fire in the room suffered under our onslaught of water.

Water from our Turntable Ladder nozzle soon subdued the angry flames. The jet of water from the ladder was then turned off. This allowed the crew, already inside, to have an easier ingress. Black smoke turned grey as water from the jet inside the building hit and finally killed a fire, which had been fuelled, by paper bags containing garden fertiliser. On further inspection we found, in an adjoining room at the rear of the premises, fifteen drums of sodium chlorate just waiting for the opportunity to join in the fun. We counted our blessings as the damping down operations commenced.

Two reporters pushed through the gathering crowds and approached our Assistant Chief Officer.

"We've pictures of the rescue," one of them said.

Our senior officers regarded all members of the press as loathsome creatures. The local journalist and his companion, who carried a large plate camera, were familiar faces at incidents throughout Torridge City. But they were always shunned and treat like undesirables.

"No comment." Assistant Chief Officer Carp said, addressing the man with a note pad and pencil. The

Assistant Chief turned and walked away with Station Officer Charr running at his side.

With the Metz Turntable Ladder no longer required, Maurice rehoused it. The hundred-foot extension ladder was safely returned to the gallows, the four screw jacks were wound up and the appliance was made ready to return.

The truce created by the fire ended as soon as the appliances reversed into the engine house. As the engine house doors slammed shut, the outside world no longer existed.

Buttons Charr resumed his officious and demanding attitude.

"The appliances were not clean enough! You took far too long for your dinner break! And there are Station routines still to complete," he informed us.

Our moment of glory had gone. One minute we were chivalrous heroes rescuing a person in distress the next we were mopping floors and suffering again under the threat of further disturbances from our supposed flooding.

In the papers next morning, our dramatic rescue and fire was given front-page prominence. An action picture showed us rescuing the old man and walking him down our Turntable Ladder with Maurice operating the controls.

Were we heroes again we wondered?

A telephone call, from our Chief Officer, soon brought us down to earth.

"Who's the civilian operating our Turntable Ladder?" Chief wanted to know. The picture on the front page showed Maurice still dressed in his full-length canteen coat. In the black and white print the dramatic photograph did look as if he was a passer-by wearing a raincoat. And, as Station Officer Charr was quick to point out, Maurice's coat was not fastened properly. And even worse his buttons were still missing.

Two long tours of duty eventually ended when our own Station Officer Finnan returned from his annual leave. Buttons as we had now christened him left us to inflict 'flood' damage elsewhere. Normality resumed.

Station Officer Andrew Charr never did get everybody to wear their full-button allocation. Nor did he get his cups of tea delivered personally. But he did not leave us empty-handed. Maurice surreptitiously, using a pipette, deposited drops of battery-acid on the threads of cotton behind every button on his brand new uniform.

Until the next visit by Buttons Charr we were safe from flooding and a peaceful flow resumed.

Chapter 10

An excess of soot, the residue from domestic coal provided a bevy of chimney fires.

Twice a day during the working week thousands of families coughed into life as the coal-fuelled open fires in their house spewed out smog, which blanketed the City in a blue haze. These fires first burst into life in the morning and then repeated the process at teatime. Torridge City Fire Brigade attended well over five hundred chimney fires every year. They often disrupted our essential cleaning duties on the Station. Chimneys allowed the accumulated soot to choke their flues before catching fire. Our management and senior officers regarded this type of turnout as a nuisance. But for crews destined to be imprisoned on the Fire Station, these calls provided a welcome relief from station drudgery.

A call to a chimney fire, which dispatched our Pump Two to forty-three Colligan Terrace, came just after our 0900 hours Monday morning parade.

We approached the Colligans, an area not known for social graces, without making a sound. Brigade orders specified bell and siren was never to be used on such trivia as chimney fires or grass fires. Dressed in helmets, tunics and rubber-soled shoes (the smooth leather soles of our fire-boots were useless on slippery roofs) we sat on the rear bench seats for our Pump to arrive.

We could see thick white smoke, mixed with red sparks from burning soot in the distance. It spewed high into the grey October sky. Imitating a small volcano, a plume of smoke slowly descended and covered the surrounding streets in a thick acrid blanket. At the front door of number forty-three a young scruffy man stood. Sporting dirty trousers, which had been once white, and a brown jacket with the remains of food on both front lapels, he screamed at us as we stopped.

"You took your time," he yelled, every other word an obscenity.

Sub Officer Gardon, now back on duty from sick leave, did not reply but grimaced, keeping his feelings hidden. One of our most experienced and hardened Sub Officers; he rolled his eyes as we entered the house. I followed him, brushing close to the young man who was still in the doorway. A sweet smell filtered up my nostrils as we shuffled through the open front door and into the house. Still lashing us with his tongue, he followed us down the passage and into the front room.

The room reeked. Even taking shallow short sharp breaths produced a feeling of nausea. The room was packed tight with rubbish; partly eaten pieces of discarded food were sandwiched under a tower of plates, cups, and mugs all were stacked high on every available surface. On a partly hidden table in the centre of the room a mountain of cardboard boxes were piled high. Underneath them layers of filthy clothes were seen and muddled together in a messy pile. An old butcher's bike was propped upside down, its black greasy chain, broken and dangling, poking through the mess.

Every square inch of the floorboards was taken over by discarded pots, pans and bottles. Everywhere was filthy. In the hearth a fall of soot was piled high, like a black mountain. As we walked further into the room through the maze of filth we placed our feet with great care. Our shoes squelched through damp partly solid objects beneath our feet. We did not dare to investigate closer.

Sub Officer Gardon looked at me but said nothing. He tilted his head as an indication that we should leave the room. His black fire-helmet with its two red bands, indicating his rank, rocked slightly. He rarely fastened the leather straps and they hung loose and dangled under his chin. The sulphurated air from the burning chimney outside felt kinder to our lungs than the atmosphere inside the house.

"Ladder up, hose-reel down the chimney," our Sub Officer instructed. He removed a silver-coloured tin box from his trouser pocket and proceeded to clear his vocal chords from the stench by taking a pinch of snuff. The rest of our crew, driver Fireman Trevor Tailor and Barry Bleck stood outside, away and free from the stench.

Removing it from the back of Pump Two, three of us carried the hundred and thirty pound; thirty-five foot double extension ladder to the side of the house. The heel or base of the ladder was held securely by Barry and

Trevor as I pushed up on the two strings, or sides, until it stood upright and vertical. Barry came round the heel and pulled on the extension line. The head of the ladder extended, clearing the house guttering by three clear rungs.

Trevor, his uniform cap covering his short-cropped hair, pulled on the extension line to activate the pawls, a hinged securing device fitted on the top extension. Barry lowered the top extension until it came to rest on the pawls locking the two ladders together. Together we leant the ladder gently against the guttering. Being the youngest and therefore the obvious candidate, I collected the roof ladder, put it on my shoulder and began to climb.

The roof ladder was a piece of equipment designed to rest in the guttering and then to be laid across sloping roofs. Light in construction it provided us with easy access and prevented damage to the fragile slates.

Carrying the fourteen-foot roof ladder on my right shoulder I began climbing our main ladder. Glancing through a stained smashed window, I noticed that the bedroom contents were as awful as those were in the downstairs room.

When I arrived at the guttering, belching smoke from the offending chimney blew back down the roof and engulfed the top of the ladder. Almost blinded, I fed the roof ladder off my shoulder and slid it up on the tiled surface. Placing the heel, or base, in the guttering directly behind the strings of the extension ladder I waited for Barry to climb up behind me with the hose-reel. This process needed the weight of someone at the head of the thirty-five foot ladder to prevent the roof ladder from slipping off the roof.

Barry gave me the end of the rubber hose-reel from the drum on the Pump curled in a loop. I transferred this loop onto my left shoulder and, pulling the hose-reel tubing, I clambered up on the roof. When I reached the ridge I sat astride the apex and shuffled towards the chimneystack. Dirty grey smoke oozed freely from the chimney pot, shooting up into the sky as I stood alongside it.

Mortar crumbled in my hands as I held onto the stack. Suddenly the direction of the wind changed and I became engulfed in a thick fog of choking smoke. Coughing and with my eyes smarting I stood perfectly still until the fog cleared.

"We're not sheeting the inside. Just put water down the chimney," Barry relayed our Sub Officer's orders, which indicated that there was to be no protective sheet held over the fireplace.

When Sub Officer Gardon, a man of few words at the best of times, was annoyed his lips tightened to resemble steel pipes. With a face full of thunder, his eyes became ever more prominent and bulging as he stood in centre of the cobbled street looking up at me through the swirling fog.

Trevor, our driver, with the appliance pump now in gear and its engine ticking over, opened the water tank valve and allowed the eighty gallons of water carried in two on-board tanks into the water-pump. He increased the revs.

"Water on!" Trevor shouted up to me. He was holding his uniform cap in one hand. I shuffled up close to the stack, stood on my toes and just managed to push the hose-reel nozzle outlet down the chimney pot. Amidst all the hot choking smoke still jetting out, water shot out of the end of the hose-reel. The chimneypot hissed and crackled as the cold water went in.

We were using only a fraction of our eighty gallons of water, but the thick choking smoke soon gave way to white steam.

"Knock off and make up," the Sub Officer shouted up from below bringing to an end to the incident.

I went back along ridge tiles. My feet were the first things to go down the roof ladder as I gripped the strings of the extension ladder from the ground before I passed the hose-reel tubing to Barry. He grinned.

"The Sub's not too pleased with the occupier," Barry said as he took the tubing from me and climbed down to the road below. I lifted the roof ladder from the guttering and slotted it over my shoulder. With both ladders replaced the hose-reel wound back on its drum. Gardon fastened every tunic button for protection and looked up at the offending chimney pot. There were no signs of heat but only a whisper of gentle steam, which fluttered out in a single gossamer thread.

The Sub Officer once more bravely ventured into the filthy house. Trevor and I followed staying close. The front room did not look affected at all; the falling soot that had been disturbed by our water just blended in with all the rest of the accumulated filth.

"At least the room's now covered in pure sterile soot," Trevor commented as he brushed his fingers through his short stubble of blonde hair.

"It's self-inflicted filth," he stated solemnly.

We returned to our Station and reversed the appliance into the engine house. We washed it, topped up the water tank and wiped the rubber hose-reel tubing clean, before we made a close examination for any foreign bodies, dead or alive, originating from the house at Colligan Terrace.

The stench lingered for hours in our nostrils, and no amount of washing seemed to eradicate it.

Returning to Monday and our daily chores meant emptying and polishing the long-room, our main recreation room. We had a different floor to clean on each day of the week. By now, as I had completed nine months in the Fire Service, these daily rituals were imprinted as important and essential tasks.

As each of the three watches, Red, White and Blue, worked through the week, competition arose to achieve the highest shine on the red linoleum floor in the long-room. We polished the floor all afternoon. As we made the final buffing strokes across it using polishing rags under an old heavy table, alarm bells sounded for Pump Two. It was another chimney fire and we used the same appliance with the same crew as Sub Officer Gardon took the white piece of paper with our fire message from the Control Room staff. Another chimney fire this time at number 14, Girvan Place.

Once again the chimney wagon, as Pump Two was sometimes known, pulled away from the engine house.

"That's all you're fit for," the rest of our crew shouted.

"Chimney fires are about your level. We'll stay behind for the proper fires," the guffaws echoed as we went down the street.

Girvan Street and Girvan Road were situated close to a large clothing factory. Rows and rows of neat back-to-back terrace houses criss-crossed acres of land. Clean tidy washing, draped on thin clotheslines, hung high across the streets. Large white bed sheets flapped merrily in the wind as we approached Girvan Place.

Hundreds of chimneys began their second life that day and threw out fresh smoke as people from the nearby clothing factories arrived home. Every chimney looked to be on fire as the fires were rekindled.

Outside number 14 Girvan Place a small petite woman stood anxiously. She was dressed in a spotlessly clean pale green cotton housecoat and was wringing her hands in obvious grief. She stepped back nervously and climbed up the three outside steps.

"I'm Mrs Thrasher, I'm very sorry to have to call you, but the fire in the grate is making an awful noise," she said, standing on her top step. Every edge of her three steps was scoured to a bright yellow with pumice stone.

"I've just this minute began to light the fire," she sobbed, "and my husband will be home soon," she added in a whisper.

Sub Officer Gardon, behaving in an entirely different way from the way he had done at the chimney fire earlier in the day, attempted to comfort her.

"Not to worry, Mrs Thrasher," he told her, "it's no problem. Let's have a look."

I followed him up the neat front steps and through her front door and into her living room. The house was neat and tidy. There were four chairs set around a square dining table; each chair was perfectly placed at each side. A brown chenille cloth was draped over the centre of the table. Neat folded corners, measured to the inch, were draped and reached the floor. A new brown carpet sat in the middle of the room, edged by polished linoleum. The floor shone brighter than the one back at our Station. The walls were covered in fresh wallpaper from which a large yellow and brown flower pattern shouted out.

"We've only just had the new fireplace fitted. The room's been completely decorated," Mrs Thrasher said. She held back a flood of tears.

"Have you had the old oven range removed?" Sub Officer Gardon asked.

"Yes," Mrs Thrasher answered quietly.

She produced a clean white lace handkerchief from her green housecoat and patted her nose. "My husband completely re-decorated the room and now it's all for nothing," she said, her voice trailing off and becoming barely a whisper.

We heard a noise, almost a groan, from behind the new fireplace as we stooped to listen.

"Have you any newspapers?" Sub Officer, asked.

Mrs Thrasher chased off into her scullery and immediately returned with a pile of old newspapers.

"I keep these for the fish and chip shop," she said, her hands shaking as she held them out.

We laid the sheets of paper carefully to form a pathway from the front door to the fireplace.

"Whoever fitted the new fireplace left parts of the old chimney stack still harbouring soot," Sub Officer went on to explain as I went outside. We placed our thirty five-foot ladder against the house and extended it to rest against the guttering.

All the houses in Girvan Place sprouted tall chimney pots, colloquially known as Long Toms. Some were more than six feet high and stood too high to be reached from the roof ridge tiles. To enable water to be poured down these pots we carried a chimney hose-reel adapter, a steel tube extension similar in shape to an up-turned umbrella handle. Fitted on the end of our hose-reel tubing, in place of the hose-reel nozzle, it was hooked over the high standing chimney pots.

I balanced on the ridge tiles, held the hose-reel adapter, and slotted the curved open end down the chimney pot.

The Sub Officer and Barry Tailor, working inside the room, first cleared the mantelpiece and placed a steel bucket in the hearth. Then they draped a chimney sheet, an old piece of canvas sheeting carried for this specific purpose, over the fireplace completely covering it.

Our Pump sent a quick burst of water through the red hose-reel tubing and up the thirty-five foot ladder, over the roof and out of the hose-reel adapter. A spray of water shot down the high chimney pot. Standing beside it I heard the water flushing down the chimney.

"And another," came the order.

The engine raced again, as more water went down the chimney. If there were too little water the accumulated soot would continue to burn. Too much, and excess water flooded into the living room. On the third attempt trickles of cold black water dripped into the bucket, waiting in the hearth. I was told to come down from the roof and Trevor, his uniform cap still protecting his blonde short stubble, climbed up the ladder. This provided ballast and support and allowed me to climb down.

Replacing all the equipment, we went back inside the house. The amount of dust and damage from the flying soot was minimal. Mrs Thrasher was satisfied as Trevor comforted her.

"Sit down, luv," he said, "we'll make you a cup of tea." He walked into the scullery.

But Mrs Thrasher was horrified and insisted she would make the tea and quickly chased Trevor out of her domain.

Gardon first asked permission and then went upstairs to check the chimneystack. Using a lamp, he checked the roof space in the attic for traces of soot that might have escaped from damaged brickwork.

"You want to get the people who fitted the fireplace to have another look," he told Mrs Thrasher he returned. He hunted for his snuff-box.

"They've removed the old range but they've left crevices where soot can gather," he said.

He inhaled a potion of snuff and undid his tunic.

Mrs Thrasher carried her best china cups and saucers in on a tray and deposited them on the table. The handles were so delicate and small that our sooty fingers could hardly poke through their holes.

"Will I have to pay a fine?" Mrs Thrasher's parting words as we climbed aboard our appliance.

"No, luv," Trevor began hoping to comfort her. He stroked his fingers through his blonde hair and leaned out of the cab window.

"It's a myth, luv," he said, "in 1892, in Queen Victoria's reign, there was an Act of Parliament with a ten-shilling penalty for allowing chimneys to catch fire!" He rubbed his hair as he gave her this remarkable piece of knowledge.

"But not these days," he finished. His left hand reached over and put the gear lever into position as he smiled at Mrs Thrasher.

Barry and I sat on the outside bench on the appliance and waved goodbye.

Mrs Thrasher gently waved back at us until we disappeared from her view.

Chapter 11

Dark winter nights threatened, and the legalised arson of the annual bonfires brought our usual crop of street fires. For an added measure of lunacy, potassium nitrate became available at corner shops and allowed anyone to become a pyromaniac.

The yearly ritual of retrieving household rubbish which had been stored for months in back yards, in middens and on bits of land ready for the fifth of November celebrations created many dangerous fire scenarios. Boxes of fireworks, often stored by children at home, created an even better recipe for tragedy.

The build up to this yearly pageant began weeks before Guy Fawkes Night, and we began to turnout to several instances of prematurely lit bonfires. Autumn approached and as daylight hours diminished the Station bells sounded for a house fire in the Breamish area. This area was a district densely populated with back-to-back terrace houses, separated by once cobbled streets which had recently been covered in tar and gravel chippings. The Breamish area was within a mile of our Station and we soon arrived there.

Lines of washing were still draped high above the streets as we hurriedly looked for Breamish Grove. Washing hung, pulled up high from the ground on pulley systems. Riding on our two appliances, Pump One in front and Pump Escape behind, we crept underneath lines of clothes, all hanging lifeless and still.

At last we located Breamish Grove tucked away at the end of Breamish Terrace. The eight houses were some distance back and almost completely hidden.

A woman, a headscarf covering rows of curlers, stood on the pavement. She was breathless and agitated.

"Our young kid has set fire to his bed in the attic," she screamed.

"Hose-reel," Station Officer Finnan demanded his usual North of the border brogue more pronounced than usual. The order was unnecessary. Fireman Barry Bleck had already uncoupled the small leather securing straps from the hose-reel of Pump One; the red tubing peeled easily off the drum. He dashed for the house door, the hose-reel nozzle in one hand and a heavy hand-held searchlight in the other.

"Anyone inside?" Someone shouted.

"No!" came the reply.

"No. Simon has run off. His father'll kill him!"

From the rear cab of the Pump Escape I ran to join Barry as he entered the house. I followed him up the freshly scoured stone steps and through the open door. Barry, tall and wiry, barged confidently into the living room without hesitating for a second.

An uncovered single ceiling-lamp flickered through hazy smoke. It cast just sufficient light to show a brown painted door in the far corner of the small room. Was this the door to the upstairs rooms? The smoke over the tight twisting stairs thickened as we climbed to the first floor. We were in total darkness.

"The staircase to the attic is directly above this." Barry coughed as he spoke.

I followed him. The hose-reel tubing dragged behind and needed more and more effort as we twisted our way up the stairs. On hands and knees we crawled through the smoke-filled first floor bedroom and across it to another door to which gave access to the attic stairs. The temperature rose as we shuffled up each wooden step and the smoke made breathing difficult. Barry, an established smoke eater who was reared on the tradition that the more smoke a man can take the better the Fireman, inched up the bare wooden stairs in front of me. His tall lanky frame was flat on the steps and the heels of his leather boots brushed against my face.

Every intake of breath brought sharp pains to my chest as I gasped for air. It was difficult to keep my eyes open, and I blinked constantly.

Staying close to the floor and so hiding from the dense smoke we groped our way upward like two slithering slugs. We clutched to breathe in the small pockets of clear air, which remained close to the floor, as we crawled up the stairs, which ended at the attic floor.

Barry shone his hand-held searchlight forwards through the swirling smoke. The beam of light was stopped dead by smoke. As the smoke swirled around through pockets of moving air, we could see a mattress glowing in front of us. Barry turned on our hose-reel nozzle and aimed the jet of water at the glow. A solid wall of smoke hit us. Breathing was impossible. For protection I chewed on my tunic sleeve as the damp wool filtered some of the acrid smoke. I bit harder and coughed. Barry continued to drench the bed. At first he seemed unaffected by the choking conditions.

"Get downstairs," he grunted at last. The two of us crashed down the stairs, our boots scraping on the bare wood floor. From the first floor bedroom, our lungs momentarily replenished with air, we made a final effort and climbed the narrow twisting stairs to the attic once again.

At the top of the stairs Barry made a dash for the attic window. In one quick movement he forced up the thick heavy glass window and opened it. It fell back on the slated roof with a thud. I joined him at the opened skylight. We took huge gulps of fresh air to fill our punished lungs. We jostled together, competing with the smoke escaping out into the night air. Refuelled, we continued to direct the spray of water onto the smouldering mattress.

"All right lads?" Station Officer Finnan shouted up the stairs as we turned off the jet.

"Come down for a rest," he coughed.

Outside we staggered as our boots crunched on the new gravel road chippings. The clean night air eased the sharp stabbing pains in my chest as the welcome supply of fresh oxygen-rich air flooded into my lungs.

"Get Stuart and Malcolm up here," the Station Officer shouted from inside the house to the rest of the crew, who were grouped round us on the road.

Stuart Cale, a fireman with nearly six years service, was not the keenest of men on the Watch. He was never a front man, and he was a born moaner; with two brown sad eyes he was our professional pessimist. From the tips of his black oily hair to the soles of his pale-grey woollen Fire Brigade socks, Stuart was always the Job's comforter on the Watch. He worked part time for the local undertakers and this was his ideal niche in life, fulfilling his insatiable appetite for disaster and providing a constant supply of morbidity.

Malcolm Cackerel, fresh from his twelve weeks at the Training School was still suffering from an outburst of boils. His neck sported a white bandage, which ended in a large reef knot tied under his chin.

Reluctantly Stuart, followed innocently by Malcolm, answered the Station Officer's command and entered the smoke filled house.

Standing outside we listened to the mother of Simon, the young boy who slept in the attic. She told us why she had called us.

Simon, nine years old, had dashed home from school. Intrigued and fascinated by the box of fire-works, he tried lighting a thunder flash. In an instant the whole box burst into flames.

"Where's the young lad now?" Barry asked.

"Probably at his nanny's, up Breamish Mount," his mother said, "his father will sort him out," she added wiping her face with soot stained hand.

Refreshed by the fresh air outdoors we returned upstairs. The mattress was now scorched and burnt. We parcelled it up in one of our salvage sheets and together we carried the awkward parcel downstairs and dumped it near the outside toilets, where it added to the heap of bonfire material.

Enroute back to our Station we noticed that the Pump One crew in front of us was gesticulating about something on our cab roof. As we reversed into the engine house, Malcolm climbed up and retrieved a large pair of pink bloomers. It was obviously captured from someone's washing line, and we thought it prudent to say nothing; we deposited the bloomers in our rag cupboard.

The end of the Thursday day shift arrived at last. Thursdays meant a night out with the Watch. This was a weekly ritual when we were not working nights, and it was an occasion never to be missed. Dressed in my one and only suit, a quick sandwich having been forced down while I dressed, I took a short bus journey to the centre of Torridge and by seven o'clock I was downing my first pint of beer before anyone else had arrived.

'Bag a Granny night', as some senior members of the watch called Thursdays, always began in the Torridge City Tavern. A couple of pints of beer and then en masse, we waltzed to the Wine Lodge for some white wine. For just ten shillings this intake of alcoholic courage was sufficient to make any girl unable to resist our advances. That was the theory, anyway.

"Where's Barry?" I asked. Barry, normally one of Thursday's regulars, was not present.

"He's not coming tonight," Trevor Tailor said, standing alongside Stuart Cale, full pint glasses in their hands.

"It's all that smoke he ate this afternoon," Stuart said, his car keys dangling from his hand. In spite of his miserable outlook to life, Stuart believed passionately that he was sent to Earth as a gift for every woman. His new Morris Traveller Estate was his door to success. He openly flaunted his car keys to impress any potential female in sight.

After a few drinks my world glowed. As the evening progressed we staggered onto the local dance hall, just in time to grab any willing female. But again my success rate was zero. The night ended with me happy but single. I staggered down the steps of the last bus, trying to explain politely if a little incoherently to the conductor that passengers needed careful handling. The conductor just laughed. I jumped off the rear platform onto the pavement and staggered home to my flat.

The following day Barry Bleck was off work, sick. Patricia, his wife, came to the Station straight from the hospital. He was coughing blood when he got home from work. They called the doctor who ordered Barry to go to hospital.

"Told you Barry should have worn a breathing set," Stuart Cale said, "we carry breathing sets on appliances. Why don't we use them?" Stuart as usual talked the loudest. No one disagreed.

"The Proto-oxygen sets do take an age to put on properly, but our new Siebe Gorman sets are easy," he continued.

The Siebe Gorman compressed-air set weighed about thirty pounds and the air lasted for about thirty minutes. The apparatus consisted of a compressed air cylinder and a demand regulator valve in the facemask. Unlike our oxygen sets, the air-set did not have to be completely bled free of air when starting up. The starting procedure was simple in comparison with that of the oxygen sets.

Assistant Chief Carp suddenly appeared on the Station. With the news of a fireman in hospital his visit was expected. But he arrived with the excuse to tell us there were still not enough new recruits to implement the forty-eight hour working week, regardless of demands from our Union. This new shift system, already agreed by other Brigades, provided an extra day or night off duty. The Fire Brigade Union had been negotiating for some time to achieve fewer hours in Torridge City Brigade but always the answer was no: there were not enough men.

"Bleck is going to be all right," the Assistant Chief said dodging any questions about when and if the new shift system would come into effect. He made a quick exit.

"Who wants to go and see Barry from work tonight?" Trevor Tailor asked.

"Count me in," David Capelin said.

Straight from work, the three of us piled into David's old Ford Zodiac and set off on our mission of mercy. We went to the hospital, but we were told that he had been discharged and was now at home. We piled back into David's car and set off again.

"Nice to see you all," Patricia, Barry's wife, greeted us, "he's in the front room. Go through."

Barry sat on the sofa. His face beamed. His red curly hair was groomed and tidy.

"Young Michael's here too!" Barry spotted me.

"Cup of tea, lads?" Patricia enquired.

"No thanks, Pat, we just called to see how Barry is," David answered.

"Michael, do you fancy doing my coal job?" Barry turned to me and asked. Always on the look out for more money, I accepted at once without thinking twice about it. Most men on the shift did extra work to provide additional money for a better life style. As I was still a probationer, such work was frowned upon but my take home pay barely covered my basic living expenses and any extra income would be welcome.

"My brother needs a mate when he's delivering coal," Barry said as he gave me the address of the coal-yard.

After my shift on Friday, Saturday and Sunday nights I arranged to meet Barry's brother, Gilbert, on the following Monday, a week before Bonfire night. The going rate was four shillings per hour, and with no one to know about any deductions this was more per hour than my Fire Brigade pay.

Meeting Gilbert for the first time I was startled to see that they looked identical. Same colour hair. Both tall and thin.

"This is Barnacle Bill; he's worth his weight in gold." Gilbert said, introducing a big heavy yellow Labrador. The dog took centre spot in the front cab of the coal lorry. Perched behind the gear lever, he looked out of the cab window and drooled as he watched the world outside. He displayed several lumps on both front legs. Gilbert explained

"The vet says the lumps can come off. But Bill's too old for operations," Gilbert said as we drove away.

Barnacle Bill knew somebody was talking about him. The dog looked at his master with his mouth open, his tongue out. He understood every word.

We first drove to a railway siding to bag four tons of loose coal into large waist high hessian sacks.

"Barnacle Bill stays in the cab," Gilbert said as we climbed down from the cab so that the empty lorry could be weighed. Then we drove off the weigh-bridge towards the railway trucks, stacked with mountains of coal.

"Hold the bags wide open but tuck your thumbs underneath out of the way of the shovel," Gilbert advised.

The large steel shovel scraped on the floor and pieces of coal flew into the bag without pausing. Gilbert lifted each bag when it was full on to a set of scales. There were two fifty-six pound weights on one side, and each bag was adjusted with an odd piece of coal until it tipped and balanced one hundredweight exactly.

It was nearly mid-day before we had filled and stacked eighty-one bags on the back of the lorry. On the way out of the coal yard Barnacle Bill was allowed to run about. He was not in the cab for the out-going weighing and he was indeed worth his weight in coal!

As we arrived at our first customer I strained to carry a bag of coal on my back. The savage lumps of coal dug deep into my back. I thought it was easier to carry someone down a ladder than to have such an inert solid mass bearing down on a pair of unsteady ankles. No wonder Barry and his brother Gilbert were so strong!

In front of every terrace house in the Breamish area was a tiny grate at floor level. We first emptied the sacks onto the paving stones and then the loose coal was slotted by shovel into the cellars through the tiny grate.

"Do I know you?" A customer asked Gilbert as she paid her money.

"Were you in a fire-engine the other day? You came rushing along here and took a pair of my new pantaloons from my washing line," the old woman said as she put her change into a tiny purse.

"You went to our kid's house further down in Breamish Grove didn't you?" Simon's Nan said. I suddenly remembered Simon's escape from the fire on our fire-call earlier.

"Not me, Misses," Gilbert replied.

I did not have the courage to explain that her bloomers were in our rag bin. I quickly joined Barnacle Bill in the lorry.

After a full day of bagging, carrying, and shovelling coal I was exhausted. I climbed into the cab after we had finished the final delivery and stroked Barnacle Bill with my dirty hand. I was filthy from head to toe and I ached all over. But I collected my hard-earned twenty-eight shillings. Night duty began on the fifth of November began, and we expected to be busy. The first call came, to an unlit bonfire under some electric power lines.

Sub Officer Kevin Gardon, in charge of Pump Two, rolled his eyes as Pump Two stopped alongside some waste ground. Slowly he dismounted and walked towards a policeman sitting astride his police motorcycle.

An unlit bonfire towered into the night sky between two overhead high pylons. Six heavy cables, draped between the pylons, could be seen in the dark sky.

We dismantled some of the large wooden crates and spread the material away from possible danger. Leaving the policeman to trace the culprits we returned to the Station and had just begun to clean the appliance when the bells went again. Breamish Place. A bonfire.

"That's where we were the other Thursday!" Fireman Stuart Cale said.

"That was the Grove," Sub Officer Gardon corrected.

"Breamish Place is the next street."

The dark night air was filled with the smell of bonfires as residents all over the City began their Guy Fawkes celebrations. We passed several fires. Groups of people were standing around and an odd rocket shot up, leaving a trail of sparks.

Turning into Breamish Place we were suddenly confronted with a whole road on fire. A molten river of burning liquid tar ran down to greet us. A bonfire at the far end of Breamish Place was well alight. Flames fanned by a good wind, showered sparks high into the sky.

"Get a line on," Sub Officer Gardon ordered meaning we should get water from a street hydrant.

"And keep the appliance well clear!"

He strolled up towards the bonfire.

"Who's in charge here?" He asked. Everybody looked unmoved; their eyes were uncommitted. The glow from the fire was reflected in their vacant faces.

"You can't have a bonfire here!" Gardon's eyes nearly popped out of their sockets. There was no response. Picking on one person, he asked his question again.

"We've always had a bonfire here, in this street, since I was a lad," the reply came.

"But the road now is covered with tarmac." Sub Officer Gardon appealed for reason.

Together with Stuart Cale we helped our driver, Trevor Tailor, to locate the nearest hydrant and ran out a line of delivery hose.

"Water on!" A solid jet of water from the open end of the delivery hose soon curtailed the stream of fire. The liquid river of molten tarmac froze solid and stopped dead. But the new road surface was now scarred and ruined.

"Fancy some pie and peas?" The old woman asked as we prepared to leave. I recognised the woman from when I had delivered her coal and tucked my head out of sight into the top of my open tunic.

"Simon, go get these firemen some food for your Nan," the bloomer-missing woman said.

Simon looked none the worse for his escapade earlier in the week. He ran off and brought each of us a basin containing a pork pie, covered with a lump of mushy peas and swimming in vinegar.

"Find another site for your bonfire next year," Sub Officer Gardon said. We stuffed our mouths with food and left. Until next year.

Chapter 12

There was no public transport on Christmas day. This meant walking to the Fire Station.

It was a mile-long walk through the empty, cold deserted streets, which gave the impression of a world on holiday. It seemed that only firemen worked during the festive season. As a bonus for receiving no extra payment for working on Bank Holidays, we were allowed to stand-down and the Station cleaning routines were deferred.

Living on my own, I welcomed the comradeship and the chance of being with others as well as the promise of a turkey dinner. I looked forward to being on duty.

Normally the senior officers made a point of visiting Fire Stations at Christmas, but the latest decision to delay our reduction in hours to a forty-eight hour shift system caused problems. Many Fire Brigades nearby already worked fewer hours for the same pay, and our rumblings of discontent went on bubbling under the surface. Extra recruitment had still not reached the required levels, and so our Chief Officer and Fire Brigade Watch Committee refused to discuss the matter any further.

Christmas dinner, complete with all the trimmings, was to be ready by one o'clock. Maurice Grundel, the canteen man, wearing a fresh clean brown coat, complained in his usual droning fashion that he needed assistance to prepare the dinner.

I was volunteered for this with Malcolm Cackerel, another probationer. We were immediately detailed to the canteen where to prepare, cook and serve a full Christmas dinner for eighteen men seemed a formidable task.

The vegetables, bacon, sausages had all been dumped on the kitchen table. In the centre of the table an enormous turkey sat with its legs trussed, abandoned on a thick wooden chopping board. Acres of cold white skin covered the twenty-five pound bird. Roads from its blue-blood veins spread round spikes of stubble.

Maurice disappeared, leaving just the two of us to attack this mountain of uncooked and unprepared food. I peeled my way through the heap of potatoes, using a knife that would have trouble slicing soft cheese. Eventually two large pans were filled with rocks of roughly hewn potatoes. They stood on the stove waiting to be boiled.

Maurice reappeared.

"There's more potato thrown away than for eating," he said, peering in the waste bin.

Malcolm meanwhile took charge of roasting the massive turkey, plastering its white skin in inches of lard. Then he slotted the bird into the oven.

"Where are the giblets?" Maurice asked.

"What giblets?" We asked.

The turkey, which was heating nicely, was immediately retrieved from the oven. Malcolm slid his hand inside the warm rear-end and retrieved a paper parcel containing a heart and pieces of liver.

"We'll need that for the gravy," Maurice said.

Unknown to us help was on the way. The ex-chef, Fireman Peter Margot was our saviour. Everyone but us knew Peter would be the master cook for the day. He had worked in the catering trade before joining Fire Brigade and when he arrived on the scene, he considered all our toils and troubles absolutely useless. The potatoes were not peeled properly, the Brussels were untidy, and the carrots not clean.

A white tea towel wrapped around his waist, Peter set about methodically redoing all our preparations. The potatoes were re-eyed, reshaped and sorted into four different pans for boiling. Each Brussels sprout was inspected, washed and manicured with his personal sharp knife to look neat and presentable. The carrots were given the same fastidious treatment; after being sliced diagonally they sat in their pan like works of art.

Now relegated to being mere assistants, we willingly carried out every order Peter gave us. He removed the turkey from its premature incarceration, scraped off our coating of grease, filled the inside with handfuls of stuffing, re-coated the skin with a layer of butter and herbs and placed the bird back in the oven. Malcolm's task for the rest of the morning was to nurse this twenty-five pound monster into a golden roasted offering. He was still suffering from boils and two new plasters adorned his forehead as more ulcers sprouted. He guarded the large oven with his life all morning. His face glowed from the ensuing heat as he regularly opened the oven doors to baste our enormous bird.

Under the ever-watchful eyes of our Chef-cum-Firemen, dinner eventually arrived; complete with an aroma that tantalised every taste bud. The rest of our watch, who had already enjoyed a few pints of beer from the Station bar, waited like hungry vultures.

The officers on duty, Station Officer Finnan and our two Sub Officers, took it upon them to serve everybody's dinner as we all sat down. This was a Christmas ritual and a break from our normal procedure, at all other meal times there was a segregation policy. Officers always ate in the officers' mess, an adjoining room that was specifically for Station Officers and above. In the Station canteen there were tables used only by Sub Officers and Leading Firemen. As Firemen we normally sat on our own.

But this was Christmas and for this one mealtime the privileges of rank were relaxed.

Station Officer Finnan carved the huge roasted turkey, producing a stack of white meat. Meanwhile Sub Officer Gardon poured thick vegetable soup from a pot jug into our empty dishes as we sat, our spoons rattling on our tables.

The flat ten-inch plates were too small to accommodate the enormous dinner that followed the soup. Sub Officer Latchet gingerly carried our heavy steaming plates from the kitchen to our tables. Thick slices of white turkey meat, its edges crispy brown, draped themselves over the sides of our plates. Mountains of roast potatoes, green vegetables, sausages, creamed potato croquettes, bacon, bread sauce and finally, on the slices of turkey, a puddle of rich thick gravy completed the meal.

Just to be Peter's assistant felt good. Showers of gratitude and praise greeted us from stuffed mouths. The dinners slowly disappeared, eaten with enormous relish. The room fell silent. The scrape of knifes and forks on plates were the only sound to disturb the silence.

The noise from the tiny bell high on the canteen wall tinkled, rudely interrupting our dinner. Chairs scrubbed across the concrete floor as we groaned with disbelief.

We all dropped our knifes and forks left our dinners, and took off on the long run to the engine house. Maurice Grundel, drumstick in one hand, was the last to leave.

The control staff ladies also worked on Christmas Day. She stood waiting outside the Control Room door with a strand of silver tinsel in her hair.

"The alarm panel showing a fire at Merling's Store, Brett Street City Centre," she said as the piece of tinsel slipped over one eye.

Giving out three hand-written messages, one for each appliance - Pump One, Pump Escape and the Turntable Ladder - she stood, smiled and watched as we all climbed aboard our appliances.

In my tunic, my boots in my arms, my helmet plonked on my head, I climbed onto Pump One.

Outside the streets were completely deserted. Unlit Christmas lights were dead, draped high across the street on thick cables. In the daylight hours they lost their touch of magic.

Our three appliances quickly arrived in Brett Street and pulled up alongside Merling's, a large city-centre shop, which sold everything from food to furniture. It stood deserted for the holidays.

Station Officer Finnan climbed down from his front cab and looked through the front windows. Holding his white fire-helmet casually in his right hand, he stooped and stared through the plate glass window.

Sub Officer Latchet, in charge of Pump Escape, dismounted and joined the Station Officer on the pavement. A small red-faced man wearing an old grey raincoat puffed his way out of the store through a small side door. The remains of a thick cigar jutted out from his mouth.

"I smelled smoke," he said.

"Who are you?" Station Officer Finnan asked.

"Caretaker," he answered taking a breath around the sides of the thick cigar.

Someone else worked on a Christmas Day. Good I thought.

"When I called in to check the building," he began, "I noticed a smell of smoke." He sucked in air and let out a mouthful of smoke without removing the cigar. His words mingled with the exhaled smoke. His face was obscured behind a blue cloud.

"I broke an alarm glass. I hope I did the right thing?" he coughed.

We followed him through a door into the store. A series of coloured bulbs pulsated silently from electric bulb holders high on the ceiling. Their coloured display flickered and danced on the dark walls of the empty store. Breaking a break the glass point, the caretaker had activated a direct telephone link to our Brigade and set off the fire alarm in our Control Room.

We searched the ground floor but found no trace of smoke.

We located the point where the glass was broken. Station Officer Finnan, using a piece of cardboard, temporally repaired it and Sub Officer Latchet re-set the alarm system at the front entrance. The pulsating coloured lights on the ceiling went out.

"There was smoke," the caretaker insisted, "it was near the shop window."

We looked again and sniffed the front display windows. There was no trace of any smoke, not even a whiff.

"We'll take a look outside," our Station Officer told the caretaker, "it's more likely smoke from his Christmas cigar," he muttered under his breath as we all went outside.

Merling's shop was jammed between adjoining stores and this meant we had to walk around the complete complex to reach rear of the premises.

"There should be an alley-way leading to Moyle Yard and the loading bay at the back," Maurice Grundel told us from the open cab window.

"Can anyone smell anything?" Someone asked.

"It'll be my Christmas pudding that's burning!" Maurice shouted. He was still sporting his brown coat. He took a bite from his turkey leg as he crunched Pump One into gear. We climbed on the rear running board as the appliance moved down Brett Street. The alleyway entrance to Moyle Yard from Brett Street was not wide enough to allow our Pump to enter. We dropped off the rear platform and, thinking more of our stomachs than of a false alarm, headed off to the rear of the store, walking through a narrow path to Moyle Yard.

Nothing. No smell. No sign of anything.

"Let's get back to the Station." Station Officer decided.

Three appliances returned as fast as they had come.

The crews of Pump Two and the Emergency Tender, who had remained on the Station, salvaged the deserted remains of our dinners. Marking each plate with our names on pieces of cardboard, they had placed them in a warm oven to await our return.

Locating our half-eaten dinners, we resumed eating I was just about to stuff a fork loaded with a piece of bacon, sausage and stuffing into my mouth, when the bells sounded again.

Fortesque Hotel, Moyle Yard.

A full turnout again, with Pump One, Pump Escape and Turntable Ladder.

Once again we left our part eaten meals, this time for the Fortesque, a three-star, hundred-roomed city centre hotel which was fully staffed, even on Christmas Day. Access was at the rear of Merling's store. As we turned into Moyle Yard, the approach road was blocked by a couple of taxis and an ambulance.

More people who had to work at Christmas.

We ran the last few yards and entered front foyer of the hotel to find an anxious manager waiting.

"I didn't want to bother you on Christmas Day, but there's a smell of burning in the cellar," he said.

I followed Station Officer Finnan. We trooped down a flight of deep piled carpeted staircase, through a staff entrance, along a dark corridor and entered a wired-caged wine cellar. We looked and sniffed around. There was no trace of anything. The manager insisted there had been a smell and even a trace of blue smoke, but there was nothing and he apologised profusely all the way upstairs.

In the hotel foyer a group of his inebriated guests cheered the rest of our crew waiting outside. The ambulance departed, taking an expectant mother to Torridge City Maternity Hospital. Two taxis, crammed with the rest of her family, followed in hot pursuit. It was, they drunkenly shouted, a possible Christmas Day birth at the hospital.

More Christmas Day workers.

Once again we were tucking into the remains.

Blanche Spurling, our faithful cook, had left us one of her famous Christmas puddings. Steaming all morning, the end result was a rich, solid lump of piping hot concentrated fruit, drenched with brandy. Each spoonful was covered in an avalanche of brandy butter sauce. The last mouthful took some forcing down. After consuming more than enough I felt and looked like the pudding heavy, rich and oozing with goodness.

The mountain of washing up was stacked high and filled every conceivable spare inch in the kitchen.

Peter Margot was indeed a good chef and his presentation and his food was excellent. But the number of plates, pots, pans and other crockery swamped the entire kitchen. A good hour elapsed before everything was finally washed and replaced. We all collapsed in a heap. But our rest was short lived. Bells sounded again. And again the call was to Merling's Store, City Centre, Brett Street. Only Pump One, with the Station Officer was to attend this time.

I grabbed my fire-uniform and we left once again for Brett Street where we found exactly the same conditions. The caretaker again insisted he could smell fire. This time he did not break the glass of an alarm but rang nine-nine-

nine. The cigar in his mouth looked no different. Still gripped tight between his lips, it stuck out like a thick stubby carrot.

Station Officer Finnan stood in the middle of Brett Street, his arms folded. His white helmet under his arm, his feet apart, he listened patiently to the caretaker. Again we searched the building. But we still could find no sign of anything untoward.

We returned to the Station as daylight faded.

The appliances, even on Christmas Day, needed to be washed-down with soap and water and leathered dry for the night watch, which would take over. Even the floor of the engine house needed its obligatory mopping; we glossed it over with water. As all hands busied cleaning, the bells sounded for the fourth time.

"Brett Street near Merling's Store again. It's a call from the police!"

Torridge City Centre streets now sparkled with Christmas lights. The roads were still deserted as we sat outside on the bench seats on the back of Pump One; strings of lights dazzled above our heads. On the pavement outside Merling's Store a policeman and his sergeant were standing waiting for our arrival.

A hundred yards away from Merling's Store, the policeman on his Christmas Day beat found that a steel inspection lid set in the pavement was breathing out a whisper of smoke.

Using our crowbar we lifted the lid and exposed underground electric lighting cables and found the problem. The extra power required for the festive illuminations had allowed a cable to overheat, causing the protective bitumen to melt and then to smoulder. Smoke percolating through pipes below ground had seeped into

Merling's Store and eventually, through the ducting, underground into the cellar of the Fortesque Hotel. Using the appliance's radio, Station Officer Finnan requested the attendance of street lighting electricians.

Someone else was working during the festive season!

The electricians arrived and soon isolated the supply. Lines of Christmas lights went out all along Brett Street. But the City was now safe.

Chapter 13

Amos Sturgeon, Scrap-Hoarder Extraordinaire. Every city has one!

Amos Sturgeon stored anything and everything, old furniture, obsolete stock and bankruptcy throw-outs, were kept in a number of old part-derelict properties, old disused chapels, run-down warehouses, underneath railway arches...anywhere.

And what a good customer of the Fire Brigade he was! At regular intervals fires just occurred in his many properties, usually at week-ends and always at night. He eventually arrived at the fire in an old blue Bradford Jowett van. He would stand, dressed like a tramp in old tattered clothes, and stare in amazement, mumble a few swear words and leave. It was rumoured he changed out of his old clothes, swapped his old van for a brand new Daimler and went home to a luxurious detached mansion in the well-to-do part of Torridge City.

My first introduction to the trouble and work that attached itself to Amos Sturgeon began in the early hours on a bitterly cold January morning in another Station's area.

Two Pumps from Weaver Road Fire Station, the first on the scene, requested that two more appliances came to their assistance. Chasing over icy, cold streets, our Pump One and Pump Escape came to a huge old building which was once a Trinity Methodist Chapel but which had been acquired by Amos and used as one of his many storehouses.

Smoke poured from an impressive clock tower its hands long gone, its clock face now broken. The green copper dome now disappeared in a swirling grey blanket, which hid any embarrassment from its change from its former glory.

Four huge stone pillars framed the impressive front entrance of the building. A line of delivery hose was draped across the wide steps and disappeared through the front doors. The two Pump crews in attendance had already got water going into the building.

Station Officer Finnan announced our arrival and decided we would attack the fire from the other side. The seat of the fire appeared to be behind the front doors.

"Get down the side road and into the building at the back," he told us, screaming his commands in his Scottish accent.

"The fire needs to be driven out, not in!"

Our Pump One moved off to rear of the chapel.

"Hydrant?" Someone shouted.

"Get a line on," chorused everyone on our crew in unison, like a rallying call.

Riding on Pump One, I dropped off the open rear platform before the appliance came to a stop. The delivery hose sat in a side locker curled in neat rolls and ready to be used. I pulled one length out. The female couplings with their instantaneous sockets had two protruding brass cylindrical lugs. With constant movement these lugs often interlocked, digging into each other in the hose locker. I tugged at one length of the hose. Three lengths of delivery hose came crashing out, falling and landing on the road in a heap. I picked up one length and set off for a hydrant.

Someone had already connected a standpipe to the street water main. Connecting the male coupling to the stand pipe and gripping both handle lugs, I ran my length of delivery hose from the street hydrant towards the rear of our appliance. The delivery hose spun from the female hose coupling as I held the hose length high above my shoulders. Connecting the female coupling to the male outlet of our Pump completed the circuit. The hydrant was turned on and struggled to fill the delivery hose from the poor water supply.

The hose from one of our two outlets from was already laid out to the rear of the burning chapel and disappeared over a locked wrought iron gate where it stopped. I picked another length of delivery hose from the pile on the road and ran to the gate with it.

"Let's get back inside," Malcolm Cackerel said in his Irish accent, appearing from the darkness of the graveyard and asking for a special outlet that connected into the end of the delivery hose. It was the first time Malcolm had appeared without any plasters. There were no longer any visible signs of boils sprouting from his face.

I dashed back to Pump One and selected a controlled nozzle which slotted into the female end of our hose and enabled the water flow to be turned on and off. I ran back, climbed over the iron spikes on top of the gate and dropped heavily into the chapel yard.

"There's a side door here," Malcolm screamed, "gaffer's finding a way in."

The delivery hose went to a side entrance, running over old gravestones, which were now used for paving. A large hand-held lamp flickered in the dark as Station Officer Finnan and Leading Fireman Bret struggled to gain entry through a large solid door. Bret tapped the side of the door with a sledgehammer.

"Here, give me the hammer!" Station Officer snatched the large sledgehammer from the Leading Fireman.

"You hold the lamp. The door needs hitting, not kissing!"

Finnan swung at the door hinges. Church buildings were notoriously robust with every door unique in design, and it needed several swings of the sledgehammer to make it surrender. The entire door surround at last gave way, crashing inwards with a sound of splintering wood.

"Remember what I told you about hammers?" Station Officer said to me.

The corridor inside was empty of smoke and the beam of light from the hand lamp easily pierced the darkness.

I picked up the sledgehammer as Malcolm peeled off more delivery hose. We all shuffled deeper into the chapel. We arrived at another door. More demolition was needed.

"Hit the door around the door handle," the Station Officer told me. I lifted the heavy sledgehammer and gripped the well-seasoned straight- grained ash handle. Everyone stood away from the metal head as it swung back. It crashed against the brass handle.

"Again. It's going!" Station Officer Finnan encouraged us.

With the second swing, the door-latch broke free. The door moved slightly inwards. We all pushed, but the door barely opened.

"There's a load of stuff behind the door." Malcolm peered through the gap, using the hand lamp to see inside.

Connecting the nozzle to the end of the dry delivery hose, I waited.

"I'll have another look outside." Station Officer said. He took Leading Fireman Bret with him and left us in the dark, taking the only light.

"Come on," Malcolm suggested, "let's get another lamp."

We retraced our steps to the outside door. We were dressed completely in black and we experienced difficulty seeing each other before stumbling on the outside door as we felt our way along a wall, treading over our hose line.

Outside the chapel our driver, Fireman John Scar, complained that the incoming water supply from the hydrant was not good enough.

During his seven years Fire Service John had been posted on a regular basis, serving time in nearly all five Stations in Torridge City. Well known for his outspoken views, he never showed any weakness when he addressed senior ranks. This, no doubt, was one of the reasons for his constant transfers.

The white helmet of our Station Officer danced in the dark. His hand lamp flashed a pencil of white beam in John Scar's face as he listened to John's request for more water.

"I've sent P.E. down the main road," the Station Officer gasped, indicating he had directed our Pump Escape to find another water supply. His words shot out of his mouth in sudden spurts.

"This hydrant must be connected to the same water-main as the other crews are using. They're attacking the fire from the front of building and driving the fire inwards. We need to be inside driving the fire out."

"Four Pumps for one of old Sturgeon's jobs." Assistant Chief Carp arrived, taking his oil-skin raincoat from the boot of his car he quickly dressed.

"Aye! But there's no water," answered the Station Officer, "and the fire's getting hold."

The delivery hose appeared through the dimly lit street. It had been run out by our Pump Escape crew and soon connected into our Pump One.

"I've found a six inch main," Fireman Barry Bleck announced proudly, "Bernard's bringing up a second line."

Leading Fireman Bernard Loche unrolled his length of delivery hose and snapped the female connector onto the inlet. His big round face beamed with satisfaction.

"Water on!" John Scar shouted, wanting the supply of water turned on at the six-inch hydrant down the road.

"I'll go," Bret volunteered. He waddled off down the road to the Pump Escape.

Taking two small rechargeable hand lamps, Malcolm and I retraced our steps into the chapel, taking two more lengths of delivery hose with us.

"The place is bursting at the seams. It's full of something." The Assistant Chief greeted us in the dark corridor. As he pushed past us the bright beam from his large hand-lamp highlighted his thin lanky shadow on the wall.

We located the end of our original length of delivery hose, removed the nozzle and in the dim light, provided by our small lamps, we connected another length of hose. Pushing on the jammed door, we made sufficient room to be able to squeeze through. We climbed up a tight twisting staircase before joining our second length of hose. We penetrated deeper and higher into the chapel. At the top of the stairs we were stopped again by another closed door.

I shoulder-charged the door. Surprisingly, it flew open and we shone our small lamps into the abyss inside. Our tiny beams of light stopped at some high wooden seat ends. Above the seats, at the far end of the auditorium, we could see a deep red glow.

Station Officer Finnan joined us as we pushed our way through the door, dragging more delivery hose with us. The entrance led us onto a balcony with rows of pews, which overlooked the main body of the chapel.

Suddenly and without warning the fire flared up, lighting the inside of the chapel in yellows and reds. Clouds of dense smoke curled upwards before stopping against the high vaulted ceiling. The smoke cloud slowly descended upon us.

Coughing and choking, Malcolm suggested using Breathing Apparatus sets.

"But it's only an old chapel," Station Officer Finnan at first hesitated, then said "yes, all right, go get couple of B.A. sets," using just the initials, indicating Breathing Apparatus, a term well known in the Fire Service.

Once again we negotiated our way back down the twisting staircase, sliding and falling over the delivery hose, still empty on the steps, and ran back to our Pump One. There we removed the two Siebe Gorman Compressed air-sets hung in the crew cab.

We began putting the air-sets on. Feeding my arms though the harness that felt like donning a heavy cumbersome haversack, the two straps dropped on my shoulders. The air-cylinder, now heavy and solid sat in the middle of my back. I turned on the main valve at the base of the cylinder. With my helmet temporally removed I slotted my face into the facemask and pulled the straps tight at the back of the head trapping strands of my hair. The clear plastic face-visor, edged with a rubber seal, now covered our eyes, mouth, and nose. Now with our helmets replaced we were ready.

"I'll turn your water supply on in a few minutes," John Scar, the Pump operator said as we gave him our yellow air-set identification tallies. With the added weight on our backs we hobbled into the chapel.

Our cylinders clanged on the narrow corridor walls as we climbed the twisting staircase once more. We went through the smashed door and again into the main body of the building. Heat and smoke engulfed us as we extended our delivery hose further along the pews towards the glow of the fire.

The delivery hose ended at the balcony edge. Before we could slot our nozzle into the end of the delivery hose, water began to trickle out of the open end..

"Hurry," shouted Malcolm, his words muffled and barely audible through his facemask. The water pressure grew and water shot out from the open end of the hose.

"Kink the hose!" Malcolm cried.

I struggled desperately to stop the flow of water leaking from the open end, drenching us both. Bending and twisting the hose to restrict the flow of water, we grappled with the delivery hose outlet until at last the nozzle pushed into the female outlet. We heard the familiar click as it was rammed home.

Immediately the water pressure built up, and made the delivery hose turn rock hard. The jet of water shot forwards and crackled; the air trapped inside the delivery hose freed itself as we pulled back on the control lever opening the outlet fully.

Across the chapel the powerful jet of water hit the seat of the fire with damaging force. The sound of splintering timber mixed with the sound fury of the lashing water. Under this serious assault, the fire fought back, spitting angrily at us. Our water struck at the heart of the fire. We struggled as the pressure from the force of the jet forced us backwards. We continued to aim our jet of water in the direction of the fire. In a final act of defiance, the whole chapel filled with acrid smoke and steam.

Our breathing apparatus protected us from the filthy, obnoxious atmosphere. We breathed in easily, taking in fresh air from our pressurised cylinders. The demand valves in our facemasks clicked repeatedly and this constant clicking provided comfort and assurance.

"You can come out now," Assistant Chief Officer Carp told us, coughing as he struggled to breathe through a rag he held close to his mouth. Unlike our senior officer we remained protected from the polluted atmosphere by our breathing apparatus.

"And take those sets off!" He added sarcastically.

The cold air in the street outside felt good as we removed the rubber seals from our sticky sweat-covered faces. Heat from our hot damp tunics drifted up to our faces. In the headlights from our Pump One we seemed to be supported by a mythical steam sky-harness. Removing the heavy sets from our backs we placed them on the rear of Pump One. We were cold and wet, but at least we were free from the usual chest pains of breathing in smoke. Water poured freely out of our boots as we removed them.

A noise, like that of a large motorised lawn mower, put-putted up the road from Amos Sturgeon's old van as he arrived. Big and fat, he had difficulty climbing out of it. With one arm folded over the roof he levered himself slowly upwards before allowing one foot at a time to grip the road. Our Assistant Chief greeted him with a hint of annoyance.

"Another load of rubbish causing us trouble, Amos?"

"Full of valuable stuff," Amos replied in a gruff voice, "worth a fortune that stuff in there." He ambled off to inspect the damage.

The chapel was certainly packed solid with something, valuable or otherwise. The fire was now considered to be under control. A message was dispatched to Brigade Control to confirm that no further assistance would be needed. We just caught the end of the message sent by John Scar over the Pump's radio '...fire extinguished by three large jets' it concluded.

The crews from all four Pumps gathered together for warmth, company and a quick cigarette. All of us were now wet, miserable and cold.

"Two of you wore B.A.s," guffawed someone from the Weaver Road Fire Station.

"We thought men from Torridge City Station were proper firemen, not cissies." Another added the banter increasing.

"In future leave your trouser legs outside your boots," John told me, ignoring the comments, "then the water goes down the trousers and not straight into your boots." The brief respite over, the unenviable task of damping down commenced. Every piece of damaged stock had to turn over to make sure there were no hidden pockets of fire left.

The chapel was filled to the brim with wood from old school desks. Desktops together with hundreds and hundreds of planks from their bench type seats stacked in enormous piles all over the disused Chapel. No doubt rescued, on the cheap by Amos Sturgeon, they now piled high waiting for a future when fashion would return and people wanted to use real wood again. Apart from some of the edges, charred from the fire, underneath, tons of the oak-planks remained clean and marketable if and when the right time arrived.

Dawn lightened the eastern sky as we loaded all our used wet hose onto our appliances. We returned wearily to our Station.

Chapter 14

"You actually wore B.A.s at one of Sturgeon's derelicts!" We were taunted continuously. No mercy was given.

"You can't be real fireman."

"Real firemen can eat smoke!"

The ridicule continued as crews changed over at parade time.

"Everybody in the muster-room, now," the ever demanding Leading Fireman Bret shouted to us as we finished our night shift cleaning routines.

"The Assistant Chief wants to speak to you," he told us.

Official visits to any of the five Fire Stations in Torridge City by our senior officers were rare, and were usually for one of five reasons: to gloat; to admire themselves; to deliver some form of reprimand; because they wanted something or because they were about to retire.

Assistant Chief Officer Carp demanded us, his captive audience, should attend and soon got us. We shuffled slowly into the muster-room, grouped together for safety.

The muster-room, the axis of Torridge City Fire Station, was behind and slightly below the engine house.

Forever dark, the square room supported three exits. One was a large brown door from outside, constantly polished from men rushing through to answer the fire-bells. The second was a narrow rear entrance from our canteen. The third consisted of two blue swing doors, which led directly into the engine house up three narrow steps. On the four walls of the room our fire-uniforms hung. The high top shelf above them displayed a line of mostly black fire-helmets. Each helmet shone and the line strained upwards like rows of nesting ravens and reflected the harsh light from the two fluorescent tubes which were left on all day. The helmets all sat brooding, waiting patiently for the next call-out. Most helmets were black, some with a single red band for Leading Firemen and some with two red bands for Sub Officers.

Occasionally a white helmet sprouted to break the black monopoly. The white helmets were for the three operational Station Officers in charge of the three Watches. Underneath the fire-helmets on large hooks our individual belt and fire-axes hung wrapped in our fire-tunics. Below these our clean and shiny fire-boots sat erect on a shelf above central heating pipes. A large wooden table with two long bench seats occupied centre stage in the centre of the muster-room.

Rumours had spread for years which said that our eighty year old Fire Station was, at long last, to be replaced.

Stour Crescent Station, one of the Torridge City outer sub-stations, had recently closed while a new one grew on the same piece of land. Their only remaining Pump was now temporarily housed in a small shed adjoining the building site. News that this new Station was to be completed later in the year revived speculations that our Station was next in line for renewal.

John Scar, well known for his outspoken views, was the last to arrive; he strolled casually through the swing doors from the engine house.

"Glad you could join us, laddie," Assistant Chief Carp said, obviously annoyed at John's late arrival. Underneath his arm Carp carried a roll of paper, which we discovered were the plans of a proposed new Fire Station.

The latest proposals looked very impressive, as the tightly rolled plans were unravelled on the muster-room table. To prevent them curling back into a tight roll, Carp placed his uniform cap on one end. The single row of silver oak leaves on its peak bristled with newness as it sat there acting as a paperweight.

John offered to hold the other end and placed a willing hand carefully on the table. Carp stood back and glowed with pride. No one, he knew, could fail to be impressed by these latest proposals.

But John Scar was not impressed. Suddenly he lifted his hand and the plan curled, springing towards the Assistant Chief's cap.

"There's no point in building such a fancy place at all." John began.

"Such a fine looking Station is no use to us firemen."

The room went deathly silent. There was no sound at all. I had never experienced such open confrontation with a senior officer before, and I gasped my mouth wide open.

"All that's needed is a big hole in the ground," John went on, "with a big heavy lid. As firemen arrive for work we can all live in the hole. When there's a fire, the lid comes off, and we hear 'come out lads we need you'."

The muster-room hummed. I smiled nervously.

"After the fire we'll hear 'get back in your hole. That's where you belong!'" John drove his message home forcibly.

Assistant Chief Officer Carp went pale. The air went glacial. He picked up his treasured plans deliberately and rolled them up slowly and carefully. The crisp noise of the paper was the only sound to break the pregnant silence. Carp collected his uniform cap from the muster-room table and carefully placed it on his head.

Before anything else happened the fire-bells sounded and all eyes turned to the indicator board. 'Pump Two' shone out from the indicator board. I thankfully recalled that this was my allocated appliance for the night.

"Stand-by at Ellen Approach." A voice shouted from inside the engine house.

All the appliances at Ellen Approach Station had been called out to an incident leaving their station area with no appliances. Our Pump Two was sent to their Station to provide cover until they returned. Leaving behind the electric and stunned atmosphere I grabbed my fire-uniform from its peg and joined the crew on the Pump Two. John Scar, who was our driver, found it convenient to leave. He quickly started the engine.

On our way to Ellen Approach Station, the appliances radio crackled with our appliance call sign.

"Tango One-Two. Receiving?" A man's deep voice demanded.

Sub Officer Latchet, sitting in the front of the appliance, reached for the mouthpiece. Pressing the small microphone at the end of the black cable, he said,

"Go ahead with message."

"Return to base, Tango One-Two!" It was the voice of our Assistant Chief.

When we returned, we learned that one of the two women in Control was ill and had gone home. Since it was never thought proper for a woman to work all night with a man, her partner was also sent home, so two Firemen would have to man Brigade Control for the remainder of the night.

Housed in a long thin room at side of the engine house, Brigade Control received and handled all incoming fire calls for the whole of the City. Normally the Control Room remained forbidden territory and out of bounds for firemen.

Assistant Chief 'volunteered' John Scar for control duty and, perhaps because I had dared to smile, I was delegated to be his assistant. John, who had spent time on Watchroom duty at the outer Fire Stations, knew something about telephone systems and Control Rooms.

The switchboard displayed three red coloured flaps. They were direct lines from the General Post Office and indicated incoming fire calls. Direct lines, on another part of the switchboard from our four outer Fire Stations, operated via a series of jack-plug connections and eyeball indicators.

The large revolving chair swung easily as I took basic instructions from John. The intricacies of using the hand set, connecting the cord and jack-plug into the correct socket, operating the switches, accepting calls as the eyeballs clicked down were all second nature to John.

"The red flaps are the most important." John emphasised.

"They're incoming fire calls. When one drops, it buzzes. Answer it immediately."

Radio equipment at the side of the switchboard showed a chrome mouthpiece that stood upright. It provided instant communication to our appliances, which most were fitted with radio receivers.

The Control Room also housed the 'bible', the occurrence or logbook. Fourteen by seventeen inches in size, it weighed over seven pounds. This green leather-bound book containing three hundred, individually numbered pages recorded everything, in ink. It recorded every coming and going of senior officers and every vehicle movement.

Fire calls were underlined in red ink. Every call was faithfully recorded, and would be until Judgement Day. This logbook was a legal document and could be called upon as written evidence of disputed fire attendance times. The correct time was obtained from a large brass maritime clock hanging on the wall above our heads.

John chose to be the entry officer and promised to record every detail in the 'bible.' My task was to operate the switchboard. After my brief introduction I tried to remember all the complicated instructions and procedures. John suggested we had a pot of tea and disappeared into a small anti-room. Immediately he disappeared, a red flap dropped and a buzz shattered the peaceful air. John dashed back.

I pressed the key that let me speak to the caller.

"Fire Brigade?" I said. "Fire Brigade?" I repeated the question.

There was no answer. Line went silent.

"This is the G.P.O. operator," a voice interrupted.

(G.P.O. General Post Office, forerunner of British Telecom.)

"The line's gone dead. The caller's rung off. It was the 'I can see flames,' idiot who rang yesterday. He's a real nuisance with his malicious calls!" The telephone exchange operator monitored every call from their switchboard.

The Control Room again went silent, waiting.

Another red flap dropped and buzzed, indicating another incoming fire-call.

"The road's on fire!" A woman's voice screamed.

I asked for the name of the road.

"Waveney Close," woman answered, "there are sheets of flames all over the road. I can see it from my front window." The woman's voice raised an octave.

"Can you give me your telephone number, please?" I asked.

"3 0 7 5 2!" The women screamed her reply. I wrote down the details as quickly as I could onto a loose sheet of paper.

"We will attend. Thank you," I told the caller.

Spinning the street index drum that listed all Torridge City's addresses, John shouted across the room.

"Waveney Close is off Waveney Road, in the Ellen Approach Station Area. Send both their Pumps."

I contacted the Ellen Approach Station, using the direct telephone line.

"Send your Pump and Pump Escape to road on fire, Waveney Close, off Waveney Road."

Meanwhile John contacted Assistant Chief Carp and Divisional Officer Chad at their homes.

The Fireman on Watchroom duty at Ellen Approach rang back to confirm that both appliances had left the Station.

John meticulously wrote the details into the 'bible'.

'2111 From 999-30752.
Road on fire. Waveney Close Waveney Road.
Ellen Approach Station instructed to send
Pump and Pump Escape.

Assistant Officer Chief Carp
& Divisional Officer Chad informed & attending.
'2112 From Ellen Approach Station. Pump and Pump Escape
Sub Officer Allice in charge, left for Waveney Close.'

We waited for further information. The radio eventually crackled into life.

"Message for M 2 X F from Zero Tango Two." This was the call sign from Assistant Chief Officer Carp's car radio.

"Go ahead with message, Zero Tango Two." I pressed the transmitting button and spoke hesitantly into the microphone.

The reply was duly recorded into our 'bible.'

'2120 From M 2 X D Zero Tango Two. A.C.O.Carp.
Stop for Waveney Close. Proved to be a spilled
workman's paraffin lamp
Out on arrival.
All appliances returning.'

The 'Stop' message indicated that no further assistance was required.

As all appliances and officers returned to their respective stations and homes, the fire-call chapter was recorded neatly into the 'bible'.

'2131 From Ellen Approach Station,
Pump and Pump- Escape
returned from Waveney Close.
Sub Officer Allice o/i/c.

__2133__ A.C.O. Carp returned home.
__2135__ D.O. Chad returned home.'

As the hour hand crept to midnight the Control Room took on an eerie silence. John explained his embittered outburst to the Assistant Chief. He spoke with genuine belief and commitment, but he sounded strained and unhappy. At incidents firemen were instant heroes he said. But once they were back on their Fire Stations, attitudes changed dramatically and firemen became a nuisance having to occupy their waiting time with enforced menial cleaning duties. As he spoke strands from his thick black hair fell across his face. He spoke with great passion and feeling. Eventually his words drifted off as he slumped down in his chair.

Sitting alone in front of the switchboard, I held the whole Brigade at my fingertips. All the appliances were safely tucked up in their engine houses. The brass clock ticked as seconds became minutes and minutes made hours. The radio transformer was disconnected, its deep hum silenced now.

Around two o'clock a red flap dropped and a buzz indicated that a fire-call was coming in.

The sound brought John instantly awake. He threw off his grey woollen blanket and stood next to me as I answered.

"Fire Brigade?" I said. Before the caller answered a second red flap dropped. John grabbed a spare handset to take this second call. But a third flap fell at the same time. Now all three incoming lines indicated there were other callers.

"I can see flames," my caller said.

"What's the address?" I asked.

156

The buzzing continued over our conversations as an unanswered call waited to be answered.

"I can see flames from a building, down Brett Street." The young voice repeated the message.

John took his message and wrote on his piece of paper, 'House fire, 17, Irwell Crescent.'

I knew Brett Street was in the City centre and would require a full turnout. I reached out to activate the Station bells and the switches to show Pump One, Pump-Escape, and Turntable Ladder on the indicator board in the muster-room.

I wrote the address on three separate pieces of paper, producing one copy for each officer in charge of each appliance.

John had also found located the address for his house fire on the street index.

Irwell Crescent was also in the Torridge City Station area. Pressing the switch for Pump Two John took both fire messages and stood waiting at Control Room door for the crews to wake up. Within seconds hands were grasping the loose pieces of paper with their fire messages.

The appliances whirred into life in the distant engine house.

The fire at Irwell Crescent needed another Pump. I consulted the street index and found the next available Station to be Stour Crescent Station. I rang through to the Station. The fireman-cum-Watchroom-man on duty at the end of the telephone said there was only one Pump at Stour Crescent Station, which he reminded me was being rebuilt.

"Send it," I told him as he repeated the address.

John returned from giving his fire messages to Pump One, Pump-Escape and Turntable Ladder, sending them to

Brett Street and sending Pump Two to Irwell Crescent. He reached over me to answer the next fire call.

'House fire, 12 Leam Place.' Another fire in Torridge City centre, but now no appliances were available.

"Two Pumps from Ellen Approach, the next nearest," he said reaching for another piece of paper. As he did so, another call came in. I pulled out my plug from the connection to Stour Crescent Station, slammed it into the socket for Ellen Approach Station ready to turn them out to Leam Place.

John again answered another call, and wrote down another address, 114 Mount Ribble Flats.

He knew at once these flats were in Torridge City Centre area. He consulted the index again to find the next available Station.

It was Nethan Street Station, and he instructed the fireman on duty in the Watchroom to send both their Pumps to Mount Ribble Flats. Four Stations had now been now mobilised, all of them to fires in the City centre.

"Weaver Road Station to Stand-by at Torridge City." John said.

"Now every station's on the move," he added with a smile.

Yet again we received more incoming calls as the red flap dropped and buzzed again.

We both answered, only to find two further calls to the house fire at Leam Place.

"Number 12? Yes, we are already attending this fire," John told one of the callers.

As the men on Watchroom duties at the outer stations rang back to confirm their appliances had been mobilised correctly we made telephone calls to Divisional Officer Chad, and Assistant Fire Chief Officer Carp.

"Carp here," the Assistant Chief answered, "yes laddie?" He asked me. I relayed the fire messages just as another red flap dropped and buzzed. John confirmed this was the fourth call for number twelve Leam Place.

"We've just received a fourth message for the house fire at Leam Place," I told Carp.

"I'm on my way," he responded, "send D.O. Chad to cover the others."

I switched on the transformer for the radio set to warm up and waited to learn the results of our labours.

Brett Street was a malicious false alarm. Irwell Crescent was a chimney fire and Mount Ribble Flats was a paraffin heater, which had been on fire but was out before the appliances arrived.

The message from the appliances from Ellen Approach Station, which had gone to Leam Place, took some time to arrive, and were no better for the wait. Finally we received the message

"The house is well alight. Two jets are in use, but there are people unaccounted for."

Two bodies were found behind a bedroom door. They might have been saved if the nearest appliances had not been sent on a false errand elsewhere.

Daylight dawned before all radio calls came to an end. The ambulance, the police and eventually every appliance returned to their respective Stations. John and I felt proud at our organisation, until we discovered no one had written anything in the 'bible'.

Since 02.00. every page in it had been left completely blank..

Using leftover scraps of paper we found some notes of what had happened. The times were not exactly correct, but we guessed they were within a minute or so of the correct time. Eventually we produced two pages of entries, nearly every turnout underlined in red ink. We thought it looked very impressive.

Our fifteen-hour night was nearly completed but even the Control Room did not escape routine cleaning. There was the floor to mop. The only difference from Control-mopping and Station-mopping was that we painted a pleasant pine-perfumed disinfectant onto the bright red linoleum floor and filled the Control Room with an aroma of woodland.

Feeling tired and bleary-eyed but proud that we had handled the night with competence and flair, we completed the cleaning with relish and with a feeling of satisfaction. But a telephone call from Assistant Chief Officer Carp soon shattered our misplaced contentment.

He told us that we should not have sent a full city centre turnout to the first 'seen flames' was a malicious call; we should have sent only one Pump. By mobilising and emptying the City Station we had left the area vulnerable and subsequent delay in turning out to Leam Place may have made it a fatality fire.

John tried to explain, but the telephone went dead.

"Time to crawl back in the hole," he said, replacing his telephone handset on the table.

Chapter 15

A transfer-list was normally issued once a year. This list moved Firemen, usually unwillingly, from Station to Station and created a 'have a kit bag, will travel' tradition.

Without any warning Malcolm Cackerel, my probationary partner on White Watch, was transferred to the Nethan Street Station. Malcolm lived at the opposite side of the City and now had to pass two Fire Stations to reach his new posting. This of course added more journey time and extra bus-fares to his day.

Nethan Street Station, popularly known as the rest home or country club, housed two of our senior officers who lived in the adjoining property. Chief Officer Bass lived in a large purpose built detached house and Divisional Officer Chad in a cul-de-sac, which consisted of council-houses owned by the Fire Brigade. Their two staff cars were kept cleaned and polished alongside the appliances in the engine house. The Chief's car was a converted police Ford Zephyr.

To replace Malcolm, Roger Braise arrived, complete with his belongings in two old kit bags. Roger was ruby-red faced, smiled and laughed as he dropped his kit bags onto the muster-room floor. According to the Brigade's grapevine, Rogers posting was a result of some mysterious damage to the washing of the Chief's wife. The story that Roger had deliberately cut her washing line in their garden spread like wild fire to our Watch. His version was that he was only retrieving a football from the Fire Station's drill ground, when he was set on by their bull-mastiff and caught a clothes-prop as he tried trying to escape its jaws. The clothesline snapped and Roger fell headlong into the Chief's prize flowerbed, blinded by a huge pink nightie.

He took a good ten minutes relating his story complete with actions, sounds and laughter. Instantly we nicknamed him 'Dodger'. For his misdemeanour Dodger was put on the transfer list and moved as quickly as he had dashed for freedom from the Chief's vicious dog.

Roger was tall and thin, with a mop of fair hair that was combed back from a large protruding forehead. His face beamed with mischief and with an infectious giggle that filtered all over our old Station, he instantly announced his arrival in capital letters. Immediately accused of wasting time and of causing troubles by Leading Fireman Bret, Dodger just grinned.

His smile produced deep furrow marks in his impish face.

"The party's over. You're not paid to enjoy yourself. Your card is already marked young Braise" Leading Fireman Barney Bret grunted.

As his unofficial mentor, I was given the task of taking Dodger, who had not served before on Torridge City Station, on a guided tour of the Station.

I was the Yards and Fires man for our three nights on duty, and he followed me as I stuffed the various boilers with coke before damping them down for the night. As I fed Big Bernice with coke, a solitary white bulb hanging from the smoke stained ceiling shone its pathetic light over our heads. The sound of the alarm bells ringing in the distance dragged us from the depths of the dimly lit boiler house across the yard and through the well-polished muster-room door.

'Chimney fire, Mount Ribble Flats' the caller said.

Mount Ribble Flats were built in the 1930s. They were about a mile from the Fire Station and housed nearly a thousand families. Built on twenty-three acres of land, the site contained areas for communal refuse, laundry rooms, shops, a Post Office, hard surface playgrounds, tennis courts, and a football pitch. This futuristic design was unparalleled at the time when it was built. But this once modern thriving community was now suffering from neglect and human misuse.

Following the Second World War decent residents of Mount Ribble chose to live in new housing estates that were sprouting all over other parts of Torridge City. Mount Ribble Flats were now left with less caring tenants. The once neat and tidy flats now slowly sank into deprivation, dragged down by a minority who cared nothing for cleanliness and took no pride in their homes. The play areas were constantly covered in broken glass and the communal areas, suffered bombardment from brainless vandals and were a constant source of deliberate fires and turnouts for us.

Every flat contained an open fire fuelled by coal. Each fireplace possessed a chimney; the thousand chimneys poked up from flat roofs in-groups of seven, like outstretched hands. The tall black chimney pots resembled stubby fingers clawing sky-wards; each pot displayed a small metal tag, securely fastened to its base, showing the flat number. This enabled the Fire Brigade to identify each chimney.

We were manning a Home Office Green Goddess Bedford appliance because the Pump we usually used refused to start. Wider than our Pumps, the Green Goddess was stored alongside the Emergency Tender at the rear of the Station. We struggled with the two large sliding wooden doors before the appliance crept out of the Station with an inch to spare. Once it was out, our driver, Fireman Trevor Tailor, sat in the front with Leading Fireman Loche on his left; they had climbed aboard through the narrow, side entrance, folding doors. The other crew-men sat on a long bench seat that stretched the full width of the cab and gave ample room for all three of us; I sat between Dodger and Peter Margot as Trevor drove us through the city-centre towards Mount Ribble Flats. With no siren, no blue lights and no short-wave radio we set off.

Hordes of kids chased after our green-painted appliance as we drove through an impressive arched entrance and into the inner courtyard at the entrance to the flats. When we arrived we all climbed down out of the folding cab doors as dozens of children milled about, waiting to be entertained.

We all knew what to do. I went with Peter to get up to the roof, Dodger and Leading Fireman Loche went inside to the flat. The driver, Trevor, operated the pump, and hopefully prevented our appliance from becoming an additional plaything.

With Peter I made my way up the internal staircase carrying a general-purpose rope, up the four flights of stairs.

The door to the roof supposed to be locked and left secure, but we found it wide open. We climbed easily onto the flat roof without needing to use our special key. A scuffle in deepening twilight indicated we were not alone on the roof. Dark forms appeared and disappeared, playing hide and seek and hiding behind the chimneystacks. The flat roof was just another play area.

Approaching a two-foot high parapet wall alongside the edge of the flats, we looked down on our Green Goddess, fifty-foot below. Trevor, hatless and with his blonde hair just visible in the streetlights stood in the crowd of young girls and boys.

"Stand from under!" Peter shouted the Fire Service command for those likely to be in danger below. I threw one end of our long-line over the side. It slithered down the side of the building. The excess landing on the pavement in front of the Green Goddess.

We waited for Trevor to fasten the line to the chimney adapter, a large umbrella shaped tubing, screwed on to the hose replacing the usual hose-reel nozzle.

"Flat number 4-1-5," Trevor shouted up at us.

The tubing spun off its drum as we began hauling the hose-reel upwards. It scuffed the parapet wall as I struggled to pull sufficient length to reach the stack on the roof.

"Put the adapter over 415's chimney pot," Peter told me.

Several chimneys were smoking, the smoke mixing and drifting into the night sky above our heads. The smoke from one chimney in particular emitted white smoke than any other. It had an identification plate on its base of the stack but only the number five remained.

"Aren't they're any other numbers," Peter said looking around the stack.

"No!" I answered.

I hooked the bent end of the adapter over the offending chimney pot where it rested snugly in the notched orifice.

We waited for the signal from below to inform us that Leading Fireman Loche and Dodger had sheeted up the inside of the flat, and ready for water to go down the chimney.

"Water on!" Dodger shouted from a balcony window near the flat beneath us.

Trevor increased the revs on the Pump. Pressurised water ran through the tubing up to the roof and finally down through the chimney adapter into the smoking chimney pot.

The children on the roof, all with cheeky dirty faces, scuttled out from their dark hiding places. One child ran along the small parapet wall, playing a game of chicken and running perilously close to the edge. He was no more than seven or eight years old. Three other darkened images all completed their dares and grouped around us.

"More water," Dodger shouted again. The engine below raced again. More water spurted out of our chimney adapter.

"Let us have a go Mister?" One of the grubby faced boys asked, hopefully.

"Clear off you cheeky brats." Peter shouted threateningly.

"Do you know who has been removing the number plates?" I asked thinking it was better to make peace than war.

The children looked defiant and scurried off disappearing behind a chimneystack.

"More water," shouted Dodger below, and more water cascaded down the chimney.

Looking over side of the parapet, we saw Leading Fireman Loche leaning out from a window two floors below.

"Are you sure you have the right chimney pot?" He asked.

"Yes," we both replied in confidence.

"More water!"

"Mister?" A young voice said. He pointed a grubby finger. Sparks suddenly emerged from an entirely different chimney pot. Black soot mixed with dirty grey sulphur smoke floated upwards.

"You've put water down the wrong chimney." Peter said to me.

"Better go down and see," I suggested.

We climbed down from the roof and onto the main staircase. As we turned onto the third landing a flat door opened. Framed in the doorway a huge tubby man with a soot-stained towel draped round his waist appeared. Black streams of wet soot fell from his bald-head. Rivulets of water ran across his shoulders and down his chest. A slow moving mass of jet-black liquid oozed endlessly down. His only protection, the once white towel, needed constant adjustment. It slipped slightly as he opened his mouth, but nothing came out. He was beyond speech. The whites of his eyes contrasted with his black sooted face. He blinked, and his eyes widened in shock and amazement.

His soot-encased lips opened wide to show his bright red mouth. Once more he attempted to speak. Black water trickled down his body and down his legs to form black puddles on the floor. He lifted one leg. It was difficult not to smile.

Apologising to him we pushed past, leaving him speechless and entered his flat where a thick black fog hovered in the living room. The fireplace steamed profusely as the water from above surprised and extinguished the flames. The remains of the fire lay in the hearth spitting defiantly.

The heavy black fog made breathing difficult and we had to take short shallow breaths to cross the room and open a window to allow in a supply of fresh air to come in.

Leading Fireman Bernard Loche, alerted by the ever-inquisitive young onlookers came into the room, passing the soot-drenched fat man. The pools of black soot underneath the man's bare feet grew to near lakes.

Perhaps swear words were the only way to describe the utter chaos. It was impossible to speak normally in the thick heavy black choking atmosphere. Obscenities became the language of the moment and were uttered between coughs and gasps for fresh air.

"We'll have to get this place cleaned up before anyone finds out what we've done," Leading Fireman Loche said. But our young onlookers spread the word and before many minutes had elapsed a crowd had assembled outside the door to the flat.

"But first go and find the right chimney pot for the flat we have already sheeted up that's on fire." Loche ordered.

We meekly retraced our steps to the roof and poured more water, hopefully down the right chimney pot spewing out a stream of sparks before we attempted any cleaning.

Soot at any time is difficult to clean. When it is wet cleaning is impossible. Before we arrived the flat was one of the well groomed and unlike some of the other properties in the complex, an obvious homely much-loved treasure. The widower lived on his own and was very house-proud. We retrieved some of his clothes from a bedroom. As he dressed, he told us he had only recently lost his wife. A collection of photographs of his wife and children, on the mantelpiece, were now covered in inches of soot. We desperately attempted to clean the avalanche of destruction from the soot from the whole area and to bring some decency and order back into his life.

We struggled for two hours. We brushed the floor, wiped down the walls, washed the ornaments and took the carpets outside and shook them. But the room still reeked of soot and was still badly stained; as our cleaning water congealed created slurry that went everywhere. We returned in shame to our Station.

Leading Fireman Loche reported our mistake as soon as we arrived back. Although we looked like chimney sweeps we faced an onslaught of questions. Why the wrong chimney? Why not the correct one? Why had we thought the wrong one was on fire? Why? Why? Why?

Each question was repeated at every level of the rank structure as our fault went up the chain of command. In less than thirty minutes it reached the very top. We were summoned before the Assistant Chief Officer, Mr Carp.

We expected a severe roasting after he had made a visit to the unfortunate man's flat.

The Assistant Chief seemed remarkably calm about the whole episode. After seeing the damage to the flat he agreed with the widower that the Fire Brigade would meet the claim for the cost of re-decorating.

"Learn by your mistake laddie," he began, "don't let it happen again. The child that never stumbles never learns to walk."

When we arrived for our next tour on duty, a list of extraordinary transfers appeared. Leading Fireman Bernard Loche was transferred from White to Red Watch; Trevor Tailor was packed off to Weaver Road Station and Peter Margot to Stour Crescent Station.

The transfers were not retribution, of course, but for unforeseen manning difficulties within the Brigade in preparation for the forthcoming reduction in hours.

For some unknown reason both Dodger and I escaped the transfer market.

This time, at least.

Chapter 16

'Man stuck in wagon,' the message read.

We could hear screaming before we got there. The loud agonised shouts led us towards a large yellow van. Crouched inside, under the front seats, a large man screamed in pain. One arm was trapped beneath the dashboard. The noise of his and screams reached fever pitch.

"It's big Harry." We were informed.

"It's big strong Harry. He's got his fingers stuck in the windscreen motor," our informer said with a hint of amusement in his voice. The air was blue with swear words. Harry, removing the windscreen wiper motor forgot to disconnect the vehicle's battery. Somehow power to the windscreen motor was activated and like Sod's law, Harry's fingers were caught and locked within the vice-like grip of the lever mechanism.

The screeches of pain rose to glass breaking pitch. It sounded as if Harry was being murdered. I grabbed our wooden box containing the hearth-kit and ran towards the pitiful sound with the rest of the crew.

Station Officer Finnan, who had gone into the van through the passenger door, shuffled in and came face to face with Harry.

"Let's see if we can deal with the wiper mechanism from the outside of the vehicle." Turning his head, he spoke softly in his Scottish twang.

The hearth-kit, a title from the old days, originally comprised tools for cutting open the hearths of fireplaces to provide access following a chimney fire when the fire had spread under the floorboards. Our hearth-kit, although still containing the original bricklayer's bolster, cold chisels, a club hammer, a floor-board saw, a hacksaw, pliers and screw drivers had additional equipment which had been added during the passing years.

The hearth-kit contents were kept in a large flat wooden box, which opened like a thick book. I looked inside and among the tidily positioned tools I found a hammer and chisel. The hammer and steel chisel would be the quickest way to cut a hole through the vehicle's front panel. I thought.

"What do you think you're doing?" A voice shouted, stopping me dead.

The owner of the scrap yard approached. Tall and spindly, wearing a full-length coat plastered in years of grease and oil, he bore down on me.

"Making a hole to get into the motor," I answered confidently.

"You're not cutting into my van. Harry or no Harry." He snatched the hammer and chisel from my hands and threw them down on the ground.

"Just a moment," Station Officer Finnan said, pulling himself out of the cab.

"I'm the one who gives the orders round here to my men. No one else does." The tall owner stood back and mumbled something under his breath.

Finnan grabbed my shoulder, dragged me to one side and told me to think first before I acted.

"See if the inspection panel will screw off," he whispered.

Below the windscreen on the outside of the van an oblong panel was held in place by two screws. I pushed the end of the screwdriver into one of the screws and turned. It moved a fraction before the head of the screw snapped off. Screwdriver in the second screw also moved but then seized solid. The panel now held only by one screw now felt loose. I prised it up a fraction and pivoted it round on the remaining screw. A curved scratch-mark gouged into the yellow paintwork as the panel swung round.

"You're a bloody vandal. There'll be nowt left of van when you've finished," the owner said, oblivious to his mechanic's agony.

Looking through the small opening I saw Harry's trapped fingers curled like a snake in among the wiper mechanism. Two of the stubby fingers were sandwiched, caught between the steel linkages.

"If this linkage could be moved slightly, his fingers would be free," I prophesied.

Probing inside the mechanism, my hand suddenly touched a trapped finger. Harry let out an even louder scream. His injury was not life threatening, but the pain must have been excruciating. His verbal complaint left no one in any doubt of his suffering or what he thought of my parentage.

"What about a bit of oil?" Fireman Jeffrey Twaite, a crew-member, suggested. It was a good idea. Old oil can, complete with a long narrow spout, was inserted through the inspection hole. Oil ran down the long narrow outlet in the direction of big Harry's fingers.

"Can we get some sort of wedge against the linkage?" Jeffrey enquired as he looked inside. But the chisel I produced from our hearth-kit was too big and too clumsy to manoeuvre through the narrow hole.

Big Harry was still in an awkward flat curled position and began to feel faint. His loud complaints subsided and the abusive language eased.

Jeffrey climbed in through the offside door and shuffling on the floor to ease into a position under Harry's legs.

"Get in the other side," Jeffrey told me.

I crawled in and came face to face with Harry. Our faces were almost touching as I reached inside and followed Harry's trapped arm under the dashboard to reach his hand. His face moved and touched mine. His skin was cold and clammy, and his breath stunk of yesterday's beer.

He closed his eyes and his body relaxed. I yanked on his hand. He recovered immediately. A finger moved and his oil soaked hand came free and he slipped slowly from his uncomfortable crouched position, stiff and embarrassed. The tears pouring out of both eyes must have been the result of perspiration.

We collected all our tools, packed them back into the hearth-kit and returned to our station.

Reversing into the engine house, we found young curly headed recruit standing and watching anxiously.

Rodney Rudd was the latest addition to join White Watch for his few weeks on trial before training school. Rodney listened intently as Jeffrey went into precise detail of how big Harry had been reduced to tears.

At the end of our day shift a Union Meeting had been organised. Normal branch meetings were usually poorly attended. But with the introduction of a forty-eight hour week by other Fire Brigades, and without plans imminent, for us our large recreation room burst with impatient and angry union members.

The Torridge City Fire Brigade Branch Secretary, Fireman Norman Sterlet, tall with a thin frame and dressed in his off-duty civilian clothes, found great difficulty controlling us as we all packed densely into the smoke filled atmosphere.

Most Firemen were members of the Fire Brigade Union, but our Chief Officer and many of his senior officers thought the Union always meant trouble. Men wanting promotion in the Brigade were overlooked if they involved themselves in the Union. While car and dockworkers led the country in pay, hours and conditions, firemen fell way behind. At the bottom of this pyramid the majority of firemen needed money from other work just to bring their pay up to a decent level and many resigned for greener pastures elsewhere. Most of the time it was felt the paying public did not know a Fire Brigade even existed, and with a Union impotent against strong senior officers who dictated policy and ruled supreme, morale plunged. There were always plenty of moans and groans out of earshot of our leaders, but not many working on Fire Stations expressed criticism openly.

Fireman John Scar on our watch was an exception and soon made his presence known. He stood up at our meeting and in a loud voice challenged Norman Sterlet how we were treated by our senior officers.

I remembered the previous outburst he had made to our Assistant Chief. I had never seen anyone take on our senior officers, and now our Union officials, with such passion.

"For most of the time we're an embarrassment," he started "all we do is clean and clean until there's a fire. It's Fireman this and Fireman that and Fireman go away, but it's thank you brother-Fireman, when the flames begin to play."

The meeting hummed with amusement at his misquotation of Kipling.

Norman Sterlet intervened with difficulty and shouted above the noise. He informed us that the Union's National General Secretary had expressed a desire to attend this meeting but that Chief Officer Bass had refused to allow him to do so.

"There were to be no outside Union men coming on any of my Fire Stations," Chief Officer had told Norman.

Eventually the meeting was concluded by the announcement that the General Secretary would address us on neutral ground about the problems of the delay in introducing fewer hours. This would be at the top of the agenda.

With most Fire Brigades in the country already in agreement in implementing a reduction of working hours from a fifty-six to a forty-eight hour week, we were repeatedly told that Torridge City could not recruit enough men and so could not reduce our hours.

The meeting dispersed with those of us off duty going to the City Tavern. After a pint or three flowing down our throats like nectar, alcohol loosened our previously restricted tongues. But deep down there were signs of a cancerous tumour eating away. During the next few weeks any strong militant views faded and the tumour benefited from a welcome remission as life continued as normal.

"Roger can lift three men," Jeffrey Twaite announced, in the hearing of Rodney Rudd, our new recruit as we sat in the canteen having our tea break one Saturday morning.

"Never. No man can lift nearly four hundredweight," Rodney said, taking the bait.

"This man can lift three men," Jeffrey offered another tempting morsel. He pointed to Dodger, Fireman Roger Braise, describing him as super-human.

"Why isn't he in the weight lifting championships?" Rodney gulped down the hook, complete with bait.

Cross-questioning and the challenge were left to simmer as the alarm bells sounded.

Full turnout, Pump One, Pump-Escape, and Turntable Ladder to a fire alarm at Torridge City Meat Market.

We dashed through the city centre with bells ringing and sirens wailing. Pump One in front, the other two appliances in convoy behind. We noisily cleared a path through the busy traffic, which gave way. The Saturday shoppers looked and stared in blank amazement as we raced by.

"Sorry, there's no fire." The announcement greeted us as we arrived. A man dressed in a bloodstained brown coat greeted our arrival as our three appliances drove through the gates of the meat market.

"A young lad has his hand in a meat mincer," he said, "I'm sorry about the fire-alarm. Somebody must have panicked."

"Somebody get the hearth-kit and the first aid-box," Station Officer Finnan shouted. He, Jeffrey Twaite and I followed the man through a wide double door and into a large open warehouse, Rodney Rudd our new boy was close behind.

Passing dozens of animal carcasses, all hanging motionless from a high steel track on steel hooks, we ran to enter a small door at the far end of the warehouse. It led into a back, almost secret room.

In the centre of this hidden room a large cast-iron meat mincer was fastened firmly to the end of a large wooden table. Alongside this sat a small young lad. He looked at us and smiled pathetically. He did not look in any pain; he even smiled at Station Officer Finnan as we approached. But poking down into the throat of the electric meat mincer, which had been adapted from an old hand mincer, the end of his arm disappeared into a mass of blood stained meat.

We could see a huge electric motor fastened to the workbench providing power via a rubber belt and a pulley wheel.

"Is the power turned off?" Station Officer Finnan asked, cutting the drive belt with his personal knife.

Jeffrey Twaite slowly removed large handfuls of raw lumps of meat from the mincer. The young lad chattered away as if nothing had happened. He even apologised for all the fuss.

"Get a message back to Control," Finnan told Sub Officer Gardon, who was in charge of Pump Escape "and ask for an ambulance. Tell Control the situation and return Pump Escape and Turntable Ladder to the Station." His words were brief and to the point.

With all the pieces of unminced meat carefully removed, we could see a hand disappear into the Archimedes screw, which fed raw meat into the cutting blades. The minced meat produced a mixture of mashed flesh, making it impossible to distinguish any difference between that of an animal or a human. Jeffrey screwed off the cover to remove the large disc, full of small holes, from which strings of meat emerged. The disc showed a small square shaft, the end of the Archimedes screw.

"Can we reverse the screw?" the Station Officer asked. He opened our hearth-kit and found a pair of our new Mole-grips.

Mole-grips, a new conception, were similar to a pair of pliers and had jaws, which tightened and locked themselves in position when they were gripped together.

Adjusting the width of the gaping jaws by turning a small knurled nut, I squeezed and locked the jaws onto the square end protruding out of the meat mincer. Blood seeped out, coating the end of the grips in a sticky mess. But which way must I turn the nut? Clock wise or anti-clock wise?

"Try clockwise," Rodney, our latest recruit, suggested. I turned the Mole-grips clockwise. Slowly the thread moved. Suddenly my hands slipped off. The handles were smothered in thick sticky greasy blood.

Gripping again, I turned them slowly. Slowly, ever so slowly, I turned. Slowly the square end of the Archimedes screw moved.

Station Officer Finnan held the young lad firmly in his arms. Lad's eyes rocked backwards as he fell limp. Not a whisper of complaint emerged from his gaping mouth, with no obvious signs of pain.

"He's passed out. Be as quick as you can," Station Officer said, in his usual soft twang.

I urged the handles to turn but the small narrow opening and the greasy meat covered in blood made a firm grip almost impossible. It was a full turn and a half before the Station Officer; Jeffrey and recruit Rodney could lift the young lad upwards, free at last. His hand, now clear, revealed a mangle of flesh, meat and blood.

The ambulance crew arrived as we carried him outside.

"Two fingers missing," one of them announced, glancing at the damaged hand. The ambulance doors banged shut and they quickly left for the hospital.

Joined by a police officer, we followed our Station Officer back to the mincer.

"Who knows how to dismantle the mincer," he asked the abattoir workforce.

Although they dealt with carcasses most of their lives there seemed to be reluctance for anyone to come forward.

"I can," our own Rodney Rudd offered.

Within a few moments he had disentangled all the parts of the mincer and put them on to the bench. Prior to joining the Fire Brigade, he informed us, Rodney had worked for an engineering firm, which manufactured meat mincers among other things.

Poking around, Jeffrey first noticed a wrist watch with both leather straps chewed off. Then from inside the red mass, came one fingernail and then bits of fingers. With all the bits pieced together, we found one half of a finger and another finger cut into six separate pieces.

With the pieces of human limbs wrapped in a clean bandage we carried the remains out to our appliance. Leaving the policeman to deal with the legality of such a dubious piece of apparatus, we left the scene with our blue light turning, our bell ringing and our siren wailing and raced to the Torridge City Casualty Department with our precious cargo of dismembered fingers.

"About this strong man on the watch?" Rodney asked for the third time as we waited outside the hospital.

"Wait and all will be revealed," Jeffrey answered as we set off back to the station after the Station Officer climbed on board after delivering the pieces of fingers.

Every member of White Watch gathered eagerly in the muster-room for the demonstration of supreme weightlifting. There was Jeffrey Twaite, keen to organise everything, Dodger, our strong man and lifter, and the three men needed for the lift. Rodney had to be one and John Scar and I volunteered to complete the trio. It was almost a ritual procedure in which all three men needed to be correctly positioned to ensure an even distribution of weight. A sheet of newspaper was placed carefully on the floor to be pulled free in order to prove that sufficient clearance had been achieved.

The three of us lay close together on the floor, with Rodney in the middle.

Jeffrey placed each of Rodney's arms across our two outer shoulders. We then gripped Rodney's loose hands and held them tight. Then Jeffrey intertwined both

Rodney's legs around one each of John's and mine. The three of us were now entwined and locked together as one. We lay motionless on the floor. Rodney was now completely immobilised and primed.

A concoction of sauce, soap and cold tea, which Dodger ceremonially poured over Rodney's private parts through an opened trouser-fly, brought guffaws and cheers from the onlookers. For a brief second, with a supreme effort and struggle, Rodney - not Dodger - actually managed to lift all of us briefly from the floor. Realising he had been set up he smiled ruefully, taking it all in good humour as we released him from our vice like grip.

A bucket of cold water soon washed him clean drenching him in the process. A mop and bucket was hurriedly produced and we finally cleaned up the mess.

Chapter 17

"They're short of men at Nethan Street Station! Pack your kit bag, young Fairn. It's your turn for relief duties."

As I arrived to report for duty just before 1800 hours on the second of our three nights on duty Leading Fireman Bret, who had a flair for issuing such commands, greeted me with this order. He looked down his stubby nose and his close-set brown eyes danced with delight.

Relief duties were becoming common as more and more men resigned to get higher wages elsewhere, thus creating acute shortages of manpower. The Brigade tried to increase recruitment in the struggle to achieve the numbers required for the introduction of the shorter hours but was not having much success.

Relief duties were never popular. They meant working with an unknown group of men at an alien Station and usually needed more travel time to get to a Station, which was often well away from our homes. A minimum of nine men was needed for a Station with two main line Pumping appliances. One Fireman was on permanent watch-room duty and four on each appliance.

"You'll get two nights in bed," Leading Fireman Bret sniggered. Curls from his fair hair bobbled as he turned and walked almost waltzed, away.

Still a probationer, I was nervous and apprehensive as we arrived at Nethan Street Station. Having delivered me in the Brigade's red van the driver unceremoniously dragged my blankets and fire-uniform out of the two rear doors. He slammed both doors shut and sped off, leaving me to find an entrance.

Nethan Street Fire Station was built and opened in the late 1950s, and was colloquially known as the country club or the rest home. Some of the firemen who manned the station had been posted by our high command as a punishment for their misdeeds in the past. It was not a busy station and only had about four hundred calls a year. Houses in an exclusive area of Torridge City surrounded Nethan Street Fire Station. It also housed the latest and finest fire-appliances. Our Chief, Mr Bass, lived in a large detached house next door to the station. He also happened to be Leading Fireman Bret's uncle. There was no doubt the station was a jewel in Torridge City Fire Brigade's crown.

Inside I found Sub Officer Dace, the duty officer in charge of the Station. He looked old and well past retirement age. He glanced up from reading something, glared at me, grunted something under his breath, and resumed reading.

A Leading Fireman sat to his right. He stood up and without saying a word pointed with his head, indicating that I should follow him into the watchroom.

"Give the watchroom-man your name for the log book," he said briefly, as if each word was precious.

In the watchroom I recognised Fireman Norman Sterlet, our Brigade's Union Official. He sat at a telephone console, pen poised in one hand and his long-stemmed pipe in the other.

All outer Fire Stations deployed a fireman to man the watchroom for twenty-four hours a day, ready to receive fire-calls from Brigade Control. The firemen on watch recorded everything in the Station's own logbook.

Norman Sterlet had been subjected to transfers several times in his nine years service, a hazard of serving as a Union Official. He put the long thin stem of his pipe in his mouth and inhaled, his cheeks indented to form two deep caverns. The bowl of his pipe, shaped like a decapitated egg, glowed bright red as clouds of blue smoke lazily left his lips and fogged his face.

He wrote neatly in ink in the logbook,

'1831 Fm Fairn reported on relief duty from Torridge City Station.'

"Were you on watchroom duty a month ago?" I asked.

"Not me." Norman's reply was short.

My attempt to explain that I had served in Brigade Control on a previous occasion met a stony silence. Further conversation seemed pointless.

It was a different station, a different world.

"If you want supper you'd better see the canteen man," Leading Fireman told me.

"Where's the canteen?" I enquired.

"Put your gear on a peg in the muster-room," he said, ignoring my question.

I went into the muster-room, a room to be found in all Fire Stations, and arranged my fire-tunic, respirator, belt and axe on one of the several empty pegs. With my fire-helmet on the shelf above them and my boots on the floor, I was ready to turnout. Glancing into the clinically clean modern engine house, I saw two appliances, which looked brand new and resplendent.

Norman rose and opened the narrow door leading from the watchroom into the engine house. He stood framed by the open door and unexpectedly, without my asking, reeled off the appliance specifications.

A Dennis F24 Automatic Water Tender and a Dennis F12 Pump Escape stood alongside each other poised for action. Both were gleaming and looked ready for turning out. The Pump Escape looked identical to the one we manned at the City Station, and was complete with two large carriage wheels suspended from the rear. But the Dennis F24 looked entirely different from the ones I was used to. Both appliances had fully enclosed cabs and inside seats for all.

The Water Tender, Norman explained, was only five years old and carried five hundred gallons of water, providing an instant supply. Appliances carrying such huge amounts of water were a new concept.

I thanked Norman, impressed by the freshness of the appliances and equipment. Nethan Street Station looked like a showroom. It looked brand new and almost unused compared with the ancient grubby and well-battered station I was from.

We went out of the engine house again and through the two swing doors of the muster-room, which led into a dormitory. Four beds were folded up neatly against a wall. Again, compared to my Station, the dormitory looked neat and comfortable.

A flight of polished stone stairs trailed from the dormitory to a landing and a corridor with a floor that gleamed like flat water. My shoes kissed the floor surface leading me to a door marked 'Kitchen.'

Through the door a voice shouted.

"Hello, Michael."

Malcolm Cackerel, who had been posted to Nethan Station two months earlier, struggled with a huge tin of corned beef on the table in front of him. Using a large carving knife he slid the pointed end carefully inside and slowly eased the red chunk of meat onto a waiting wooden carving block.

"You here on relief duties?" Malcolm said in his Irish lilt as he wrestled with the hunk of meat. He was brandishing fresh plasters on new boils on his chin.

"I'm the canteen-man and part watchroom-man, with Norman, for the night," he explained.

The meat suddenly slid out as the tin casing released its grip. The solid red mass plopped out and sat upright proud, edged in white-yellow fat.

"Remember Christmas dinner?" Malcolm asked. I remembered.

"I've got this recipe for a corned beef stew," Malcolm said.

His large knife came perilously close to my face as he turned round and pointed it at me. He chattered away excitedly as he explained that he had just got back from a visit home to Ireland and that he had returned to Torridge

City complete with his wife and with some of his mother's secret recipes.

"Sludge for supper," he said. I watched as he prepared thick slices of corned beef and sandwiched them between layers of sliced potatoes and onions. Eventually the large steel dish was stacked to the brim.

"I have a magic potion from home and a secret additive." He bowed his head allowing one of the plasters on his neck to gape and display a large angry red spot. From a cupboard he produced a small paper bag, containing a concoction of spices and two bottles of stout.

He mixed his mother's secret ingredients into the Guinness and poured the concoction over the corned beef, drenching and soaking the contents. When the dish was filled to the brim, he carefully put his offering into an oven. As the stew cooked for an hour or so, a pleasant aroma filled the kitchen and the rooms upstairs. A brief announcement over the loudspeaker system brought the rest of the crew in search of the tantalising smell.

The result of Malcolm's culinary offering looked ghastly as he ladled the sludge onto large white plates and handed them through the serving hatch to grasping hands. Deep pudding plates, filled to overflowing, needed carrying carefully as we all found a place to sit and eat.

Malcolm disappeared, allowing his watchroom partner, Norman to enjoy his supper. Eight of us sat there, our spoons digging in.

Surprisingly, the supper was well received. Second helpings were essential, and we went on eating until all the sludge had disappeared and the dishes were scraped clean.

The sign on the canteen wall told us that 'Empty plates are proof indeed!' We agreed.

Our stomachs were filled to capacity, and not a morsel was left. The food on Fire Stations once again proved to be an occupational delight.

As the hour crept to the allotted permissible time for the official boots off period, at 2300 hours I prepared for a night guaranteed to be quiet but collected my boots from the muster-room just in case. With my blankets arranged on the mattress I slipped into bed.

Bells broke the guarantee around three o'clock in the morning. The large, heavy, and rarely used brass bells seemed to shake the Station as they rung with ferocity.

Having had plenty of practice at jumping out of bed from busy nights on my own Station, I soon slid on my waiting socks, both feet into the boots poised at the side of my bed. I yanked up my trousers and with my braces on my shoulders, dashed off towards the engine house.

The Station alarm bells were still pounding the walls.

Malcolm Cackerel, still on watchroom duty, stood with two fire messages.

"Both appliances to farm fire, Araglin Road," he shouted, though he hardly made an impression above the noise of the bells.

Araglin Road ran beyond the Torridge City boundary and went for ten miles to Araglin Town, which sat, nestled in the folds of the countryside. The Town had its own County Fire Brigade and, by tradition, county men were never thought to have the experience and skills as we city Firemen did. Inadequate and often part timers usually manned their old and decrepit appliances.

Our driver opened the pair of large polished wooden engine house doors. They sprang back smartly and with a clang clipped into retaining brackets. The Station broadcasted the sounds of efficient activity.

I climbed into the rear cab of the Water Tender and waited for the rest of the crew. The engine raced as we waited for everyone to climb aboard. We moved out slowly into the dark morning. The Pump Escape followed us immediately, the noise of its engine competing with ours.

The cold air of an early May tore through the open side window as Malcolm and I sat close together on the rear inside bench seat. Malcolm, relieved from guarding telephones for the first half of the night, now found himself enroute to a fire.

The single blue light on the roof of the appliance stroked the country hedgerows as we raced along at full power, eating the miles along Araglin Road to the farm. The thirty-nine horsepower eight-cylinder Rolls Royce engine filled the internal cab with its thrust of supreme power. The glow in the sky behind us faded as the streetlights disappeared over the horizon.

Suddenly a woman with an unusually large head appeared in the light of our headlights. She waved frantically at us, standing in the centre of Araglin Road. Her white coat flapped open revealing a long pink nightdress underneath. As we approached we saw that a scarf covered her head. Underneath we saw curlers protruding from the front, making her head twice the normal size.

"Come through," she shouted as we reached her farm gate. Our appliance crept through the opening and stopped. Malcolm opened his cab door and helped the woman aboard.

Glancing back up the main road we saw no sign of our slower Pump Escape. So we moved off through the gate and up a narrow lane towards a farm.

"The barn's on fire," the woman said, gasping for breath, "it's next door to the cowshed!"

The dark shadows of farm buildings were etched against a yellow sky as we roared up to the farm. We continued through a narrow gap between two outbuildings into a yard. Directly in front of us a white-orange sheet of flames spiralled upwards from a Dutch Barn. Steam and long fingers of flame fanned upwards from a huge stack of straw.

The farmer stood in the middle of the yard holding a hosepipe. The water from the hosepipe fell short of flames as he glanced quickly over his shoulder at us. The half of his face we could see glowed with light reflected from the fire.

All our doors flew open as we ground to a halt.

"Water, we need water!" Someone shouted the obvious.

Just as had happened at other incidents, no specific orders were given. Everyone knew what was required, and pooled their ideas to help the others.

The Water Tender carried five hundred gallons of water. As soon as we ran a length of delivery hose from the pump outlet, fitted a hand-controlled nozzle into the end, and water arrived instantly. All the other appliances in our Brigade needed an augmented supply from a hydrant or from open water to provide such a sudden large jet of water.

The jet hit the flames. A rod of water three-quarters of an inch wide gouged into the haystack. But the on-board five hundred gallons of water would only supply water for about ten minutes. However, the Pump Escape arrived at this moment. Their flat windscreen mirrored the scene as we welcomed their arrival.

A small lean-to shed, painted with bitumen, steamed with the reflected heat. Suddenly it caught fire as we watched and the roof exploded in flames.

We turned our jet of water and directed it onto the shed. The flames struggled under our deluge.

"We'll need more water soon," our driver screamed above the sound of the racing engine and the thrust of our water jet.

"There's a stream at the back of the cowshed," the farmer shouted.

The Pump Escape drove round our delivery hose as the farmer's wife pointed the way. The appliance splashed through the gathering water on the cobble yard and disappeared.

The heat, which was reflected from the stack, scorched our tunics as we turned and faced backwards to give ourselves some protection as we continued to direct the jet of water on to the roof of the shed. The farmyard was now in darkness. Belches of smoke and steam had replaced the light, which initially came from the fire. The whole farmyard was filled with a deep choking fog. Water from our jet stopped the fire on the roof from spreading but the fire continued to take hold of the stack of hay. Mixed with choking smoke, the flames etched further and further into the stack.

The appliance water tank was now empty and our jet trickled to a stop.

"We're getting the P. E. into the stream," a Fireman from the Pump Escape shouted through the smoke.

Finding ourselves surplus to requirements, the two of us went looking to assist the Pump Escape crew. Guided by the headlights from the Pump Escape we could see a shallow stream which had already been damned, using piles of unwound delivery hose placed an arc to form a semicircle and halt the flow of the water which smelled of sewage.

Four lengths of hard suction hose were screwed together to make one long length and connected to the side-mounted pump-inlet point, on the Pump Escape, eventually went towards the rising stream. The loose end of the suction hose capped by a huge brass basket was thrown into the water and the driver began to prime the pump, extracting the air and allowing the polluted water from the stream to replace the air in the suction hose. Excess water now shot out from below as the pump was filled with water. The flow of water soon charged through the delivery hose back to the fire. The delivery hose stretched and curled along the farm yard as we tripped and stumbled in the congested dark alleyway and returned to the fire.

The delivery hose we had abandoned earlier on the farmyard spluttered and gasped into life as water from the Pump Escape recharged our empty Water Tender. The fire now attacked by two strong jets of water soon showed signs of weakness.

Another appliance arrived in the yard. The County men from Araglin Town had arrived.

The newly arrived crews dismounted and joined us in the attack. They carried a portable pump on their bright new appliance; in fact all their equipment looked newer than ours. Shiny aluminium couplings gleamed from lockers that illuminated when opened and made all our Torridge City brass equipment look ancient. With relative ease they soon provided extra water from their portable pump, working alongside our Pump Escape at our dammed stream. In the face of all this extra assistance the fire slowly submitted.

The early morning ball of sun was slowly creeping upwards before we dismantled the Dutch barn and split it up into individual bales of straw. Each bale was dragged from the high stack, split open and its fire quenched with the filthy stinking water. The farmyard became knee-deep in burnt black straw and stunk like a sewage-farm.

The farmer, with assistance from his neighbours, used a mechanical forklift and piled the steaming straw onto a tractor and then transported the burnt and stinking morass into an adjoining field.

"The whole lot'll have to be burnt," he said as we huddled in-groups to have the welcome pot of tea provided by his wife.

"The cattle will not eat straw that smells of fire," he explained.

Steaming mugs of tea quenched our dry throats like water feeding parched soil. As we drank the delicious tea, sandwiches crammed with thick slices of salty bacon came endlessly from the farm kitchen.

The myths of the County men not being proper Firemen were shown not to be true here. As individuals they were the same as we were, doing the same job but with newer equipment. But they left us angry by reminding us that they worked eight hours less than we did for the same pay.

As we stowed our hose and equipment and made ready to leave the farmer's wife appeared yet again this time with three cardboard boxes containing eggs, eggs and more eggs. They were, we assumed, the spoils of war. With the clutches of eggs stowed carefully, our appliance threw out clouds of blue smoke from its exhaust as we made off down the farm lane to join the main road. At long last we returned to Nethan Street Station. Malcolm chattered all the way back to the station. His face and pink plasters were now blackened with soot, but even without sleep he could still ramble on and on.

The day shift, already on duty, awaited our return as we drove into the drill yard at Nethan Station. Our long hard night was seen on our blackened faces. The stench of sewage and burnt straw was embedded in our skin. The promise of an easy and quiet night had proved to be unfounded.

Perhaps my second and final night would continue the Country Club tradition?

Chapter 18

Standing under a hot shower in the ablutions of Nethan Street Fire Station I washed and scrubbed myself down with a loofah the size of my arm. With a second shower and a further rasping rub I desperately tried, but tried in vain, to decontaminate my whole body from the ingrained taint acquired from our previous night's farm fire.

On relief duties but with no fresh clothes, I begged and borrowed a pair of trousers, some old socks and a loose fitting red pullover to make my journey home.

From behind a pair of heavy eyelids lined with grit and rubbed red-sore I sat on the top deck of the bus feeling very uncomfortable. Passengers on the journey home stared at the state of my dress as I paid the conductor with Fire Brigade-issued plastic bus tokens and sat, glowing with embarrassment, low on my seat.

I still lived on my own above a greengrocer's shop. Eventually I arrived home after two bus journeys and dropped onto my bed too tired to undress. The door to the land of nod opened easily as I fell instantly into a deep sleep.

I awoke in the late afternoon, absolutely famished. With potatoes from the shop below boiling away and a large frying pan stuffed full with fat beef sausages from the local butcher, I boiled, fried and then devoured a heaped plate of 'bangers and mash'.

Then I had another wash, this time in my kitchen sink, in yet another attempt to rid my skin of the lingering obnoxious sewage stench. I dressed and set off for my second night on relief duties at Nethan Street Fire Station. I sat alone on the upper deck of the bus peering through the steamed front windows, looking for the appropriate stop.

I recovered my drying fire-uniform from the warm boiler house at the back of the Station. The trousers were nearly dry but my tunic still felt damp. White salt marks of perspiration showed clearly from the seams of my leather boots as I carried my uniform back into the Station. I brushed off the salt and coated my boots with a thick layer of greasy dubbin. Then I placed all my fire-uniform in the muster-room ready for action. Nethan Street Station was normally a quiet station and our previous busy night was the exception rather than the rule. Nobody expected another disturbed night for at least another six months.

I was allocated to crew the Pump Escape with the Sub Officer in charge of the appliance. I assisted with the evening's appliance check, opening every locker and counting the contents.

The day crew had obviously spent all day restoring the appliances to their former pristine condition. Every locker sparkled clean with crisp white lengths of delivery hose rolled tight and neat; they filled the hose lockers. Their bright brass male couplings dangled like heavy gleaming pendulums, catching against the inside of the locker as the hinged door clanged shut.

Fireman Norman Sterlet held the equipment check-list in his hand together we went through the inventory item by item. Our final task was to turn on the main valve of the cylinders of the two Compressed Air-sets. These were inside of the cab. The contents of the cylinders were checked to make sure they contained at least four-fifths of their original contents. When we finished we wrote our names on the set's tally.

This yellow-coloured tally measured five by one and a half inches and listed our name, the Brigade, the contents of cylinder and a space to record the time of entry into a fire. We then reported that our appliance was fully equipped to the watchroom-man, who recorded this neatly in the station's logbook.

The evening progressed with the usual dull period spent listening to the text extracted slowly and painfully from the Manual of Firemanship, Part 6b, Practical Firemanship and from a chapter dealing with Fires in Rural Areas. The Leading Fireman with the enthusiasm of a zombie read from the manual but his words drifted off unheeded to the ceiling. Considering every one of us had spent most of the previous night fighting a Dutch Barn fire, the words of advice were now history.

At the stand-down before supper, everyone gathered more eagerly around the snooker table. Two men dominated the table, Sub Officer Peter Dace, the officer in charge, and Fireman Norman Sterlet. They were well known for spending many an hour playing competition billiards, and their games had become something of a Brigade legend.

The latest score was 247 games to Peter, and 314 to Norman.

This was scrawled on the score-board in blue chalk for all to see and regularly updated. The clink of balls as they rolled effortlessly over the green baize was the only sound to disturb the deathly silence as the pair fought over game five hundred and sixty two. Norman enjoyed a hundred-point break and was well in front for yet another victory.

Norman, his political views as red as the billiard ball he cannoned for yet another two points, was one of Torridge City Fire Brigade's Union Officials.

The evening provided plenty of scope for everyone to express their political views about the forthcoming General Election in Great Britain. In my eighteen months in the Fire Brigade, firemen appeared to be dressed in all colours of the political spectrum and the difference of opinions was often a source of deep and emotional argument.

Dressed in a dark-blue bib and brace overall over his pale-blue collarless shirt, Norman completed his break of a hundred and thirty points. From his front pocket he removed a long thin pipe and an old shiny tin, now completely devoid of any of its original paint. Between thumb and forefinger he began stuffing strings of tobacco into the pipe bowl.

When the surface of tobacco was sufficiently flattened and firmed by the tin lid, he fingered his brass petrol lighter. Holding the yellow flickering flame against the ends of the tobacco, he inhaled. Clouds of fresh blue smoke danced up and filtered through the overhead snooker table lights.

"The Brigade is going on shorter hours. Next January our hours will be reduced from fifty-six to forty-eight," he began.

"But other brigades are already working shorter hours," a voice from the back of the room interrupted.

"What's the Union ever done for us?" Someone else taunted.

"A change of government won't improve anything!"

The banter continued, and Norman shook his head.

Sub Officer Dace finished his break and Norman bent over the billiard table. His chin rested neatly on the billiard cue. Baize reflected green light on his chin. He would never convince everyone. But he tried. However, he concentrated on billiards for the moment.

He deftly wrapped up another victory as words piped through the loudspeaker on the wall.

"Supper up!"

The evening meal brought any further discussion to an end as an enormous mutton pie emerged piping hot from the oven. Made in an enamel bowl about eighteen inches in diameter, the thick brown crust, propped up during cooking by stacking tea cups on top of each other, was sliced and cut into large individual portions. Complete with lashings of steaming steak and kidney and covered in thick rich gravy, everybody's plate was now full to overflowing.

Meals at Nethan Street Fire Station were enormous.

The time dragged after we finished our supper before the hands towards the time of our approved rest period, 2300 hours. The quiet undisturbed station was now living up to its reputation of being a Country Club or rest home as the whole crew looked forward to a peaceful and uninterrupted night. We waited patiently for boots off time and bed.

But it was not to be. The red lights in the recreation room flashed on as the large fire-alarm bells rattled on the walls, disturbing the expected tranquil atmosphere. The pole-shoot doors, normally kept closed, banged open. We queued, waiting to slide down the thick Fireman's pole from the second to the ground floor.

The Fireman's pole, obsolete on my own, rather ancient Fire Station, was on modern Stations still an efficient and fast method for a group of men to descend from floor to floor in reply to the summons of the alarm bells. On Nethan Street Fire Station they were made from stainless steel, about seven inches in diameter, and dropped from the upper floor to ground level and almost into the engine house. The poles were thick enough to hold on to by both hands before wrapping both legs around the pole. As we slipped down, the legs could be loosened or tightened to achieve the right amount of braking, allowing a controlled descent. With practice it was possible, after first climbing on the pole, to free-fall the first few feet and just as the ground was reached, a final nip from both hands and legs perfected a soft landing.

"It's a chimney fire," the watchroom-man shouted from the muster-room.

The Water Tender quickly left the engine house. Those of us left behind sauntered slowly back upstairs. Almost immediately the bells rang again. Once more we all slid down the pole.

The watchroom-man stood outside his narrow door and held a single sheet of paper up.

"The fire is at a Merling's shop, the one in Araglin Town. The County Brigade at Araglin have a 'make-up' demanding eight Pumps," he shouted excitedly having difficulty competing with the noise of the bells. A 'make-up', a Fire Brigade term meant that the Pumps already in attendance could not cope with the incident and additional Pumps were needed.

"One Pump only is requested from our Brigade, the other Pumps must be coming from somewhere else," the watchroom-man continued to shout his information to us.

I collected my fire-uniform from its peg in the muster-room and raced to join Sub Officer Dace, in charge of the Pump Escape. The driver and Norman Sterlet completed our four-man crew. I climbed through the rear cab doors of the Pump Escape and sat next to Norman as the appliance slid out of Nethan Street Station for the ten miles to Araglin Town.

My tunic, used on the previous night's fire, was still damp. It felt cold and stiff. My hands slid reluctantly through the linings of the sleeves. Every front chrome button resisted my first attempts at fastening it. The inside of the boots felt damp as I tugged hard on the leather loops and forced my toes down. I rolled up the bottoms of my trousers and put them over the outside of my boots. Dressed, I stared out of the cab window.

The appliance jolted and swayed as we negotiated a roundabout and headed off leaving the streetlights and into the pitch darkness of the countryside. The engine raced faster through each gear change as we surged noisily forward. We drove past the farm gates on Araglin Road and, just visible in an adjoining field, we could see dark mounds. These were from the fire of our previous night.

Araglin, a town of about 65,000 population was served by a full time operational County Brigade Fire Station. Retained Firemen, who were part timers, manned all the surrounding County Fire Stations. They were disliked and despised by full time Fireman but they were reluctantly accepted as a necessary evil to serve outlying districts.

The streets were empty as we raced towards the town centre, looking for signs of a fire. Above the noise of the engine our driver screamed a question, asking if anyone knew the town. Suddenly a standpipe poking out from a street hydrant gave the answer to the question. We slowed down and turned into a main shopping street, following the delivery hose.

We pulled in and parked behind the other appliances. The delivery hose criss-crossed all over the road; two lengths disappeared through one of the front doors into a large shop. Sub Officer Dace dismounted as we stopped. He approached a white helmeted Officer surrounded by a group of Firemen. Then he ran back with our instructions.

"The fire's below. It seems they've been chased out by a deep seated fire in the cellar," Sub Officer Dace told us.

We climbed out of our appliance and looked through the shop doors. The delivery hose disappeared into a thick fog of smoke. Several Firemen stood outside in the road as if waiting for something to happen.

"They need men with B.A.s on," Sub Officer Dace said.

Breathing Apparatus was rarely used at fires in our Brigade, but this was an incident, which was big enough to justify wearing sets.

The Pump Escape carried two Compressed Air breathing sets. With Norman Sterlet we lifted both sets clear of the cab. With the sets slotted over both our shoulders and resting on our backs, we adjusted the straps and buckle, turned on the main cylinder valves, slotted the facemask over our faces, replaced our helmets and deposited our yellow identification tallies with our driver. He put them in his trouser pocket.

For all that our training procedure had constantly impressed upon us in drill sessions that an entry control point should always be present at fires we could see no evidence of one here. The procedure was designed to store our individual breathing apparatus tallies on a clipboard with a written record of our entry and proposed exit times when our air supply was likely to expire. This was to provide crews working inside an incident with some form of protection from crews on the outside.

Our orders were to find the end of the delivery hose, which had been abandoned by an earlier crew when they were driven out by a rapid build-up of heat and smoke. Delivery hose, two and three quarters of an inch in diameter, provided a supply of water from outside, for firemen to be able to man-handle to the heart of the fire. We were informed the end of this deliver hose had been left close to an opening to a cellar down which was possibly the seat of the fire.

We waddled, with the added weight of our air-sets on our backs, through a group of firemen all standing close to the main glass doors. I glanced above the door and noticed in huge chrome letters edged with red paint the sign saying Merling the Family Store. We pushed through the group of firemen and entered the shop through the open double doors. Our air-sets clicked as the demand regulators closed and opened, feeding compressed air from the cylinders on our backs into our facemasks.

The hand-held searchlight Norman carried penetrated barely a foot or so before being stopped by a solid grey wall of fog. On the floor we crept forward on our hands and knees inch by inch. We followed the delivery hose line deep into the shop. We felt our way and scuffled along, feeling for a path over the debris on the floor. The smoke was so dense we could only go forward inch by inch. The beam of light from the hand-held searchlight was useless against the dense thick smoke. Heat pricked our unprotected ears as we shuffled further and further inwards. We edged slowly along a wooden wall on our left. The delivery hose on the floor was charged solidly with water, guided us on and on, deeper and deeper into the shop.

The wooden partition wall came to an end and we could feel the heat from the fire through a small gateway at floor level. We inched through this opening and near a hole in the floor we located the end of the delivery hose. Water spurted out from the various holes on the hand-controlled nozzle. The nozzle, in addition to its on-off valve, also had a facility to create a protective spray jet.

The visibility was now zero. The temperature rose until my ears itched and hurt. Inside the facemask, sweat seeped out from my forehead and droplets fell over my eyebrows and into my eyes. I gripped the hem at the back of Norman's fire-tunic tightly. Nothing in my training had prepared me for anything like this. Claustrophobic, blinded and burning I felt frightened and lost. The soles of Norman's boots were an inch from my face mask, providing the only human comfort as we scuffled and edged forward and dragged the delivery hose with us. It was heavy and awkward to man-handle, and we stopped every foot or so to pull more of it free as we crawled slowly forward. Norman stopped.

"Check the gauges?" he shouted.

His order provided some voice contact as his words, even though they were masked and garbled, leaked out from inside his facemask. I grabbed the hand searchlight and read my pressure gauge, bringing the dial so close to my face that it touched my mask.

"Seventy atmospheres!" I shouted.

As we continued forward the heat increased. We seemed to be in a box of some kind. Suddenly a trap door appeared on the floor. Heat poured out of it, as if it were an open oven door. Through a break in the fog we saw steps disappearing, possibly leading down into a cellar.

As we crawled down the stairs the delivery hose jammed solid. I shuffled backwards to gain additional length. By pulling and tugging I achieved a few more feet and pushed the loop forward into this unknown box structure. Scrambling over the bight I rejoined Norman and together we half shuffled, half fell, down the wooden stairs. Heat attacked the skin on back of my hands.

Norman opened the nozzle by pulling back the on-off lever and water shot out of the end, crackling and splattering. The steel hard delivery hose now felt limp. There was no sign of any flames. Norman waved our water jet in front of us. We were drenched in scalding water immediately. The smoke completely engulfed us.

"We've got to get closer. More length on the hose," Norman shouted through his facemask.

Like a man possessed, full guns blazing, Norman pushed the delivery hose. Water poured in front of us into the smoke and heat. We attempted to injure the enemy wherever it was hidden, constantly moving the jet of water in a waving motion. I pulled and tugged at the delivery hose and managed to work a few extra feet free to enable us to go further down the steps.

At the bottom of the steps the fire was now frustrated and annoyed with us and unleashed its anger. Through a break in the smoke we saw a red haze only yards from us. Norman pointed our jet of water in the direction of this red haze. Immediately the fire disappeared, hiding behind the dense smoke.

We lay prone on the floor and continued to direct our jet of water forward through the smoke, hoping to wound the fire mortally. Our air cylinders clanged together as we wrestled in the confined space, directing our killing jet forward. The temperature seemed to drop and we thought we were at last achieving a result with our water.

Suddenly a whistle sounded! It indicated that the air supply from one of the breathing apparatus was running low.

"Let's get out!" Norman said.

Leaving the hose we retraced our steps up the steps and still close to each other we crawled out of the shop, hot and exhausted.

The cool open air outside the shop provided instant relief as we emerged from the inferno. Greeted by the other firemen, who were still grouped together, we returned to our Pump Escape. Both our whistles screamed as we removed our facemasks and breathed the welcome fresh air.

Sub Officer Dace and our driver had been waiting anxiously for us outside the shop. We thought we were the only ones inside, but now we learned of another crew, which had entered through a rear entrance. They were also dressed in breathing apparatus and had a second jet of water working inside the cellar.

For nearly thirty minutes we had been subjected to the torture of immense heat. Norman slowly stood upright. His face was drenched in sweat and strands of his hair draped down like wet string covering his forehead. I undid the steel buckle of the harness and lifted the heavy Air Set off my shoulders and placed it on the road at the side of our appliance. Originally thirty pounds in weight, it now felt far heavier.

After all our exertions, the first thing Norman wanted was a smoke. He produced his well-polished tobacco tin and a miniature stubby pipe from inside his tunic. Soon he was puffing away drawing both cheeks inwards.

As we recovered, a white helmeted County Fire Brigade Divisional Officer appeared.

"Can you go back in?" He asked.

"We have a shortage of B.A. wearers."

Suddenly a red Trojan van drove down the street towards us, interrupting our answer.

The County Fire Brigade insignia displayed on the front door looked very impressive. Fiercely applied brakes squealed the van to an abrupt stop. From an opened nearside cab door an immaculately dressed Sub Officer leaped out. His fire-boots gleamed; his helmet-lacquered black reflected the outside street light. His polished black belt supported a whiter than-white, immaculately clean axe handle. He marched smartly over to us. Norman and I sat on the pavement and looked on. The front of Norman's tunic gaped wide open as he continued to suck on his pipe.

The Sub Officer marched directly past us, stood to attention facing the County Divisional Officer and saluted in expert fashion. His right arm took the arm longest way up and the shortest way down. The Divisional Officer returned his salute enthusiastically.

"Sub Officer Peal, Sir. From Liddel," the Sub Officer shouted.

Liddel village was a great deal closer than Nethan Street Station but we noted that they had just arrived.

"Any B.A. wearers?" The Divisional Officer shouted back as if all conversations needed to be loud and deafening.

"No Sir," an equally loud response.

They turned and marched off.

"Looks like you'll have to go back in," Sub Officer Dace told us dryly.

"So much for retained Firemen," Norman said, taking a last lung full of pipe smoke.

Our driver changed both used cylinders from our exhausted air-sets and screwed on two fresh cylinders. Our harness straps were now stiff damp and wet as we reluctantly slid the sets once more over our shoulders. The surrounds of the facemask were now cold, but we pulled them over our heads and thrust our faces into position. With the straps adjusted and tightened we were ready once more.

Again we made our way through the front door of the shop and retraced our path to the end of the delivery hose. The store was still full of thick acrid smoke but our self-contained breathing sets provided life-saving air. Again we crawled on hands and knees through small opening into the box-like structure and through the hole in the floor. We went down the steps and eventually located our delivery hose in the dungeon. Smoke still blocked out our vision as we blindly turned on the jet of water. As the jet of water hit the ceiling above us and cascaded down on us, scalding water hit our bare hands. I pulled down my tunic sleeve and tilted my helmet forwards for protection.

Between spasmodic breaks in the dense smoke we obtained a fleeting glimpse of the cellar. Piles of boxes were shadowed against a glow at the far end of the room. Without warning this glow exploded and instead of being a small patch in front of us it now spread to cover our whole angle of vision. Amidst all the noise and rumbling our air-sets clicked more rapidly and provided some comfort as the valves opened and shut and as we took deeper and deeper gulps of air. The temperature began to rise rapidly. The solid jet of water from our hose continued to force forwards.

"Get out! Get out!" The cry came from above.

Immediately we dropped the delivery hose and struggled, half-falling and half-running back up the stairs. Sub Officer Dace, handkerchief clamped firmly over his mouth, had struggled through all the smoke to give us warning of a pending flash-over, a term used to describe a building on fire, reaching a critical temperature and in danger of imminent explosion. Without question we beat a hasty retreat.

As we covered the last few yards to safety, lumps of ceiling cracked from above our heads and hit our helmets.

"The roof's going," Dace said as we scrambled out through the door. The fireman, who had once all grouped themselves around the entrance, now took off, scrambling to the far side of the road.

"The roof's gone!" someone shouted, stating the obvious.

Deep inside the building there was a sound like that of a struggling jet aircraft as the fire unleashed its anger and exploded. A huge ball of fire shot up from inside the centre of the shop, accelerating and forcing a path straight upwards.

We watched. Within second's large tongues of fire lashed out from the roof of the building.

A Turntable Ladder at the back of the building began pouring water from its seventy-foot high outlet. The fire was now only under attack from outside as we stood with all the other firemen and watched. We were cold, wet, hungry and defeated. The fire had beaten us. Our feeble efforts to reach its heart and attempt to assassinate the fire failed. For four hours water from jets outside the building poured into it.

At long last the fire subsided, relinquishing its grip on life and died slowly.

Eventually the smoke inside cleared and the ground floor became accessible. Grey morning light emerged from a smoke stained sky as dawn approached.

Inside the gutted shop our original length of hose was now covered in broken glass and rubbish. The floor was awash in inches of water. We retraced our steps to examine our original position, guided by the growing morning light outside.

The small narrow gateway turned out to be an entrance through a wooden shopping counter. Steps through a manhole in the floor behind this counter led down to the basement. Our length of hose had been burned away and our nozzle outlet was now somewhere buried under tons of rubble.

The final turnout had involved fifteen Pumps, but most of these were manned by retained part-timers. Most of them only knew how to fight fires from the outside, and as we prepared to go back to our Station we talked among ourselves and questioned their ability to understand proper fire fighting.

This fire had been extinguished, killed and annihilated by pouring gallons and gallons of water from outside the building. With only a limited attempt at destroying our enemy internally, we were fighting a different war. We had been using part-time retained fire fighters rather than full-time main line troops.

During our journey back along deserted empty country roads the morning sky turned clear blue before the welcome sight of Nethan Street Station appeared.

As I packed my filthy, smoke stained uniform and wrapped my unused bedding and prepared to return to my home Station, I was told that my two nights on relief duty, at the so-called Country Club or rest home, were the worst two nights anyone could ever remember.

Chapter 19

The annual pilgrimage of Her Majesty's Inspector of Fire Services created a frenzy of extra cleaning.

During my eighteen months in the Fire Service I had realised that the majority of a Fireman's time was devoted to Station cleaning. While a privileged few, the tradesmen, (electricians, joiners, and plumbers) all went off to maintain the houses owned by the Fire Brigade, those remaining on Fire Stations were kept occupied by cleaning routines which were strictly enforced.

Weeks before this inspection, almost a Royal event, and our cleaning routines were intensified and reached fever pitch. Even the remotest dungeons of the Station were subject to a rigorous intensive cleaning campaign. It was hard to imagine anyone who did not have to, let alone such an important visitor as a Government Inspector in a uniform similar to our Chief Officer's, visiting our top yard boiler house. It was situated a hundred yards from our engine house and could only be reached after the visitor had crossed a busy public road, gone across a yard and passed beneath our hundred and twenty-foot hose tower.

Once under the shadow of the hose tower, lifting a heavy hatch-cover revealed a dark deep hole in the floor. An awkward vertical ladder with the third rung from its bottom broken, and the position of the light-switch in the depths of this abyss meant the visitor must first struggle down, remembering the missing rung. At the bottom he had to fumble in the complete darkness for a switch. When he found it and switched the light on, a solitary forty-watt bulb at last bathed the boiler house in a weak feeble glow. Like an eternal flame, this top yard boiler was never allowed to go out. The constant heat it provided dried our delivery hoses, suspended by their couplings and hoisted up the hose tower, where they stayed until they were bone dry.

Every boiler house on the Station required sweeping, the inevitable mopping, and cleaning. Even the millions of pieces of coke were arranged into neat and tidy piles. Orders for this extra purge on cleaning came from above. Such orders always arrived, finally falling on us at the bottom of the chain of command, in red and in CAPITAL LETTERS. If our Chief ever cleared his throat, by the time news of his tickle reached our ears, we were led to believe he was suffering from bronchial-pneumonia!

Leading Fireman Barney Bret was ideal to carry out these orders; he interpreted his uncle's orders with verve and vigilance. We hid from Balmy Bret in the most distant corners of our wandering old Fire Station, and this meant that he spent most of his time finding us. This game of hide and seek became something of a challenge as we regularly avoided his gaze.

Although it was often easier to clean than to spend hours hidden on lumpy coke or hiding in our disused hayloft, our actions had the welcome effect of increasing Bret's blood pressure and encouraged more evasive tactics.

Whining, he eventually told on us to Sub Officer Gardon and eventually Station Officer Finnan was brought into the picture.

We conceded defeat. So the toilets became lime-washed, every boiler house, including the obscure top yard boiler house, was tidied and made fit to accept top-notch visitors. And all the appliances on the Station were polished and polished until they all reached a pristine showroom condition.

In addition to all this intense cleaning we were on night duty for the evening exercise for the Inspector. Rumours were rife that Breathing Apparatus Entry Control was to be at the top of his agenda and our planned exercise was to include the correct procedure, following Brigade Orders.

Accidents had occurred at incidents where men wearing Breathing Apparatus were not subject to any outside control or monitoring; as a consequence running out of oxygen, or air, had occurred and men had been lost. Fatalities always produce inquiries, and a series of regulations now stated that tallies for every type of Breathing Apparatus were essential. They had to record, name of the wearer, type of set, cylinder contents and the time of entry. So tallies were issued to accompany every breathing apparatus. There were several types, each with its own significance.

The Proto one-hour oxygen-set had a white tally. The Salvus half-hour oxygen-set blue and compressed air-sets had a yellow tally. These, when they had been filled in correctly, were clipped onto a control board and kept outside an incident before anyone was allowed to enter.

This produced a written record for each fireman, showing position and status.

Breathing Apparatus Control Officer in charge of this entry control board thus monitored all operations from outside. By plotting cylinder pressure against a table of figures printed on the entry board, predictions could be made about when the wearer should withdraw before his set became exhausted.

This was the correct procedure when on a practice drill. But I remembered our fire a few weeks earlier, at Araglin Town, and noted the difference between classroom techniques and putting the theory into practice at real incidents.

Hours of extra drill, which we had to endure in addition to all the cleaning ensured that these procedures would work, like clockwork at the planned exercise to be held in an old cloth mill. As a result of our work our six year-old Pump Escape, its body built with care and dedication, shone like new. Its red side panels gleamed with many coats of wax polish; even the slots on the hundreds of round headed screws, which secured the body panels to the wooden frame, were all vertical and precisely positioned. The roof shone black, having been polished constantly with boot polish. The tyres on the four road wheels beamed as a result of our constant buffing. The chrome edging around the front windows and the large bell perched on the roof reflected objects as though they were mirrors. The mud flaps hanging from the rear wheel arches had been scrubbed, washed and painted in black gloss paint. The steel fifty-foot escape-ladder had been removed and every inch of metal rubbed and polished with oily rags. Two large carriage wheels spun freely from the rear of the appliance, their treads glistening under a film of oil.

Every appliance on every station in the entire city was subjected to this devoted attention. Cleaning had become obsessive. Even fire calls were a hindrance as we were rushed back for more cleaning. Our battered old Fire Station took on a facade of disguised sham, like rotten wood hidden under a thin decorative coat of paint.

Late on a Tuesday morning, our last on days before going onto nights and our planned exercise, the sky turned pitch black with the promise of a summer thunderstorm. In the engine house the light rapidly faded as we re-polished our already gleaming appliances. No one dared to touch anything for fear of leaving even one dirty finger mark. Raindrops began to bounce off the street outside. The roof rattled under this sudden onslaught and the pavements were awash as hailstones filled the gutters.

The bells sounded just after 1400 hours for our pristine Pump Escape to respond to a cricket pavilion, which was on fire on the borders of the City in the Stour Crescent Fire Station Area.

The dark threatening clouds floated away leaving a fresh deep blue sky. The pleasure of escaping from all the drudgery and constant cleaning was regarded as a blessing as we happily climbed aboard and raced away.

The message read 'fire at Churnet Village Cricket ground, needing a Pump from Stour Crescent Station and a Pump Escape from Torridge City Station.'

I joined Fireman Stuart Cale as the second crew-man in our freshly painted cab. The smell of fresh oily paint filled our nostrils as we struggled to dress in our fire-uniforms in the moving appliance. Leading Fireman Bret, the officer in charge sat in the front alongside our driver, Fireman Jeffrey Twaite, as he negotiated the city-centre traffic with ease.

We began the long haul to the city boundary. Stour Crescent Fire Station was set in the industrial part of Torridge and in addition to large areas of old domestic property it protected several heavy engineering works and a huge petrol-farm. The other appliances at Stour Crescent Station had all been shipped out to other stations whilst a new station was being built. This left only one Pump on call for the area.

The eight-mile chase through the industrial belt was an unusually long distance for us to travel. We left the City suburbs behind and raced out into farmland. In the fields flashing by as we left Torridge City boundary, we could see corn, which had been flattened in the recent storm.

Eventually we could see traces of black smoke spiralling into the blue sky. We slowed down and noticed an open gate and a tight country lane leading off into the distance.

C. C. C., an old battered sign precariously held up by an old rusty chain, pointed towards our fire. Our precious Pump Escape crept through the gateway with inches to spare and carried us along a long narrow lane. Branches from the overhanging trees rustled above, touching our polished black leather cab roof. Each scratch sounded painful. We had polished it to perfection and we groaned as we heard it suffering from this onslaught of hawthorn branches, which gouged and damaged it above our heads.

At long last we could see the remains of a cricket pavilion through our front windscreen. Constructed of wood, which had constantly been covered with creosote over the years, it had burned well. The Pump crew from Stour Crescent Station tried desperately to save the pavilion.

With no readily available water supply there was very little they could do. When we arrived, four charred timber trusses stood upright all alone.

Using the hundred gallons of water out of our Pump Escape hose-reel tank we too poured all our water onto the burnt carcass. The pavilion was now a pile of charred rubbish. We helped to turn over the remains in an attempt to save something of value, but apart from finding an old wooden box with a few cricket score books inside, our attendance was not much help.

"We must get back to the Station," Leading Fireman Bret said, his eyes disappearing in slits amongst his wrinkled fat face.

"The appliance has to be cleaned, now it's been out," he added.

Apart from bits of branches on the roof our Pump Escape still looked good. Jeffrey, the driver, climbed into his cab and slotted the gear lever into reverse. As the Pump Escape moved backwards, a pool of water appeared under it possible from the leaking hose-reel pump. The front wheels, black with their tyres buffed to a high lustre, sank into the mud. The appliance dipped to one side as the offside front wheel went deeper. The rear drive wheels lost their grip and turned freely, throwing up brown streams of mud from behind as Jeffrey attempted to find some grip. The appliance ground to a halt.

"Empty the lockers to lighten the load," someone suggested. Laboriously we emptied the contents from their immaculately clean lockers. The delivery hose and the other equipment were soon piled high on the surrounding turf in a huge and untidy heap.

Although we were miles from any known habitation, the cricket ground soon attracted onlookers. Several mothers with children in prams appeared and with them a retired gentleman and a group of youngsters looked on with amused curiosity.

Using Stour Crescent Station's Pump we fastened a rope to our front bumper and they attempted to pull our stricken Pump Escape free. They failed miserably. Their drive wheels spun round in a vain attempt to find some grip. Both appliances had now settled in the growing sea of mud. Our attempts became desperate as the mire splattered both our once gleaming appliances in the yellow-brown mud.

"Just concrete around the base and leave it for children to play on," the retired gentlemen suggested as he adjusted his Panama hat.

The Sub Officer from Stour Crescent Station ignored our increasingly worried Leading Fireman Bret about possible repercussions and requested using the appliance radio, Brigade Control to send our Emergency Tender. Perhaps its winch and cable might pull us free it was thought.

Eventually a staff car arrived with Divisional Officer Mullet, our Fire Brigade driving instructor, who had been sent to investigate. He wound his car window slowly down and his bright red face looked out.

The sight of two appliances, which were now, only naked shells, squatted deep in a quagmire of mud, left him speechless. Obviously annoyed, he reversed his car. Its wheels spun round and churned up more mud. We all pushed on his bonnet and just prevented another vehicle adding to the bogged-down collection. Large streaks of yellow mud from our grubby hands coated his once smart red car. He decided that the Emergency Tender was needed.

The once immaculate country cricket ground looked like a battlefield. Walking was almost impossible in the deep thick mud; we struggled, knee deep, through the now greasy terrain.

The Emergency Tender arrived at long last and charged up the lane. With a high pantechnicon body clearing a path through the overhanging trees in the lane as it arrived, it looked like some tribal chief covered in a mass of branches.

The winch was at the rear of the appliance. This, of course, meant that the Emergency Tender had arrived facing the wrong way. Wisely not trusting the soft green turf to support the appliance the driver slowly reversed all the way down the lane. Turning on the main road and returning in reverse all took time. Meanwhile our appliances sunk deeper and deeper as a result of our constant nibbling attempts to free them.

At last the steel cable was pulled from the Emergency Tender and attached securely to the rear of our Pump Escape. But the weight and strain was too much for the winch motor. The Pump Escape refused to budge an inch and rocked itself deeper.

Some other bright individual suggested moving the Emergency Tender closer and using a snatch block to double the mechanical advantage.

A snatch block, a twelve-inch pulley wheel attached to a large hook, allowed the cable to be doubled back and provided twice the pull over half the distance. By the time the Emergency Tender had manoeuvred close enough its rear wheels had become bogged down in the mud. The rear wheels clawed and spun round desperately, failing to find any useful grip.

Our Pump Escape, Stour Crescent Station's Pump, and now our Emergency Tender all sat encased in a sea of mud.

The old gentleman who earlier had sarcastically suggested a play area for the children tut-tutted. Tilting his straw boater he leant on his walking stick. His hands crossed on the ebony handle, his eyes sparkled.

"It looks as though you could do with a tractor," he said.

"My son may have something in the next field." His words implied that he was taking pity on us city folk.

"James, go and get him," he said to one of his young charges. Young boy chased off down the lane.

Within minutes an old large blue tractor appeared in an adjoining field. The old gentleman's son shut down the engine and jumped off the rear driver's seat. He carefully selected an opening in the hawthorn hedge and came to us.

"You have got yourselves into a bit of a mess. I'll bring the tractor round, "he said, going back through the hedge.

The tractor engine chugged off. Puffs of black smoke poured from the exhaust pipe as the driver bounced up and down on his seat.

Once he had reached our stranded appliances he tied a thick greasy rope around the towing eye of the tractor and then to the front of the Emergency Tender. The rope tightened and the tractor set off. The Emergency Tender shook violently, wobbled and broke free. The rope was untied tractor sped off to the outfield, where it reversed to the Pump Escape.

The Emergency Tender, now free, set off back home.

I took the loose end of the old rope attached to the tractor and struggled through the mud, crawling underneath the wheeled fifty foot ladder on the back of the

Pump Escape. Suddenly my right foot had no boot on it. Stuck solidly up to my arms in yellow slimy mud, I searched for my elusive boot. Flaying about, I floated helplessly onto my back. Staring upwards into deep blue a solitary wisp of cloud sped rapidly across the sky, blissfully unaware of the trauma below. Half swimming and half-crawling I retrieved my boot and fastened the tow-rope to one of the rear eyelets, scraping a channel through the mud.

The rope attached and with the Pump Escape in reverse gear our driver, Jeffrey, tried to help the tractor in a final effort to become free. But the Pump Escape lurched back, going even deeper. The tractor tugged and pulled until by sheer brute force the appliance came free. A loud cheer and an equally loud ripping noise accompanied this achievement.

We examined the damage. Both the rear mud flaps had been wrenched from their mountings, which were now missing. Once painted to perfection the mud flaps were now lost forever and relegated to life in the quagmire.

"Get your machine back to the station and clean it," the Divisional Officer grimaced as he gave the order.

"Drivers," he complained. He was not amused.

Leaving the muddy scene with the Pump from Stour Crescent Station still needing rescue from the muddy prison, we made a hasty retreat. Reversing down the long lane down to the road all took time, and we collected more damage from the hawthorn bushes on our cab roof.

The old cricket pavilion was now burnt to the ground as if we had never attended the fire. A hole, which was now gouged along the boundary, left a cavern deep enough for a village pond, perhaps large enough for fishing in summer and ice skating in winter! And somewhere in the pond of the future lay a pair of our once shiny mud flaps.

The dirt and mud flying off our road wheels left a trail for yards and yards on the quiet country road. Pump Escape, once a shiny example as a result of hours and hours of toil and polish, reversed into the engine house in disgrace. Every piece of equipment, which had been removed to lighten the load, was now defiled and tainted. Every locker was caked in mud. The rest of our watch looked on with a mixture of sympathy and barely hidden laughter.

It was five-thirty and close to the time for the change of crews, which meant that the cricket pavilion fire fiasco had taken all afternoon. We too were all plastered head to toe in mud and in the same state as the appliance. But for the remaining half-hour we attempted to restore the Pump Escape to its once former glory.

At 1800 hours, the night crew took over. Our uniforms, too, needed to be swilled and scrubbed with a yard brush to ease away inches of baked yellow greasy mud. Finally we showered and went off duty.

Over a period of twenty-four hours, the night crew and the day crew who followed, under strict orders from above, cleaned our Pump Escape and returned it to its pristine showroom condition.

The planned exercise for Her Majesty's Inspector at Gurnet's Mill was scheduled to start at 1900 hours. But the fickle summer weather changed again as fine drizzle descended from a dull overcast sky as we arrived for the night shift.

Our best uniforms, kept for such state occasions were produced from our lockers. Our polished axe-belts were now correctly positioned on the two small metal hooks on our tunics and rested above the two small chrome buttons on the back. A leather belt supported the axe-pouch and our axe-handles, washed white, all hung correctly on our left at exactly waist high.

We strutted about, preened ourselves and waited.

The bells sounded at exactly 1900. We were ready and waiting in the muster-room. We heard the call Pump One, Pump Escape, Turntable Ladder, to exercise, Gurnet's Mill, Fender Place, off Fender Road.

Three appliances, using blue lights only and no bell or sirens chased off to join the appliances from the other four outer Stations. In all six Pumps and a Turntable Ladder came to demonstrate our efficiency.

Gurnet's Mill, an old Victorian complex, was sited alongside an old filthy stream which had contained cellars which had been empty for years and were now dark and damp. In these cellars old sacks, stuffed and filled with bricks to imitate injured people, were hidden. Crews wearing Breathing Apparatus were to go through the entry procedure drill before searching the building and recovering the sacks.

Her Majesty's Inspector with our Chief Officer, Mr Bass stood sheltering beneath a canopy from the fine rain. The Inspector held a loose pair of brown leather gloves in his hands. Both he and the Chief had two rows of silver oak leaves on the peaks of their caps. The peaks moved up and down in unison as they chatted. They looked very impressive and important.

I lifted a Proto-oxygen set from the cab of the Pump Escape and joined Dodger, Fireman Roger Braise, at the Control Board.

The Proto-set was heavy on my shoulders. The black oxygen cylinder sat waist high on my back. The main valve was turned on and locked into the open position by a small catch. It provided two and a half litres of oxygen per minute, sending it to the rubber bag that covered my chest. A mouthpiece was placed between my teeth and a spring nose clip gripped my nostrils like a thumbscrew. All the air in the bag needed to be extracted since, as we had been taught at training school, any residue remaining would cause a severe headache. By breathing in the contents of the bag, gripping the exhalation tube and breathing out, the air in the bag was finally exhausted. A final injection of oxygen, using the bye-pass valve, topped up the bag and a last lungful inhaled and exhaled ensured that only oxygen remained within the enclosed set.

The Fireman manning the Control board took my white identification tally, checked my name and entered my oxygen cylinder pressure, and slotted the plastic marker under Fireman Braise's tally on a large white board.

The red rubber goggles over our eyes, we were ready to enter the building. With the apparatus, weighing twenty-seven pounds, over our shoulders we set off in the direction of the basement.

The mill cellar was pitch black. Gripping each other's sleeve we followed a dry line of delivery hose laid out in advance to give us the direction. We shuffled along, and the filthy conditions in the cellar soon covered our best uniforms in inches of ancient dust.

We turned on our small lamps to see where we were. Tiny pencil of lights mingled and crossed in the dark. We bumped into a crew on their way out; they gave us some indication as to the location of the hidden sacks.

The mouthpieces gripped between our teeth made communication impossible. By sign language and grunting we helped each other as we progressed inwards. At last we located an old coal sack which was solid with bricks and between us we man-handled the supposed body outside.

Each crew of two recovered a sack, until all the sacks were accounted for and the drill was declared to be complete.

We retrieved our tallies from the Control point and began taking off the Proto sets. The strong vice grips from the nose clips stung as the heat and sweat welded the rubber to our nostrils.

The mouthpieces were painfully removed from sore mouths. Our once smart fire-tunics were now plastered in basement grime.

The drill had felt like play-acting. It was nothing compared to the dangers of a real fire situation. However our superiors demanded that we acted out this farce as a drill, but when it came to real dangerous situations the idea of proper control procedure seemed to be overlooked.

Our Turntable Ladder had been elevated high enough to produce a water tower. From the stinking stream the water entered one of our Pumps and then pumped up the ladder to emerge seventy foot high. The spray from the head of the Turntable Ladder joined the rain, which was drenching us. At last the order was given to end the drill. In our dirty uniforms, wet by the constant drizzle and spray from the Turntable Ladder, we were herded together for the pep talk.

"Gather round lads," the Inspector said condescendingly. We jostled for position. He thanked us all profusely and said he thought the Turntable Ladder drill went remarkable well.

"You must use the correct entry control at all times," he said, emphasising the need for the correct procedure.

"I am very pleased."

He turned to our Chief Officer. Their eyes met in a salutary manner. He whipped his loose leather gloves from one hand to the other and walked away.

The inspection was over, until next time.

Chapter 20

The long-awaited meeting at which we were to hear from Fire Brigade Union General Secretary arrived at last. The meeting was arranged on neutral ground, at The Trades Hall, since our Chief Fire Officer adamantly refused to allow any outside Union men to speak to Union members on any of his Fire Stations.

The large hall was crammed with Union members waiting to hear the details of their immediate future prospects and also to hear about the directions in which other Fire Brigades were heading.

Normal monthly Union branch meetings, which were condescendingly allowed to be held on Fire Stations, usually attracted few members. But with some Brigades now working eight hours less then others for the same pay as a result of the introduction of a forty-eight hour week, a feeling of injustice grew to such an extent that many previously silent Union members felt angry enough to demand some action.

The air was rich in tobacco smoke. Humming with anticipation we herded ourselves together, shuffling down onto long hard bench seats. The seats were set in tiers and overlooked the platform. The room was packed solid. Impatient and restless brothers took every seat.

A table dressed in a dark-green blanket took centre stage in the auditorium. A tray of glasses and a water jug adorned it. The General Secretary looked confident as he climbed on the stage accompanied by our Torridge City Fire Brigade Union Secretary, Norman Sterlet.

Norman looked different from the way he looked when we crawled about on our hands and knees in heat and smoke at Merling's store fire two months earlier. His hair was combed neatly and he was dressed in a smart dark brown suit. His long thin pipe, gripped tightly between clenched teeth, protruded from his lips like a natural extension of them.

He pulled out a chair for the National Secretary to sit on. The chatter and buzz continued as the National Secretary meticulously took a glass from the tray and filled it carefully with water.

John Scar, never one to miss an opportunity to express his point of view, was keen to speak first. He stood up waving his hands to attract attention from the platform.

"OK Brother Scar you can have your say soon, let me first introduce," Norman began.

"We all know who he is. The problem is, what's he going to do?" John interrupted.

The room fell silent.

"Sit down, Brother Scar," Norman insisted. He introduced the National Secretary who stood, feet apart, and began a long prepared speech outlining a policy to improve the image of Firemen.

"The Union does not just want to kick out mops and buckets so that Firemen did nothing between fires. We should not be handling mops, buckets and wash leathers but making people conscious of the need for safety. The Fire Service ought to be a policing authority and we can now see a new Service emerging," he went on and on until the speech ended at last. He sat down.

Before Norman had time to ask for questions, John Scar was up on his feet and pointing his finger at the stage.

"For years now the Union has been saying that service for the sixties is coming."

He stood, rocking back on his heels, his hands on hips.

Everyone listened intently as John went on.

"But we are still poorly paid cleaners unwanted until we're needed."

"We're just cheap Mrs Mops," he repeated.

"And Mrs Mops for eight hours more than other brothers," someone stood up and shouted from the front row.

A chorus of 'Mrs Mop. Mrs Mop. Mrs Mop' drowned the response from the platform.

"Mrs Mop. Mrs Mop. Mrs Mop!"

"Mrs Mop. Mrs Mop. Mrs Mop!"

Norman Sterlet brought a brief halt to the proceedings when he stated that at the rate men was still leaving Torridge City Brigade there was no immediate prospect of a forty-eight hour week being introduced. But he promised that certain proposals would be made to the authorities.

This statement just fuelled more and more chanting.

'Mrs Mop. Mrs Mop. Mrs Mop!' The stamping of feet brought more chaos and an early end to the meeting. The seeds of discontent were finding fertile soil.

Short of money, I declined an offer to go to the City Tavern to continue the discussion over a few pints and instead accepted a lift home in Dodger's recently acquired van; he had christened 'Joseph'.

I was always short of money. Although the prospect of working shorter hours for the same pay was a promise for the future, working eight hours less would not increase my weekly income. Average weekly pay, according to Government sources was £16.14s.11d but my take-home wages of £11.1s. every Thursday, did not cover my rent and food bill. Making money from any part time work I could get was essential.

The majority of firemen had some sort of outside employment and I found casual work at the greengrocer's shop below my rented room off-loading vegetables and helping in the shop when I was off duty. This was an absolute necessity if I was to survive.

Dodger's van, Joseph, had begun life as an ice-cream van. Dodger used this new acquisition for his latest business venture, delivering wet fish from the wholesale fish market to fish-and-chip shops. The van's body was now painted in several shades of cream and blue. With the serving hatch completely removed Joseph looked like a mistake. A sheet of corrugated-steel covered the gaping hole where the hatch used to be, which was painted bright red. The driver's sliding door formerly coloured dark brown and with ice-cream advertisements, was now daubed with bottle-green paint. Joseph hit the city's streets like a spot of arterial blood on virgin snow.

Reports of the special Union meeting were relayed to upper levels of our hierarchy in record time. We were informed that plans to introduce the promised forty-eight hour week needed more transfers as we returned to our day shift. Consequently a list two pages long of firemen who were to be moved from our station to another station appeared from above.

Firemen were transferred to other stations for a variety of official reasons, including promotion and the shortage of drivers. In reality transfers were likely to be a form of punishment for such things as saying the wrong thing, upsetting senior ranks, regularly being on sick leave, not being considered suitable or being known as an active Union trouble maker.

Not surprisingly, Fireman John Scar was on the move again. He spent most of his ten years Fire Service moving from station to station, watch to watch. He took his moves casually, making friends easily wherever he landed. This time his kit bag was packed and he was off to Blue Watch at Weaver Road Station.

On my own Station, Pump One, Pump Escape, Pump Two, Turntable Ladder and an Emergency Tender needed twenty-two men on each of the three watches Blue, Red and White. The number was made up of a five-man crew on each of the three pumping appliances, two men on the Turntable Ladder and Emergency Tender and three men on leave. To introduce a forty-eight hour week meant an extra three men were needed. The transfer of John Scar, one of the drivers on our Watch left only nineteen men to provide the bare minimum of four crew for each pumping appliance and four men for the two special appliances, Emergency Tender and Turntable Ladder. If anyone went sick or if there was a driver shortage a relief Fireman from another Station had to be found. But every station and every Watch in the City suffered similar deficiencies and mastering the act of moving drivers and Firemen became a nightmare for those in command at Station level.

There were two types of drivers. Light vehicle drivers were used for vans, cars and certain special appliances. Red Machine drivers drove the main line appliances.

"Get a full driving licence and you can drive," Station Officer Finnan told me as we came on duty one Thursday morning.

I had a provisional driving licence and in the days when my finances were better I had taken driving lessons. I had even taken my driving test but failed it. Since Mother's death, now that I was living on my own, money for such extras had to be found some other way. Although Torridge City Fire Brigade could examine and pass learner drivers, this was not available for probationers.

"Take your driving test in Joseph," Dodger suggested.

"Go in your uniform. It'll make all the difference," he added.

After morning parade the privileged few, the tradesmen and those with station perks, again disappeared. The tradesmen assisted with maintenance of Fire Brigade property and those with other station perks including the canteen man, the hose man, the hydrant man and the van driver, vanished from the Fire Station or into the hideaways they had created for themselves.

Insufficient manpower now meant that Pump Two became unavailable at 0915 hours. Those of us who were left had to man Pump One, Pump Escape, Turntable Ladder and Emergency Tender. Our named tallies shuffled on the crew board on the muster-room wall from hook to hook appliance to appliance until they finally stopped and dangled against an appliance. This was often different from that to which we had been detailed on morning parade.

The first job on a Thursday was for someone to collect the money for our wages from the bank. It was then issued to each of the five stations. At our station, Station Officer Finnan and Leading Fireman Bret sorted out the notes and coins into our individual pay packets, which were to be issued at the pay parade at 1400 hours.

The men left over became an embarrassment. No one really knew how to occupy Firemen whose sole task was to be ready to turnout at a moment's notice. Work creation schemes devised through the years provided hours of occupational therapy. This was supposed to keep our idle hands busy and Satan at bay. Station cleaning was the main task and there was plenty of it. It was like sweeping a desert free of sand. The cleaning routines seemed to continue forever. We really were Mrs Mops!

Every day some windows had to be cleaned and a floor to be washed or polished. On Thursdays, the windows in the engine-house were cleaned inside and out. I began the morning's therapy with a bucket, wash leather and a short extension ladder. I started polishing the windows.

Dodger asked for assistance in removing clinkers from our top yard boiler house and so brought temporary relief from my window cleaning. Willingly I left my half-cleaned windows often known as 'diamonds' and trailed up the street, across the road and down into the bowels of the earth.

Using a rope we man-handled half-filled heavy dustbins from the depths. We began removing the clinkers from the hot cellar, which was full of sulphurous fumes with a pungent odour, which scoured our nostrils clean.

While we were carrying out this task the alarm bells rang.

The bell hammer tapped intermittently against the bell.

We scrambled up the broken vertical ladder like disturbed rats. I forgot about the missing third rung and stumbled. At my second attempt I emerged, half-crawling, and ran out of the top yard and down the street dodging between an electric milk float and a passing coal-lorry. We ran to the Station. As we arrived we saw that the engine house doors were already open. The Pump Escape and Turntable Ladder both edged out.

"It's a full circus," the Turntable Ladder driver shouted through his open cab window.

Through the engine house we chased to the muster-room to check our names against the crew board and collect our fire-uniforms. Our names hung alongside Pump One.

We raced back through the swing doors, our boots in one hand, our helmets and tunics in the other. We boarded our open backed Dennis F8 Pump.

"Where have you two been?" Leading Fireman Bret asked, his fat face showing disapproval. He did not wait for an answer as we set off with a jolt, which shook his helmet down over his eyes. Station Officer Finnan, wearing his white helmet, looked anxiously from his front seat through the sliding cab doors; we were the last of the crew to arrive.

"What's the address?" I asked Bret.

Bret, not the sort to speak to a mere fireman, said nothing. He sat already dressed in his helmet, tunic and boots, his large frame silent.

Dodger removed his helmet to allow room for his lanky frame to enter the two sliding-cab doors leading from the open back into the front cab. As he came back from the front cab he replaced his helmet gripping on to the ladder which rested on gallows above our heads.

"It's Nurse's Home at the Infirmary," he had discovered. He shouted above the noise from our bell and siren.

Torridge City Infirmary, a sprawling complex of different buildings, had several entrances. A set of traffic lights, specifically designed to assist us gave us information about which entrance to use. They were situated high on an outside wall and we strained to see these three-coloured lights as we approached.

"Red, it shows Red!" Dodger shouted as we approached.

Coloured lights, red, yellow, and white in varying combinations made up the different codes. The top light glowed.

"Red, that is the Nurse's home," Dodger shouted, confirming the address.

Sub Officer Gardon, the officer in charge of Pump Escape, and its crew already in attendance, scampered up the steps and disappeared into the Nurse's home.

Several nurses, each in varying states of undress, were in a huddle outside the building. They had come out because of the sounding of the fire alarm.

Station Officer Finnan had the cab door open before our Pump One stopped and leaped out. We jumped off the rear platform and followed him up the steps and through the large polished front door. Inside the building the loud fire-bells drowned the corridor in noise.

Sub Officer Gardon, taking everything as usual with calm and dignity, strolled back down the corridor.

"It's a chip pan, but it was out on arrival, Alec," he said above the noise of the alarm bell.

The Station Officer told Leading Fireman Bret to send the Stop Message and told me to silence the fire alarm.

Locating the fire-alarm panel, I found the system showed FIRE. A hospital porter dashed towards us. A bunch of keys in his hand. Using one of his keys we opened the glass door and I pressed the button marked 'Press to Silence Alarm'. The bells stopped ringing and silence reigned.

Meanwhile Dodger was more interested in all the waiting nurses than in any fire and soon cashed in on his luck. I joined him at the front doors as a crease developed across his face. He smiled broadly.

"Hello, Michael?" A voice cried. I looked at the sea of faces, having difficulty finding the lips to fit to the voice. I scoured the crowd seeing several bright beaming faces.

"Hello, Michael?" The repeated call brought my eyes to a girl dressed in a pink baggy dressing gown. Her damp blonde hair clung tightly to her head.

"You don't remember me? It was bonfire night in Breamish Grove last year. You were there," she said, "I was staying with friends," she added, rubbing her hair with a towel.

Dodger never missed a trick. He muscled in on the conversation, almost taking it over.

"Fancy going out? Have you got a friend? What about tonight?" His approach was abrupt and direct.

The reply, that they were all on night duty, did not deter him.

"We'll get you back before ten," Dodger insisted.

"But you're married!" I told Dodger as we sat on the appliance, returning to the station.

"So I'm married. They're not to know that," he replied smiling tightly.

Slowly Thursday ended. The windows were cleaned once more and another floor reached the acceptable shine. There were no further calls and the day dragged. Fire calls always came in spasms. Often we had days, even tours, on duty, without a wheel turned in anger and then suddenly a shift with several calls would play havoc with our cleaning routines.

Thursday, pay-day came at last. Borrowing from my weekly rent I looked forward to our night out. Leaving work at 1800 hours I went home washed and changed and just as I was about finish off a bacon sandwich Dodger arrived in Joseph.

Apart from the inside of the van reeking from fish, mini explosions and the occasional jet of black smoke from the exhaust, Joseph performed well as we drove our two nurses to the local cinema. We all left early, before the main feature film had finished, and raced back to reach the Nurse's home before their check-in time.

As Dodger made his goodbyes in Joseph, I walked, hand in hand, with my nurse to the entrance of the home.

Katherine Charlotte Gwyniad, a second year student nurse had to run the last hundred yards to escape being late. She glanced coyly over her shoulder as she opened the large entrance doors we had seen earlier in the day.

"See you at the weekend?" I arranged our next meeting before we parted.

Over the following couple of weeks I met Katherine as regularly as our different shifts allowed. Her strong personality impressed me very strongly.

At last I had enough money from helping Dodger with his various jobs to pay for a driving test, and I accepted Dodger's offer to take the examination in Joseph. I was very nervous as we approached the test centre.

Joseph announced our arrival with a bang, which was followed by a cloud of oily black smoke from the exhaust.

"Good luck," Dodger said, a smile dividing his face, as I went in dressed in the uniform normally used for our on-going and off-going parades.

I sat nervously in a small room, which was solid with other potential drivers. My name was the last to be called.

"Michael Edward Fairn," a tall smart looking gentleman said as I meekly followed him outside.

"Can you read that car number plate?" Asked my examiner, ticking off my name on his note pad.

I read out the car number. I'd got through the first part.

Passing a line of modern driving-school cars we came at last to Joseph. I thought I heard a slight sigh.

The examiner struggled with his sliding door. It took two strong hands and a hefty pull to yank it open. He climbed inside, dusting off his seat and examining his hand. I joined him timidly. He carefully placed his papers on the passenger shelf as he looked behind him into the back of the van. Empty fish crates and an old shovel was scattered around the counter, which was once for ice cream. The van was still impregnated with the smell of fish and I thought there was a twitch of the examiner's nose.

His papers fell from the non-existent shelf and settled in disarray on his pair of highly polished shoes. There was a sigh from his lips as he stooped to pick the papers up from the floor. He attempted to open his side window. Presumably to freshen the air. But it did not oblige.

I reached down to locate the starter button underneath the driver's seat. The engine turned and turned over before it started reluctantly.

Glancing out, I saw Dodger standing on the pavement, his lanky body propped against a lamppost. He grinned, both thumbs pointing upwards.

I engaged first gear. We lurched forward. I removed my uniform cap and placed it alongside the examiner on his seat. It did not seem a good idea to wear my Fire Brigade uniform but with nothing to lose I set off, confident of failure.

The examiner warned he would tap on the dashboard for the emergency stop. As he reached forward I obediently stamped on the foot brake. Joseph careered sideways as we shuddered to a halt. The examiner sighed again.

I knew I had no earthly chance of passing the test. The examiner confirmed my thoughts by ending the test early. On our return, Dodger full of confidence, waited, still propping up the lamppost.

"Just a couple of Highway Code questions," the examiner said.

I answered the questions as the examiner pulled on the sliding door handle. He sighed again as the inside handle came adrift in his hand. Without saying a word he handed me this chrome offering.

Dodger ran to the rescue and, working from the outside, pulled the door open.

Before leaving the examiner turned and handed me a slip of paper. Perhaps it was my uniform, or perhaps he was just pleased to get back in one piece, but I had passed!

Chapter 21

"D.O. Mullet is here for your light vehicle driving test." The bald statement greeted me one Friday, my first day on duty after my annual leave. The fact that I had passed my civilian-driving test was welcome news in the Brigade. Torridge City Fire Brigade required a light driving test qualification in order or me to be able to drive vans, cars and certain special appliances. It needed a retest from our Brigade examiner.

This time the test was to be taken driving a 1943 Austin truck, formerly a fire engine. This war-time appliance was a red covered wagon, which had once carried a ladder, a hose-reel, and a small tank of water and had pulled a trailer pump. After the Second World War it was kept for general use, and with its petrol engine and a crash-gearbox I found driving this monstrosity a constant struggle. My attempts were limited to going up and down the back street with anyone who was willing and stupid enough to give me tuition. Locating any gear was impossible.

Fireman David Capelin tried to explain and prevent me from damaging the gearbox, but even he, who was known for his placid temperament, must have been near the end of his patience.

"The road speed needs to balance the speed of the prop shaft," David told me a dozen times, showing a hint of impatience on the last few. He sucked hard on his pipe and then looked away, shaking his head.

I understood the theory but understanding the theory is one thing, putting into practice another. There seemed to be no margin for error. The gear lever either slipped easily into gear when things were correctly aligned or they would not.

"For your test, get into third gear and leave it well alone." David, normally calm and caring was impatient after my umpteenth demonstration of how to engage the gears without any grinding noise.

I took David's advice. The old vehicle struggled along in third gear during my light vehicle-driving test. This consisted of a quick dash round the Station area with Divisional Officer Mullet on board. Straining in third, but with an engine powerful enough to drag us around the streets, I even managed at one time to select fourth top gear. There was a wry smile on the Divisional Officer's face as I tried to wear down all the teeth in the gearbox to engage third and even worse second, gear. The smile was more in sympathy than amusement, and did not indicate approval.

"You'll do," he said as we arrived back on Station.

"We'll pick the gear-teeth up later," he announced as he climbed down from the cab. Obviously another examiner was relieved at arriving back in one piece.

The old vehicle became something of a challenge. Now a fully-fledged light vehicle driver, I thought that perhaps I could obtain some driving practice. But driving was a perk for the favourite few. During the day certain men, and only they, enjoyed the benefit of driving-duties. But during our night shifts things were different.

Just after 0300 I was shaken out of bed with instructions to take the old Austin and tow in one of the appliances from Ellen Approach Fire Station that had broken down. The excuse that I had never towed anyone or anything before landed on closed ears. A length of old rope was thrown into the back and I was soon off down the street, having no choice, and crunching into second gear. The address, written on fire-message-paper, contained just two words - Farrar Walk. Not knowing the exact location, I thought it prudent to stop and ask the watchroom-man at Ellen Approach Station. Running silently in neutral with attempts at locating any gear abandoned, I cruised to a halt outside the watchroom.

Their second appliance, Pump Escape, had returned carrying the crew from the Pump which had broken down. This had left the driver to await my assistance.

"Old Gripper Ken is waiting and getting impatient," the watchroom-man said after explaining where Farrar

Walk was. I knew the driver was an old acquaintance, Fireman Ken Chevin.

Ken was a legend in the Brigade. An ex-amateur heavyweight boxer, I had already met his bent humour at training school when he had suggested a quick way to clean the canteen floor by mop and bucket instead of the prescribed hand-cloths; I was caught red-handed in the act.

He was well known for his physical strength; reputedly he could single-handed remove a fifty-foot wooden-wheeled escape-ladder from the appliance and extend it against the drill tower. These heavy wooden escape-ladders were carried on the back of the Pump Escapes and normally needed to be pulled off, dropped onto their carriage-wheels and extended by winding a large handle. This drill normally took four men.

Once I witnessed him hand-start an appliance using the handle. The machine rocked as he turned handle the around effortlessly. The strength of the man was never in dispute. A mountain of a man, his reputation had been well earned. But for all his massive frame and size he spoke with an unusually high pitched voice.

Nervously I headed for Farrar Walk. I found the appliance standing empty, gaunt and forlorn.

Gripper Ken had persuaded the occupants of a nearby house to make him a cup of tea in spite of the hour. He came out of the house as I was looking gingerly at the broken down Dennis F8 Pump.

"Hitch up and let's get away," he squeaked as he came bouncing down the path.

"Pull the machine out backwards to begin with," he sang.

The appliance was trapped in a cul-de-sac and needed to be towed, rear end first, to the main road. Towing backwards seemed easy. Removing the tow-rope from the back I re-positioned my 1943 Austin in front of the Pump. I fastened the rope to the towing eye to the front bumper of the Pump while Ken sat in the cab waiting. Then I engaged first gear and moved off slowly. Crash. Crash. The gear lever grated as it struggled into second gear. I let out the clutch and we leapt forward. The tow-rope was now slack as we took off. Suddenly the full weight of the appliance behind grabbed the tow-rope and pulled it taut. My vehicle shook like a wet dog. Then we were suddenly free as I sped away. I stopped and leaped down from the cab. I looked up to see that Ken was aghast. He glowered through his driver's window at me as I looked back down the road.

I had not allowed the slack in the rope to be taken up smoothly and it had snapped like a piece of cotton thread. I walked back to the Pump expecting a mouthful of abuse. Ken opened his cab door, turned round and descended backwards on to the road. I could not see his face.

"I'm sorry," I stuttered.

Ken walked slowly to the broken rope and picked up the loose end with his massive hands. He looked carefully in the dim light at the two frayed ends.

"The breaking load of these ropes is nearly two tons," he said in his soprano voice. I listened carefully, trying not to get too close.

"Have you ever towed anything before?" He asked.

I muttered a negative answer.

"I'll drive the towing truck. You get in the Pump," he piped.

He walked down the road towards the 1943 Austin truck.

He reversed into position and tied the two frayed ends together. He came towards me. Expecting at least a clip round the ear, I backed off as he approached. But his manner was tame, almost delicate.

"You must do all the braking," he explained. At junctions you brake so the rope never goes slack. Understand?"

I nodded and climbed aboard the Pump, slamming the driver's door behind me. I sat and waited nervously.

The seat in the Pump, strange to me, felt awkward; it was obliquely to the left of the steering wheel. These Pumps, I concluded was certainly not designed for driver comfort.

Ken moved off in the tow vehicle. When he reached the correct distance, the tow-rope tightened and we both moved forward. Ken accelerated skilfully and changed gears with no obvious delays. He never allowed the rope to slacken.

We moved off quickly down the road. I looked at the speedometer and saw that the needle fluctuated between twenty and thirty miles per hour. At the first junction, as instructed, I pressed down on the foot pedal and braked. The towing truck in front laboured under the added weight from my braking. The rope between us stayed taut. At each road junction I applied my brake pedal and kept the tow-rope taut. By the time we had negotiated all the hazards of the several junctions, two red sets of traffic lights and one roundabout, perspiration was pouring down my face. The view of Ellen Approach Station in the early dawn was a welcome sight.

With the tow-rope still taut I braked to a final stop and climbed down out of the Pump cab. Ken approached. He thrust his arm out in acknowledgement. I held out mine in reply. It was a terrible mistake. His grip on my right hand was like a steel vice. In pain I dropped to the ground reeling under his excruciating grip. The torture continued as I squirmed helplessly on the tarmac.

"OK kid, you did really well," he squeaked. He let me go. The relief was immediate. He held out his other hand to lift me on my feet. I refused and struggled up on my own.

"You'll do for me, kid," he said, laughter in his high pitched voice.

I reported to the watchroom for my arrival and departure to be recorded and entered into the logbook. The watchroom-man must have seen my encounter with Gripper Ken (now I knew how he got his nickname.)

"Never shake hands with Ken," the watchroom-man told me, too late, "but if you have to, get your hand well into the joint against his thumb and finger."

It's a bit late to tell me now, I thought as I climbed aboard to return to Torridge City Station. My right hand still ached as I stored this advice for future encounters.

On the return journey as the sun peeped out and climbed into a clear blue sky for a promised glorious summer morning, I experimented with this impossible gearbox. On deserted roads I changed gear several times moving from second to third and back down to second. With practice my gear-changing slowly improved. Timing was one of the answers, I had gathered. The time the gear lever needed to be in neutral seemed agonizingly long. But with a quick blip on the accelerator pedal as I went down through the gears, the elusive entry into the correct gear could be achieved cleanly and silently.

By the time I reached my own Station only an hour and half remained before the 0645 hours reveille. I parked the truck and, feeling a little friendlier towards her, went back to the muster-room to find my bed.

The crew of Pump One always slept on portable beds, which were dragged out at midnight into the muster-room. From the days of the horse-drawn fire engines a crew always slept in the muster-room. The old habits persisted.

Early warning from a tiny buzzer from control indicated a fire call had just been received and a turnout imminent. I looked up at the indicator board. The light indicating Pump Two was lit up.

I stood waiting and watching as everyone was abruptly dragged from their slumber as the bells sounded. Automatically they leapt from their beds and slotted their legs into their boots, which were all ready boxed with trousers. The crew pulled their braces up over their shoulders and in same movement moved towards the two swing doors to the engine house.

The crew in the muster-room took every first turnout before the rest of our crew sleeping in the dormitory fifty yards away arrived. Still enjoying the advantage of being fully awake, I found myself surrounded by people working as automatons.

Mount Ribble Flats. Midden on fire, the message stated.

Mount Ribble Flats were good customers of ours and it was a regular occurrence for us to extinguish burning middens.

The sun was now half way up the sky. On board Pump Two we dashed through the deserted streets for the mile or so to the flats. As we turned into the complex, dense black smoke led us to the offending midden, a rectangular brick structure used for storing rubbish from the flats. Smoke poured out of the air vents and brickwork. The hydrant was located nearby and a line of delivery hose quickly ran out, going straight into the midden. The strong powerful hydrant was turned on; the delivery hose filled and swelled. Water gushed from the open end and flowed straight inside the midden. As it filled with water, soaking the tons of accumulated household rubbish, big brown rats, which were dislodged from their cosy habitat, rushed out to escape a watery grave. They scampered off; their tiny feet a blur as they changed homes.

The smoke cleared. Another midden-fire had been extinguished as we prepared to return to our home station.

In the early morning no one uttered a word. Everything was done automatically. Silence reigned as if in protest at the pointless task. We returned to grasp the final minutes of sleep before reveille at 0645 hours.

Chapter 22

Our fifteen-hour night shift always began with the same routine.

After serving together for nearly nineteen months, as a crew we could deal with majority of incidents with great efficiency. Fires cowered into submission on our arrival. With nobody suffering any injury or even being slightly scratched I began to think calling this a dangerous profession was wrong. Working alongside supermen, White Watch gave me supreme confidence and the ability to deal easily with tragedies in real life.

My confidence grew to such an extent that I came to think that men from White Watch were the best. As a team we could tackle anything, any time, I thought.

Parade and roll call was at 1800 hours. The off-going watch was dismissed and the crew coming on duty were detailed to their respective appliances.

It was a filthy miserable evening. Rain all day had left roads wet and greasy.

"Something's brewing," Sub Officer Gardon said, causing us to have a sense of expectation. He would complete twenty-five years service in two months time and was soon to retire at the age of fifty-five.

He was right. By 2200 hours we were turned out four times.

The first was a false alarm to the Torridge City Infirmary. Then we attended a house fire, which turned out to be dustbins well alight in a yard. This was followed by a malicious false alarm into the centre of Torridge, raised by someone thinking we had nothing better to do. Finally the Emergency Tender was called to a road accident, though no one was trapped, in the Ellen Approach Station area.

On our return from each of the four turnouts, every appliance was covered in filthy road grime. Washed and leathered dry, they eventually looked immaculate and expectant, ready for the next incident. As the last mop and bucket rattled into its cupboard, as each wash leather was wrung dry, the bells sounded again.

This was a call to Pickerel's Iron Foundry, in Kirtle Street.

At 0213 hours on this mid-October Monday morning, the call sent our Pump One, Pump Escape and Turntable Ladder over the damp miserable streets to an address in the heart of the industrial sector.

A patrolling policeman had noticed smoke drifting out from the roof and contacted his control. The Police passed the message to our Fire Brigade Control.

When we arrived there was no sign of any smoke. All the windows looked intact, with nothing untoward. The young policeman astride his motorcycle insisted that he had seen smoke and he flashed a pencil beam of light from his torch up to the roof. Tiles covered the pointed roof of a building and stretched a good hundred yards to the rear. Made glossy by rain, the reflection from the darting small circle of light showed that perhaps there was a trace of smoke. Or were they just splashes of water from the incessant rain?

The flat-roofed glass-faced office block built on to the front of this large warehouse looked impressive. High walls at both sides of this facade prevented the access we needed to make a complete circle of the site.

We tried all the ground floor entrances, but everything was locked and secure. The glass entrance lobby looked very expensive.

"There's a small door at one end, go get the key Barry," Station Officer Finnan said in his usual inexorable Scottish accent to Fireman Barry Bleck, indicating he wanted a sledgehammer. Calling for the key was the usual humorous way of naming the implement, which he needed.

Barry soon produced the hammer from the offside locker of our Pump. The wooden entrance door soon submitted easily to the persuasion of its fourteen pounds.

The hose-reel tubing was taken from Pump Escape. Dragging it behind us, we entered a small door on the ground floor. There was no trace of smoke inside and the atmosphere was crystal clear in the strong beam of our hand-held searchlights. A concrete staircase led upwards. The steps had obviously been unused for years and were covered in inches of ancient dust.

I followed the Station Officer as we scampered up the stairs, leaving footprints from our fire-boots in the disturbed carpet of dust. We arrived at a door. It was locked.

Another swing with the fourteen-pound sledgehammer and another door submitted, crashing open. It opened into a large dark workshop. The hand-held searchlight shone into a deep black abyss. A sheer drop of twenty feet beckoned as our toes balanced on the threshold. There was no staircase, nothing. We stood, precariously gaping into a dark hall. A slight smell of smoke lingered in the air.

"It's not the right building. It must be next door!" Station Officer grunted.

We half fell half tumbled, back down to the street in front. The prestigious glass fronted building had a small laminated window to one side of the two glass doors. It cracked with a ping with a tap from our sledgehammer. Our second tap dislodged a large chunk, allowing access through which three of us squeezed.

Inside the entrance lobby we found a reception desk and, dancing in the pencil beams of light from our searchlights traces of smoke were suspended, moving almost graciously in the air. Everyone went in a different direction. Doors led off from the corridors but there were no stairs. After we had searched the ground floor, we thought that the smoke must have been coming from the first floor.

I re-joined Sub O Gardon outside and, together with Roger Braise; we decided to pitch our thirty-five foot ladder to gain access to the first floor. Full glass windows ran the full length of the building and we pitched the head of the ladder to balance on a narrow steel window-sill.

All my training on ladders had specified that the head of a ladder needed to have three or four rungs above the entry point. But drill ground procedure is one thing, fire ground procedure is another.

Roger-the-Dodger climbed up while I stood footing the ladder and holding the base of the ladder secure.

"The windows feel warm!" Dodger shouted down.

"Can you get in?" Sub Officer Gardon shouted back.

Dodger removed his axe from the pouch on his leather belt. He prised the window open using the pointed blade, and ducked as the window-catch broke off with a crack.

"Stand clear!" Dodger shouted as bits of broken steel fell on to the road below.

The big window, hinged in the middle, tilted and swung out. Dodger crept down the ladder to allow the window to open wider. Climbing back up, he eased through the narrow gap. The window moved and tilted, rubbing his back as he entered and dropped inside and out of sight.

With Sub Officer Gardon we extended the thirty-five foot ladder. A couple of rungs pushed through the narrow gap into the first floor. I scaled the ladder, taking the hose-reel tubing tied in a loop over my right shoulder and carrying a hand-held searchlight in my left hand.

Climbing with only one hand free meant stopping, releasing my grip on each rung, leaning in close to the ladder and progressing upwards in short spurts. It was yet another non-drilled exercise.

Reaching the window, I passed Dodger the searchlight and the hose-reel tubing and tried to climb in.

Shuffling through the large hinged window that was determined to be shut, not open, I felt the broken window catch. I edged to the left to avoid tearing my tunic.

I landed face down on the floor inside. The room was hazy with smoke and warm. There was no sign of any fire. We shuffled forward as Sub Officer Gardon, behind us climbed the ladder and squeezed through the hinged window.

A current of air from the open window passed us. Holding the searchlight I scanned the room for the signs of a fire and its location if it existed. We crossed the room, bumping into chairs and tables. At far end of the room a door was locked and secure. The metal handle felt hot.

Sub Officer Gardon panted as he joined us at the locked door.

"No one has yet found an entrance from below," he spurted out gasping for breath, "I'm getting too old for all this climbing about," he added.

"It feels hot behind this door," Dodger said.

Sub Officer tried the door. He yelped as he touched the round brass handle with the back of his hand.

"Water on?" He asked.

I turned on the nozzle of the hose-reel. Water shot out from the end and splattered on the floor.

"Let's have the door open," Gardon said.

Dodger kicked once at the handle. The door remained solid and unmoved. I stood alongside Dodger. We intertwined our arms, standing side by side. Together we hit the door with our inside legs using the leather soles of our fire-boots. The door complained at first and resisted slightly but then, under the constant kicking of our two boots, a splinter of timber with the door frame still attached fell inwards.

A surge of air raced past us. Dense black smoke inside the room billowed and rolled over, disturbed and fed by the sudden entrance of the fresh air.

Sub Officer, the hose-reel turned on full, attempted to spray the water into the room. But our hose-reel jet was too feeble and the spray of water became absorbed into a sea of black smoke. The fire, which had been dormant because it was starved of oxygen, now revived and thundered with anger.

"It's going to flash over!" Sub Officer Gardon shouted.

"Let's get out! Quick. Quick!"

No one argued. The three of us made for the window, banging into chairs and tables as we went. In panic I dropped the hand-held searchlight which crashed on to the floor. Immediately we were plunged into darkness. But the fire behind the door threw out fingers of flames and chased us towards the window, giving us some light. The fire now roared with anger.

A crack of muffled thunder shook the floor. The whole room shuddered. Against the front window, flames licked the backs of our heads as all three of us jostled for the exit through the window.

Pushed and shoved by the other two, I fell out face first. Desperately feeling for the ladder below the window, my hand clasped the side of the ladder as I was forced out. I fell, clumsily, sideways and my legs hit the side of the ladder.

Recovering, I turned to an upright position and slid onto the ladder. Sub Officer Gardon and Dodger, still inside, poked their faces of the window. Dodger pushed Sub Officer Gardon face first through the small window opening. I climbed back up to the top of the ladder to assist, grabbing hold of a pair of flaying arms. The window was now filled with angry flames that licked menacingly above us.

Dodger followed, swearing as he caught his arm on the damaged window catch. In the brief second he took to pull his arm free the flames lashed out of the window. He tried to cover his face in the sleeve of his tunic as a large pane of glass from the open window cracked above us.

We half-fell half-climbed and finally tumbled in a heap on the ground.

Dodger fell the last ten feet on top of us. Lashed mercilessly by the flames that now roared out of the broken window, he had lost his grip on the ladder.

Helping hands from the rest of our crew pulled us apart. A large jet of water was directed above us as the three of us struggled to our feet. The water jet increased in pressure and shot into the open window. The cold water spray from this jet on my face felt refreshing.

Dodger, half dazed, stood up. A dark stain appeared from the end of his tunic sleeve. Blood dripped from his finger ends.

"My hands are tingling a bit!" Dodger managed to say with a wry grin.

We carried him to the front of our Pump Escape and in the headlights the dark liquid dropped steadily onto the road. His normally bright red face looked pale.

"Make Pumps four and get an ambulance?"

Station Officer Finnan appeared on the scene and shouted to me. This was an order to be relayed back to out Control indicating we wanted another two Pumps to the two already in attendance.

I propped Dodger against the front bumper bar. Then removing my helmet I climbed aboard the Pump Escape to reach the microphone for the radio. The petrol engine raced more loudly as the driver pulled down the throttle lever, adding more power to the on-board water-pump and increasing pressure to the jet.

The whole first floor now glowed with fresh yellow flames. There was a crash of broken glass as the windows shattered and a deluge of splinters hit the road surface below.

Within seconds the whole first floor was a mass of flames and well alight. The once quiescent fire now raged with malice.

"Message from Tango Zero One," I held the microphone close to my mouth as engine noise in the cab reached fever pitch as I stated the appliance call sign.

"Go ahead with your message," the reply came from our Control.

"From Station Officer Finnan at Pickerel's Iron Foundry, Kirtle Street, building well alight, make Pumps four and request attendance of an ambulance," I said excitedly.

"Repeat the message," Control requested.

After three attempts my message was at last understood by our Control.

I returned to find Sub Officer Gardon drenching Dodger's head and hands with cold water from the pump, using my fire-helmet as a bucket.

"Stay with Dodger," he told me.

The fire now raged through the roof and went on spreading. Huge angry flames shot out through holes in the flat roof for hundreds of feet into the air. The head of our thirty-five foot ladder used in our escape was still pitched against the building, but it was now enveloped in a mass of flames. Jets of water dissipated and turned to steam before they reached the fire. The three firemen holding the jet pulled back from the searing heat. The whole street glowed with orange light. The Pump, which was parked alongside the glass doors, began to smoke. The jet of water was turned from the building to the side of the Pump and soon cooled it down.

"Somebody move that machine before we lose it!" Finnan shouted.

The wet road was steamed dry by radiated heat. The flames, reflected in the wet tarmac, increased the building's plight by a factor of two.

"Water! We need more water?" Someone screamed.

"There's a hydrant at the main road, five or six hundred feet away. It's on a twelve-inch main," shouted someone who knew the area.

"Go and meet the extra Pumps. Tell them to get into the big water main and feed our Pump and Pump-Escape," Station Officer Finnan told me.

Leaving Dodger with our Sub Officer Gardon I started up the road in the direction in which the appliances were expected to arrive. My helmet it felt wet and cold inside from being used as a bucket. The heat from the fire fell away as I ran up the road and the early morning air felt fresh against my face.

A staff car stopped short and pulled up. Assistant Chief Officer Carp had arrived.

I ran past his car to the main road and searched for a hydrant plate to give some indication of the whereabouts of the street outlet. I found the yellow plate; high on a lamppost, and marked with a black 'H'. It pointed to the centre of the road.

The figure 12 in the top part of the H indicated the size of the water main. The figure 20 below showed the distance in feet from the plate to the hydrant lid. In the darkness I could just make out a rectangular steel lid in the middle of the road.

In the distance I heard a bell and the sound of a siren as additional help approached.

Two appliances came into view and careered towards me. With their blinding headlights and their engines roaring they came closer and reached me.

I stood, waving my arms for them to stop. The first appliance sped past ignoring me. The second appliance slowed down and pulled past, then stopped.

I gabbled my instructions and told them we needed more water. I explained that the large twelve-inch water main was in the middle of the road.

The crew dismounted and with apprehensive glances at the fire, which was now lighting up the horizon, opened the locker doors to gain access to the delivery hose.

The glow down the road grew as flames tore into the sky, sparks chasing the flames sky-wards. I rushed back down the street to the fire. Our Turntable Ladder was in position and waiting for a supply of water. The fire had spread further and the flat roof was now completely engulfed in a mass of flames.

We ran back up the road with lengths of our delivery hose to meet the hose coming from the appliance at the twelve-inch water main.

"What on earth are they doing with that water?" Assistant Chief Officer Carp demanded impatiently.

"They're having trouble connecting on to the hydrant," someone answered.

"Ask for another two Pumps to make it six, laddie," Assistant Chief Officer Carp shouted to the nearest driver.

All our delivery hose was on the road still empty and flat. The fire relished this delay and growled angrily.

Shaking in defiance, part of the first-floor front wall crashed down on to the road. Our thirty five-foot ladder, which was still propped against the window, moved slightly, disturbed by the falling debris. The loose end of our hose-reel tubing fell to the ground as the fire engulfed and devoured the part, which was still inside the building.

Dodger waited to be taken to hospital with a deep gash to his arm, and burns to his hands and face. He joked as an ambulance man applied a tourniquet to his arm.

"Michael," he said to me from inside the ambulance, "come see me as soon as you can. I have a job next week. It's bit of a secret. I'll tell you about it later." Wincing, he waved his arm.

"While you lot are still here in the cold, damping-down, I'll be chatting up all the nurses in casualty," he laughed, his face regaining some of its usual red glow.

The ambulance rear doors slammed shut and it sped off.

At last the water arrived. The flat delivery hose slowly filled out into solid tubes, which fed the Pumps near the fire. Several jets of water crackled as high-pressure water gushed out from their ends. Solid jets of water poured into the heart of the flames at last.

"A twelve-inch main should float the building away," Sub Officer Gardon said as I assisted him to lay more delivery hose and so attack the building from the rear of the property.

More Pumps eventually arrived, but the office block was now blazing from end to end. The fire was beating us and destroying the front part of the building with a maniacal delight.

I joined the crews inside the rear warehouse. They had gained access over a high wall and through large doors a hundred yards to the rear. Lines of hose ran through an engineering workshop, dodging between lathes and heavy machinery.

The fire at last subsided. Attacked by water from five hand held jets and a jet from our Turntable Ladder, it submitted at last. The workshops at the rear were only slightly damaged by water, but the first floor office complex had been completely destroyed and the ground floor was severely damaged by water and falling debris.

There were rumours of arson and Police specialists were requested. The times were difficult and fires a common route out of financial difficulties often using insurance pay outs. But accusations and rumours was one thing, precise proof was more difficult. Perhaps some highly skilled professional had taken an hour to fire the building, but this was of little consolation to us after our five hard hours of slog and injuries.

Damping down continued with little enthusiasm after the glory and excitement of the fury of the initial fire. After five hours our tunics were heavy, cold and wet. Our leather boots leaked and squelched as the damp socks inside chafed sore feet. Our skin was tainted with the sweet smell from wet wool. All this was the unglamorous side to the job of fire fighting.

The miserable grey morning sky matched the miserable picture of the destroyed shell of the building. The flat roof was now open to the sky as we turned over mountains of debris from roof timbers. A feeling of defeat and failure dawned with the morning light. The stairs to the first floor which had deceived us on our initial entry turned out to be a staircase which was now dismantled and unused. Inside the rear workshop a separate flight of stairs had been constructed to allow access only to a canteen above the office ground floor.

As the staff and workforce arrived for work on Monday morning their faces were filled with shock and disbelief. They stood huddled in-groups, trying to take in the damage and destruction that fire can so quickly cause.

I now realised that the arrival of White Watch did not automatically mean the end of every incident without a scar. This was my first taste of defeat and injury. I had thought that we were impregnable. Now I knew better.

As we climbed aboard our Pump, with our burnt and scarred thirty-five foot ladder rescued and tied on the gallows, we made a defeated journey and retreated back to our home Station.

Dodger was no doubt tucked up in a warm hospital bed, nurses tending his every whim.

Chapter 23

Remembering Dodger's final message, Station Officer Finnan and I went to see him in hospital the following morning. He sat propped up in bed against an enormous pile of pillows. He grinned and waved a bandaged arm as we walked down the ward towards him. His arm was bandaged from above the elbow to the tips of his fingers. His grin almost split his bright red face in two.

Dressed in our parade uniforms we first sought permission to see Dodger out of normal visiting hours from the Ward Sister at the Infirmary.

"I've seen your young nurse, Katherine." Dodger said. The words made his grin even wider.

"My Katherine?" I questioned.

"Yes, I understand you're to be vetted by her parents!" Dodger said knowingly, "and, by the way, if you see my wife don't mention about our foursome the other month," he added waving his right arm, as if he was directing traffic. His right ear, covered in loose skin, glowed like a stoplight.

"I've had ten stitches. My hand's a bit scorched and my ear feels as if it's been bitten by swarm of bees. I'm bound to get sympathy from someone," he joked as each brief sentence summed up his predicament.

"I'm glad you could come," he whispered to me as the Station Officer turned and talked to the Ward Sister. He produced a crumpled piece of toilet paper from under his pillow and pushed it into my hand.

"That's all the paper I could find," he apologised as I untangled it. In red coloured crayon he had scrawled the address of one of his many contacts for part-time work. He knew I always needed to supplement my meagre Fire Brigade wages.

"Just explain I'm otherwise engaged," he instructed, "and don't tell anyone about working for the Fire Brigade," he continued as I thrust the crumpled piece of paper into my jacket pocket.

"They pay well and the perks are good," he went on.

"Use Joseph," he ended as Finnan rejoined us.

I was always short of money and I readily accepted any offer of extra work.

"We'll have to go. The Deputy Matron's on her morning rounds," Finnan said. We dutifully left, meeting a formidable looking matron at the entrance of the ward, about to make her inspection.

With the last of our three nights' duty still to work, we continued to damp down at Pickerel's Iron Foundry fire.

Arson was still suspected and we assisted the police with their investigations. We turned over tons of burnt material in an attempt to locate more than one seat of the fire, which would give a good indication of foul play. The top floor of the office building was completely gutted and the floors beneath were covered in tons of debris. Under all this rubble we did find evidence of four hot spots where fires could have been started. Wafts of stinking steam floated out as we painstakingly pulled the burnt joists, wooden panels and the network of damaged office furniture still warm from the previous night's fire out by hand. Working in four-hour shifts, it took a second night before the senior officers decided there was insufficient evidence to prosecute anyone for arson. At last the incident was declared closed.

This was my last night before going off-duty on annual leave. My autumn-tour holiday consisted of three rota days, then a complete tour off duty (three days and three nights in lieu of Bank Holidays) and finally three rota days before I had to return on duty. This gave me the time and opportunity to earn some much-needed extra cash.

Katherine however, suggested visiting her parents for the weekend to coincide with the annual ritual of cremating Guy Fawkes. Her parents lived at Araglin, a town that was the scene of the large shopping store fire we had attended five months earlier.

Raiding my rent money to pay for the petrol needed for Dodger's van, I collected Katherine from the nurses' home and we motored to Araglin Town. Joseph behaved well and never produced any of his normal misdemeanours.

Meeting any girl's parents for the very first time meant an investigation and hopefully approval, Katherine was more special to me than any of my previous girl friends and I wanted to make a good impression.

"Better park Joseph out of sight," Katherine said as we pulled up at a Victorian black-stoned end terrace house. I did so and we went in through a set of two front doors. We stood in a large entrance lobby, I felt stupid. Katherine's Mother, small and demure, soon shepherded us down a passage to the rear of the house.

"Where's Pop?" Katherine asked her mother.

"He's pottering about somewhere," was the answer.

"So you're the Michael we've heard such a lot about," she added as she bustled past me.

The words followed her into the kitchen. Through the open kitchen door I saw Katherine's father. He was a tall man, with a bald scalp and a fringe, no more than an inch thick, which skirted around the rear and sides of his head. He stayed where he was, not even turning to face me. I stood waiting, like a work of art under the eye of a possible purchaser, as he continued to wash his hands in the kitchen sink. On the back of his head, circles of skin flexed and wobbled.

At last, after he had rubbed his hands methodically and meticulously, he turned and walked towards me. He stopped just inches from my face. From the fringe on his left side of his head several long thin strands of hair curled over an otherwise empty crown. Giving me a slight nod of acknowledgement he turned and without uttering a word he walked out of the kitchen. We all obediently followed him and went into the front parlour.

I sat down with Katherine's mother on a large uncomfortable settee. Her father sat in his armchair facing us. Katherine sat on the floor with her legs crossed, enjoying every minute of my ordeal. For an hour polite conversation dragged on. For me it felt like the dentist extracting a stubborn molar.

November the fifth fell in midweek but their street bonfire had been rearranged. The annual fiasco was to be held at the weekend but provided a chance for me to escape from the difficult atmosphere.

The glow from the blazing bonfire warmed both our faces as the fireworks; rockets, spinning wheels and Roman candles sparkled into a dark November sky.

At last the bonfire burnt down into a large red-hot mound and the neighbours drifted away. Reflected light from the low flames danced prettily on Katherine's lips. We stood enjoying our final moments together and staring silently into the deep red embers. Then we returned reluctantly to the house.

Sleeping in the attic in a single hard bed as far away as physically possible from Katherine's bedroom, I heard the house creaking and groaning all night long. The early morning, with its welcome daylight, brought breakfast and further feelings of dissension. An awkward air, which I did not enjoy, loomed at every moment.

On Sunday we all paid a compulsory visit to the local chapel. Throughout the service sly glances from the congregation made me feel like a specimen under constant inspection.

On the walk back, yearning for a Sunday dinnertime drink, I bravely suggested a visit to the local hostelry. This suggestion was not thought to be worthy of a reply, and a long pregnant silence hammered home the rejection. The yawning cavern of silence continued as I sat in the dining room alone with Katherine's father and waiting for Sunday dinner. As the ceiling-high grandfather clock continued its regular beat I sat, nervously perched on the edge of a hard chair. I had ample time to examine every piece of furniture in the room. From the highly polished surface of the mahogany dining table there was a distorted reflection of a black and white family photograph hanging proudly over the fireplace. The room also contained brown wooden chairs, a sideboard polished almost coal-black, and a dark red carpet underneath the table and brown linoleum edging along every dark-papered wall. The whole room was drenched in sombre funereal colours.

At last Katherine and her mother carried four tureens to the centre of the table. A cube of roasted beef, no bigger than six inches in length, was placed carefully in front of Katherine's father. He proceeded to carve this small joint with self-important relish, and issued each of us with two carefully selected slices of meat. From the tureens we helped ourselves to vegetables and at last began consuming our Sunday lunch. Besides the roast beef we had roast potatoes, peas, green string beans, and two small Yorkshire Puddings. We ate in total silence. Compared to meals in the Fire Brigade this offering looked minuscule.

By the time Katherine's mother brought in the steamed treacle pudding, the abyss of silence seemed bottomless. The sounds of spoons scraping plates and the tick-tock of the grandfather clock's constant rhythm were the only sounds to be heard. I tried to alternate the swings of the pendulum with an intake of breath followed by a spoon of pudding, but I missed the timing completely and tried to swallow a mouthful of hot sticky treacle at the same time as I inhaled. The result was an explosive cough. A hefty tap between my shoulder blades from Katherine's father, his hand heavy and more forceful than really necessary, soon dislodged the offending treacle but deepened my hole in the ground.

At long last we left before teatime for our journey back to Torridge City. The escape felt as refreshing as a spray of cold water onto a fire-scorched face.

"They don't approve," Katherine stating the obvious, "my father thinks I could do better than just a fireman."

She went on to explain that her father had lost a brother during the Second World War and that he did not approve of my German and single-parent background. His fine position (he had worked all his life in banking) Katherine's private education and their resistance to my class left me in no doubt our friendship must end.

"Take no notice. My father believes we are quite rich. He's a bit snobbish but he means well," Katherine continued defiantly above the noise of Joseph's engine.

We arrived at the nurse's home and Katherine struggled to open Joseph's sliding side door before managing to escape. There was nothing I could say to improve my financial circumstances, and I felt robbed and cheated.

I moved the gear lever into first gear. Joseph coughed in sympathy as I accelerated away.

The next day I went to the address on the piece of toilet paper, Dodger had stuffed into my hand. This brought me to a tree-lined avenue, snuggled in the richest district of Torridge City.

The detached house looked massive and had a drive flanked by huge hydrangea bushes. Chimney pots, poking erect and proud from the green slated roofs, closely resembled the candles on a teenager's birthday cake. Driving past an impressive Gothic-arched front entrance, Joseph and I entered a cobbled enclosed yard. This is real wealth, I thought.

I parked the multi-coloured van round the back of the house, hoping that out of sight was out of mind, although you got used to Joseph's glaring colours in time. As I turned the ignition off, the noise of a large gunshot coming from the exhaust announced our arrival.

The tradesman's door opened. I did not need to knock; the explosion had given notice of my arrival. A smart woman in her late fifties, wearing a red dressing gown, stood on the top step. A long silver cigarette holder in one hand, she slowly and deliberately held it up to her mouth. Her hair settled gently on her shoulders; her free flowing brown hair bracketed her middle-aged and lined face.

"Where's Roger?" Her voice croaked. "I was expecting Roger, the little sweetie..."

I explained Roger the Dodger was with an Aunt who was seriously ill.

"Just like my Roger. He's always so considerate. Please do come in. And what's your name, pet?" She said.

Cigarette smoke from her open mouth cascaded out in a white fog and misted her bright red lips as the trails of smoke danced and curled up over her face. Her lip-matching red dressing gown parted slightly as she opened the door and allowed me to enter. Liberally applied perfume floated around and, mixed with sugary scented cigarette smoke produced a rich thick odour. Tantalizingly she revealed the briefest glimpse of a nude torso through the opening in her dressing gown as I passed her.

She held her arm straight out straight and tapped her cigarette deliberately. Ash fell silently onto the tiled kitchen floor.

"Make yourself a pot of tea, pet. The daily woman's off today. You'll find things around here somewhere."

She waved her cigarette holder in a sweeping arc and floated out of the room.

I began opening the cupboards that lined every kitchen wall to try to find any tea making utensils. There were so many cupboards that this took some time. Eventually I poured boiling water into a silver teapot containing some odd looking sticks I found in a tin marked tea.

The woman returned and produced a sheet of paper containing my list of duties. She carefully flattened the sheet of paper on a scrubbed sycamore table top.

"So pet, you like Darjeeling tea? You have expensive tastes," she said.

Not wishing to show my ignorance I nodded politely. I had never experienced Darjeeling tea before and I thought it weak, tasting like perfumed water.

She left the kitchen as quickly as she had arrived.

The list of jobs was written on the piece of paper in neat handwriting. It began:

Sweep and tidy leaves from drive and lawn.
Wash and polish the cars.
Clean wash house.
Clean and polish front porch.

I gulped down my cup of tea and went outside to begin my tasks. The white ash remains of their bonfire at the far end of the garden looked to be a reasonable place to burn leaves. After I had collected and carried the leaves to it, the pile stood well over a yard high. I placed some old newspapers I had found in the outhouse under the pile, and realised I needed a match to ignite the paper.

I shouted at the kitchen door several times, but got no reply, so I went on to another job on the list. I began clearing out the wash house. It looked clean and tidy, but I found a mop and bucket began washing the floor. My Fire Brigade training as Mrs Mops came in very useful.

"No, pet. Walls need white-washing or whatever," the woman said standing in the small doorway filling the space.

She was now dressed in a green two-piece suit. Her hair was tied in a neat bob at the back by a black velvet ribbon and she rocked on her high black stiletto heels. Although she was twice my age, she was very attractive.

"My daily woman's back tomorrow. She'll find you paint and things. Do you need matches, my pet? They're in the kitchen. I'll be back later, after my luncheon club and a few drinky-poos."

Casually she left me in charge of this huge house. I watched her leave, sedately driving a white sports car.

Finding the matches in one of the kitchen drawers, I soon set fire to the pile of dry leaves. I piled more and more on top of the pile collecting and carrying bundles of leaves to the fire until the added leaves choked and killed the fire. Before I lit it again my empty stomach told me it was food time.

I found a latchkey for the kitchen door hanging on a hook and locked it. Joseph and I made off in search of a local pub. About half a mile down the road I came across a small old village inn nestled in a row of terrace houses, opposite two shops. I parked at the rear of the pub and Joseph coughed his usual announcement of our arrival.

"Nay, lad," the landlord said peering at me through his spectacles that were blurred by greasy finger marks.

"Food? This is an alehouse. Go over road and get yourself a pie."

With a pork pie from the butcher opposite and a pint of draught beer, I sat contentedly in the taproom. A couple of white haired retired gentlemen rattled their dominoes in an otherwise silent room.

One pint went to two as I relaxed.

The sound of a high revving engine outside sounded a familiar note. A red flash of paint, which was just visible through the frosted windows of taproom, looked familiar too. A Rolls Royce Dennis F8 appliance raced past.

A bell sounded as a second appliance followed.

The sight of a pair large carriage wheels confirmed that a Pump Escape also went past the pub windows. The noise of the bells subsided as both appliances raced into the distance.

"Another pint, lad?" The landlord asked.

Reluctantly declining his offer I made my way back to the house for the afternoon tasks. I jumped hard on Joseph's foot brake at the sight of a parked Pump Escape. Joseph slewed off at an angle as I stamped on the brake pedal. The brakes had still not been adjusted since my driving test.

One of the machines stood blocking the entrance to the big house and the other was parked in the driveway. Smoke billowed all around the house.

Had I left something burning in the house? My heart thumped and a multitude of questions darted through my brain.

I parked Joseph on the road and peeped over the garden wall. The Pump, its single blue light turning on the cab roof, stood partly hidden by smoke. Through the fog a couple of firemen ambled back into view.

"Some idiot's burning off pile of garden rubbish. He's left it unattended." A Sub Officer I never seen before opened his cab door and climbed in.

I skulked down the driveway and hid among the hydrangea plants, crouching down as the Pump drove past.

From the rear of the open backed appliance a voice shouted out.

"Its young Fairn," a red haired Fireman shouted, pointing at me. Ginger Saury, one of the men with whom I had joined the Fire Brigade, had discovered my hiding place.

By the time the lady of the house roared down the drive in her white sports car there was no evidence of any smoke. She braked causing grit and pebbles to fly into the air. With a wave she tottered into the house and was not seen again that day.

Next morning the daily help arrived. She was a kind old lady. Her hands constantly smelled of bleach, and the smell reminded me of my mother.

This grand old lady knew exactly my tasks for the week. The first thing was that the inside walls of the garage needed repainting.

Laboriously I emptied everything off the benches and moved them away from the walls. Using several coats of paint I worked until the walls shone snow white.

I worked until Friday midday, when my remuneration came in a small brown envelope. Five crisp pound notes and two shiny half-crowns slid neatly into my hand as I opened the envelope. Less than thirty hours work, painting and carrying out menial tasks, had earned me three shillings and sixpence per hour.

In contrast, my Fire Brigade wages that same Friday produced weekly pay of £11.3s.7d. For working days, nights, weekends and Bank Holidays on a fifty-six hour week. This equalled two shillings an hour.

The promised reduction in our hours from fifty-six to a forty-eight hour week would only provide more time off duty to do other work. It would do nothing to increase my status as a Fireman.

Chapter 24

The last few weeks to complete my two years' probation arrived and White Watch was on duty for the last of the three nights. It was Christmas Eve; time to celebrate Christmas and to regret the parting from two colleagues.

Sub Officer Kevin Gardon, born in 1909, retired at compulsory age of fifty-five. He had joined Torridge City-Police Fire Brigade in 1939 and served through the Second World War, through the formation of a National Fire Service in 1941 and to the change back in 1947 when the Service returned to the control of individual local authorities.

Fireman John Scar was the second valuable colleague to leave us. Although he had been posted to another Watch four months previously, he had promised to call and say his goodbyes. John had eight years experience in the Fire Service, but he found working for the local Bus Company more profitable.

There was no extra pay for working Bank Holidays. But living on my own with my prospects with Katherine wrecked by her parents' attitude; working during the Christmas holidays had many advantages. Working with Firemen with whom I had shared tragedies, sorrows, personal injuries and even death for the past two years, had given me experiences which produced an inner glow of warmth and comradeship I had never experienced until then.

1800 hours. Parade and roll call, allocating each man on duty to his appliance for the fifteen-hour night shift.

Following appliance checks to ensure that the equipment matched the lists on the check sheets, our time was considered a stand-down period. There was no work to be done unless we were called out on an emergency.

Plates of food were carried carefully from the canteen, down the flight of stairs, and along the back street and eventually to the four waiting trestle tables in our recreation room.

With the licensed bar for pints of good ale, good congenial company and organised games, we were prepared for a festive night.

Thick succulent slices of roast beef, chunks of cooked pork, a hock of ham, pickled onions, red cabbage, stilton cheese, boiled eggs and four large stand pies all stood on the four tables itching to be consumed.

Blanche Spurling, our ever-faithful canteen woman, had prepared a leg of ham with her usual love and care and had also provided us with an extra gift of a Christmas cake. Dark with currants, sultanas and raisins, it sliced like Edam cheese and was as black as coal.

A single red bulb hung from the ceiling. Accompanied by a silent bell stuck on the wall, the unlit bulb was the only item to disturb our enjoyment and perhaps turn us out to work.

The trestle tables sank under the mass of food as the evening progressed. The complete Watch came to play the usual knockout games. It cost a shilling to enter each game. The winnings were split between the finalist and the semi-finalist. We played snooker, table tennis, dominoes and darts, the regular games that occupied our stand-down periods. Every player's name was chalked on a blackboard and deleted as each winner went through to the next round.

"Enjoy yourselves," were the orders from Station Officer Finnan.

"But no one is to let me down if we are called out," he said.

He joined the queue as we filled our plates from the Food Mountain.

Ex-Sub Officer Kevin Gardon, dressed in civilian clothes, looked strange and different. He had always been dressed in his uniform and not many had seen him outside the Service. His thinning mat of hair, his criss-cross lined face and protruding eyes were now seen above his grey civilian jacket, which displayed the same snuff stains on both lapels as those on his Fire Brigade uniform.

John Scar, also dressed in civilian clothes arrived with Dodger Braise, still displaying the white bandages protecting his right arm. Dodger still required hospital treatment following the accident at the fire that got away. He gave his usual grin.

Station Officer Finnan called for silence and gave John an inscribed beer tankard as our parting gift to him.

John replied by telling us how sad he was to leave, but he also said that he was disillusioned by the mean and petty attitude of some of our senior ranks. He said he could no longer accept their feudalistic practices. A moment of awkward silence followed his speech.

"And I cannot survive on the wages," John added with a wry smile.

Kevin Gardon mumbled something as his turn came and he was singled out for his leaving present. He was a man of few words, but one who was admired for his enormous wealth of experience at fires. He fondled his retirement gift, a gleaming silver snuff box, as he tried desperately in vain to find words of thanks. His eyes swelled with unshed tears and rotated nervously in their sockets until Fireman David Capelin ended his torture by applauding. We all joined in.

"Buy everyone a drink on me," Kevin blurted out as we cheered.

Bells interrupted the proceedings and our chance of a free drink. We chased out of the recreation room and banged the swing doors repeatedly against the wall. Each crew-member rushed outside, across the yard and down the street through a passage and at last into the muster-room to read the indicator panel.

Pump One, it read.

I grabbed my helmet, boots and axe and with my fellow crew-man, Rodney Rudd, I charged through the two swing doors into the engine house.

"Assisting Police in Torridge City Centre," Station Officer Finnan shouted his Scottish accent a little easier to understand after my nearly two years of practice.

We sat on the back of the open Pump as our driver, David Capelin, engaged first gear and we jolted forward. It was unusual for David to be driving any of our front line appliances, since his troublesome right hip was a handicap.

A single policeman stood holding a string of Christmas lights on the pavement as we stopped. One end was detached and broken off a lamppost, the rest hung precariously across the road.

"Get the ladder off," Station Officer Finnan shouted.

The thirty-five foot ladder, which was kept on a gantry on top of the open appliance and stretching from the cab roof to overhang at the rear of the appliance, created a convenient place in which to stack other long and clumsy equipment. Our short extension ladder, the roof ladder, the ceiling hook, and the applicator were all tied to the ladder by a leather belt.

The short extension ladder consisted of a main ladder and a sliding extension. Each section was seven foot six inches in length and weighed about thirty pounds.

The ceiling hook consisted of a pole seven to eight feet long with a steel point and a four-inch spur on one end at right angles. This was a Fire Service tool, similar to a boat hook and used mainly for removing fire-damaged ceilings.

The applicator was a ten-foot long aluminium tube (3 metres), two inches in diameter. On one end was a brass outlet with hundreds of small holes drilled at different angles. Connected to delivery hose in place of a branch outlet, high-pressure water was forced out of these fine holes. The water jets impinged on each other and created a fine fog like spray.

I had already witnessed the use of the applicator during a drill and I remembered how efficiently a drum of burning oil could be extinguished. But I had never seen it used at a fire. The fine jets of water created an emulsion of flammable-oil forcibly mixed with water. The mixture was unable to support ignition; the flames went out.

I untied the leather strap securing these unused items and balanced them on the outside locker top. None were needed this time.

The thirty-five foot ladder, now freed, slid easily from the back of the appliance and was carried to the offending lamppost. The ladder was extended and Rodney Rudd was sent up with a pair of pliers and rubber gloves to cut the cable and bring down the damaged lights.

When the lights were considered safe, we left the length of cable and the broken light bulbs for the Police to deal with and set off back to the Station, returning to our celebrations.

Our three guests eventually departed, Kevin taking John and Dodger home in his car. Gathering outside, the whole Watch cheered as the hands on the Town Hall clock were clasped together to show it was now midnight, and Christmas Day. As Kevin's car turned out on to the main road, the alarm bells tinkled in the distance.

The message read Pump One, Pump Escape to house fire, at Endrick Mount.

Our laughter melted in the cold night air as our two machines burst out from the engine house doors. We roared away, putting our fire-boots on first, and then our tunics and helmets with the leather straps pulled tight under our chins. Our axes in their pouch were positioned waist-height on the left and now we sat dressed and ready. The Pump wasted no time as we raced off down the street. David showed skill and dexterity in obtaining maximum effort from the engine.

Pump Escape followed close behind, and we sat on the open bench seating looking backwards to it. Two ghost-like faces stared through the cab windows of the Pump Escape, the driver and the officer in charge. They disappeared from view as we accelerated leaving them trailing behind.

Endrick Mount was about a mile from our Fire Station.

"What's the number?" I asked. But there was no need for a number. We could see a house on fire two streets away. Flames licked ruthlessly high into the sky, bursting from a rear bedroom window and clawing upwards from a tiled roof.

We turned left into Endrick Road and right down Endrick Mount but were stopped short, our access blocked by a parked car.

"Get a line on!" An obvious order shouted somebody.

All our Pumps carried only eighty gallons of water and Pump Escape carried another hundred. Both amounts together would be insufficient to extinguish this fire.

We jerked to a sudden stop at least twenty-five yards from the front entrance to the burning house. The parked car prevented closer access.

Several neighbours were gathered standing in the middle of Endrick Mount. Some even spilled over on to the footpath.

Rodney Rudd untied the securing strap that fastened the hose-reel tubing to its drum. I jumped off the open rear platform on our Pump and set off, dragging the tubing with me.

"Where have you been?" A man shouted standing blocking the footpath. "It's taken you ages to get here!"

It hurt that people thought we had taken more time than necessary to arrive.

The garden path leading to the front door was jammed solid with people, all anxious and angry. I struggled, dragging the hose-reel tubing behind me, to make a gap through the crowd. Many willing hands came forwards to help. But the tubing suddenly caught around the gatepost and jammed solid. People crowded closer, all wanting to help. I pushed back through the crowd to free the tubing.

The Pump was already pumping and water trickled out of the hose-reel nozzle. As I turned to push another path through the crowd I could see David open one of our appliance locker doors as our Pump Escape arrived. With the stand pipe, a key and bar, under one arm, a length of delivery hose under the other he disappeared up the road looking for a hydrant lid. He ignored any pain from his awkward hip.

Station Officer Finnan and Rodney at last pushed a path through the milling crowd and joined me at the front door. The Pump Escape crew ran down the street to join us. They also had trouble with the crowds of people.

The locked front door did not give much resistance. One meaty shoulder charge and the door flung back against the inside wall.

We dragged the hose-reel tubing up over the bare wooden staircase immediately behind the front door. The tubing jammed again as we reached the top landing. We pulled hard on the tubing and gained sufficient length to reach top of the stairs. Wisps of smoke leaked from a door in front of us. The Station Officer pointed his hand-held searchlight at it. The beam stabbed the door. Ink-black wisps of smoke drifted out from the door seams.

We pushed on the door. It was locked. Turning the hot door handle we tried again. Still locked.

The beam from the searchlight darted about, at last locating a bolt high at the top of the door. It was hot to touch, but I reached up, lifted it and slid it back. The door moved inwards slightly. A bright orange light appeared from inside.

As we pushed the door wider open, strong light from the inside bounced on our faces and streamed out into the staircase, bathing us in bright reds and yellows.

"This tiny hose-reel jet won't put this out. Get a full size jet," Station Officer Finnan screamed in his Scottish accent.

I half-fell, half-slithered, back down the bare wooden stairs to the front door. A female coupling from the end of a delivery hose sat waiting on the doorstep. Both appliance drivers were outside, trying to get a supply of constant water from the town mains to supplement our meagre water supply.

"My babies are in there!" A woman suddenly appeared running down Endrick Mount. "My babies! MY BABIES!" she screamed.

"Here, take the applicator," David said, passing the shiny tube to me. I saw his face tighten as he shuffled towards me, pushing two members of the milling crowd onto the front garden.

I slotted the applicator into the delivery hose and scrambled back upstairs.

At the top of the staircase I passed the applicator to the two firemen on the floor opposite the burning bedroom. They were still directing the pathetic jet from the hose-reel through the partly opened door.

"There's somebody inside," I screamed.

"Check the other bedrooms," Station Officer Finnan's muffled voice came through the dense acrid smoke.

Rodney and I crawled close to the floor in an attempt to grab the last remaining inches of unpolluted fresh air. We crawled over bare floorboards to reach another door on the landing.

Again the door was locked. We reached it and felt in the dark for a second door bolt securing the bedroom door. The dry delivery hose on the landing behind us suddenly cracked as it filled up with water. The water from minute jets on the brass outlet on the applicator gushed out. The cold mist of water gave us a welcome relief from the seething heat.

We pushed the door to the bedroom on fire open and our long aluminium tube injected water into the mass of flames. A sudden rush of air behind us followed as the door opened wide. Static smoke swirled and parted as the light from the fire momentarily filled the top of the staircase. The two firemen holding the applicator crawled into the inferno.

With Rodney, I turned to the other bedroom door which needed a strong push before we could edge the door wide enough to enter.

The layout of the room was unknown and the room black with dense choking smoke. We stumbled onto a bed. We both felt for any sign of life along the top. Still close to the floor, Rodney grunted as I stabbed his back with my helmet.

I felt underneath the bed. A large enamel bucket moved as I jerked forward. It was too late. Bucket rocked and toppled over. Contents spilled. I felt water trickling over my tunic sleeve.

"Over here!" Rodney cried.

I crawled through the spilt liquid in the direction of his voice.

"No. No! It's a child's teddy bear." He swore loudly.

I continued to feel along the wall and behind the open door. With one hand I groped through dense smoke and heat. Both our faces were inches from the floor, breathing as much clean air as possible.

A bare foot? Yes. A leg? My fingers dreaded feeling further. Gingerly I slid a shaking hand forward, discovering first an ankle, then a bare leg, then a knee and then a piece of ruffled clothing. Yes, it was a child.

"Here, here, here!" I coughed as loudly as the smoke allowed. Rodney turned and joined me.

Between us we dragged the lifeless form from behind the door and shuffled with it to the staircase.

On the stairs I took the tiny frame in my arms and slithered two steps at a time, down to the front door.

Pushing through the crowd outside and along the garden path once again I carried the limp child. A woman, presumable the mother, followed behind. She was now stunned and silent.

At the gate David, in the centre of the crowd of people that seemed to have grown in numbers, took the motionless child from my arms. A slight movement, a cough and a sputter indicated life was still present.

"She's breathing!" David said.

We carried the limp form to the front of our appliance. Both headlights shone onto a head of damp hair, which covered the young girl's face.

Using a cylinder removed from one of our Proto-breathing apparatus sets left hanging, idle and unused, on the Pump, David turned on the main valve, allowing pure oxygen to drift across the young girl's mouth. In our headlights we could see signs of returning life. The child's eyes flickered.

"She's alive," David said quietly.

The child awoke and instantly began to sob and cough. Before either of us could take any evasive action, she coughed again and a fountain of sick was ejected from her mouth.

At one end of Endrick Mount a Daimler ambulance was waiting, its single blue light turning slowly, almost lazily, on the cab roof.

The small girl, who we learned was only three years old, was last seen bundled up in the arms of an ambulance man and being carried away. The mother was encouraged to go with her daughter and followed reluctantly telling us there was another child still in the house. I went back to the house to join the rest of our crew in the search.

The applicator worked well. The bedroom, once a solid mass of heat and flames and now hot as an oven showed no sign of the fire. The fine mist of water removed the intense heat and quelled the angry flames, using less water and being more efficient than our normal three-quarter inch jet.

The bedroom was hot and gutted. Plaster on the walls was missing and had left several patches of red brick.

A member of our Pump Escape crew was the first to spot the remains of the missing boy.

Station Officer Finnan folded back a charred blanket from under a pile of burnt wood. The tiny frame of the young boy appeared covered in plaster and debris. As Finnan moved the bundle we could see two tiny hands clasped tight together over his face as no doubt he had tried to save himself from the inferno. Leaking wheals on his head looked wet and greasy. Both bare legs were swollen and resembled inflated sausages. The tight skin across his torso had split and broken in two places as his internal organs, pink in colour had burst out from the inside. The distinctive aroma of burnt human flesh, like roasted pork, joined the cocktail of odours of wet wool and charred wood. Fresh cold air wafted in through a smashed window and provided some slight relief to the stench as the sweet body-smell lodged in our throats.

The remains of a soft and mangled candle, a charred crushed paper box and spent wooden matches which were found underneath the body provided damming evidence of how the fire had started.

"There's nothing we can do now," Station Officer Finnan said.

"The police will want photographs," he added.

The accusations that we had arrived late did not agree with the explanation obtained from our Torridge City Fire Brigade Control. Everybody at Endrick Mount thought someone else had been sent to make the 999 call. It was the 'anybody but not me', syndrome.

There were questions about why we found both bedroom doors locked and bolted, why no one responsible was left in charge of two young children, why was their mother out, leaving her children alone in the house? Why, finally, were there matches and candles in a two-year old child's bedroom?

Why? Why? Why? But there was no answer to our questions.

After the police had recorded the grisly scene in photographs we cleared the bedroom completely. The dead child was wrapped in a sheet and carried through the gawking crowd, now shocked into silence, to a special ambulance and transported to the mortuary.

We stripped the ceiling in the burnt bedroom completely, using our ceiling hook. By thrusting the pointed end upwards into the remains of the plastered ceiling, twisting ninety-degrees and pulling down, narrow wooden strips from the lathe-and-plaster ceiling crashed down, dislodged from the roof joists. Eventually the bare joists and the gaps in the damaged roof gave a clear view out into a starlit Christmas Day sky. We collected all our equipment and prepared to leave.

For us this was just another house badly damaged by fire, just another statistic. We returned to our Station leaving behind us the scene of the tragedy.

The smell that came from my tunic as we drove back to the station confirmed the contents of the spilled bucket.

"You can stay outside on the back of the Pump," Rodney said with a smile, replacing tragedy with urinary humour.

Christmas morning reveille arrived and the whole crew was subdued. A depressed air lingered as we reflected at the waste of young life. Although death is a way of life on a busy Fire Station, it was Christmas and the thought of the imprisoned babies hard to accept.

But life must go on. The professionalism of the senior members of our crew soon changed the subject, replacing tragedy with humour. The negative atmosphere was not allowed to fester.

Chapter 25

My two years probationary period ended with the news that Torridge City Fire Brigade was to adopt a forty-eight-hour working week in the coming year after a long uphill struggle.

To achieve this, each watch was divided into seven groups and each group was allocated an extra day, or night, off-duty.

Group one was off-duty the first day of the tour, group two the second day and group three the third day. Group four took the first night, group five the second night and group six the third night. The seventh group worked a full tour. At the next tour on duty each group advanced one, taking turns from having the day off to the night off. Extra men were needed to implement this system. They had not yet been fully recruited, leaving a shortfall.

Working fewer hours for the same pay was welcome, but most of us needed more money. Our weekly wages were still below the national average. Extra shift off-duty would make it easier to take outside employment to supplement our income however.

The low pay and the constant battle against our officer regime tarnished a worthy occupation. With morale at a record low I felt no particular concern about whether I passed or failed my probation examination. But following the briefest of tests sandwiched between essential station cleaning routines, and one fire call, I received the following...

Fire Brigade Headquarters

Torridge City
1st January 1965

To   Fireman M.E.Fairn C 435

PROBATIONARY PERIOD - CONFIRMATION OF APPOINTMENT

This is to certify that, having given satisfaction in your personal bearing and in the carrying out of your duties during the period of two years probation in Torridge City Fire Brigade, your appointment as a Fireman has now been confirmed.

A Bass.
CHIEF OFFICER

I never did discover what the 'C' stood for!

Printed in Great Britain
by Amazon